Breach and Adaptation of International Contracts

An Introduction to Lex Mercatoria

Breach and Adaptation of International Contracts

An Introduction to Lex Mercatoria

Ugo Draetta
Ralph B. Lake
Ved P. Nanda

Butterworth Legal Publishers

The Butterworth Group of Companies

Butterworths is a worldwide publishing group with companies in the United States, Australia, Canada, Ireland, Malaysia, New Zealand, Singapore, and the United Kingdom. In the U.S. there are legal publishing branches in Clearwater, Florida (D & S Publishers); Orford, New Hampshire (Equity Publishing); Salem, New Hampshire; St. Paul, Minnesota.

Butterworth publications are designed to provide accurate and current information with regard to the subject matter covered. They are intended to help attorneys and other professionals maintain their professional competence. Publications are sold with the understanding that Butterworths is not engaged in rendering legal, accounting, or other professional advice. If legal advice or other expert assistance is required, the service of a competent professional should be sought. Attorneys using Butterworth publications in dealing with specific legal matters should also research original sources of authority.

LIBRARY OF CONGRESS
Library of Congress Cataloging-in-Publication Data

Lake, Ralph B.
    Breach and adaptation of international contracts: an introduction to Lex Mercatoria/Ralph B. Lake, Ved P. Nanda, Ugo Draetta
      p.   cm.
    Includes bibliographical references and index.
    ISBN 0–88063–750–1
    1. Law merchant. 2. Breach of contract. 3. Conflict of laws–Contracts. 4. Contracts (International law) I. Nanda, Ved P. II. Draetta, Ugo. III. Title.
K1005.4.L35 1992
341.7'53–dc20
                 92–14274
                 CIP

Printed in the United States of America.

For our daughters

Eleonora Draetta, Evelina Draetta, Anna Lake,
Elizabeth Lake and Anjali Nanda

UGO DRAETTA

is Vice President and Senior Counsel, International Operations, of the General Electric Company (U.S.A.) in London and an adjunct Professor of Law at the Catholic University of Milan. He was formerly the General Counsel and Secretary of FIAT s.p.a. in Turin. Professor Draetta studied law at the University of Naples and was admitted to the bar of Milan, Italy.

RALPH B. LAKE

is Associate General Counsel, International of the Promus Companies Incorporated in Memphis, Tennessee, U.S.A. He was formerly the European Counsel of Holiday Inns, Inc. in London. Mr. Lake studied law at the University of Denver and the London School of Economics, and is a member of the bar of the State of Ohio, U.S.A.

VED P. NANDA

is Thompson G. Marsh Professor of Law and Director of the International Legal Studies Program at the University of Denver College of Law, Denver, Colorado, U.S.A.

CONTENTS

INTRODUCTION

The purpose of this book is to discuss the legal "pathology" of international business contracts, i.e., those aspects of the contractual relationship which arise when contract performance does not actually develop as the parties originally contemplated.[1] We group these concepts under the general rubric of breach, remedies, excuse, self-help mechanisms, and contract adaptation to changed circumstances.

As in the previous collaboration of two of us,[2] the analysis here seeks to identify practices and usages which are widely and uniformly recognized and applied in international transactions as practical norms and expectations of international lawyers. These practices and usages will be compared with common law and civil law municipal rules to determine whether an international business practice has evolved as a norm which is autonomous with respect to municipal rules, or whether it is still firmly rooted in domestic legal concepts.

The basic assumption is that there are a number of customary principles and detailed rules which are generally applied to international business contracts. This body of principles and rules, the *lex mercatoria* or new merchant law, has been identified by some scholars, particularly in continental Europe, as an emerging legal system distinguishable and autonomous from national legal systems.[3] Other academic commentators have strongly opposed the proposition that the *lex mercatoria* is a system of law capable of being enforced by its own terms. The opponents maintain that "delocalization" is impossible: contracts must be governed by a specific national law, either selected by the parties or determined by applicable conflict of laws provisions. According to this line of thought, any application of international trade practices and usages to a particular contract must be made within the context of the proper municipal law of the contract.

---

1. The term "pathology" with respect to a contractual relationship has an incongruous sound in English, but is regularly used by civil lawyers. See e.g. Bernardini, *La patalogia dei contratti internazionali*, 1984 Giurisprudenza Piemontese 799 (1984).

2. Ralph B. Lake and Ugo Draetta, Letters of Intent and Other Precontractual Documents (1990).

3. *See infra*, Chapter 1.

The debate has occasionally become rather heated. With a few exceptions, however, it is of a theoretical nature, centering around the question whether the *lex mercatoria* exists as law or as a system capable of autonomous enforcement. Those arguing in favor or against the *lex mercatoria* as an autonomous legal system have not spent much energy assessing the specific general principles to which the theoretical dispute actually refers. The main purpose of this book is to fill this gap. We do not take a position as to the theoretical nature of the *lex mercatoria* as law. Our approach is both more modest and more pragmatic. The development of an international trade law appears to be better served by identifying whether, and to what extent, some specific emerging international trade usages and practices generally applied by the international business community have an autonomous character distinct from municipal systems. Others can undertake the change or determining whether the body of rules so identified can rise to the dignity of an autonomous legal system.

Although it must seem contradictory for any book with the words *"lex mercatoria"* in its title to claim a practical orientation, we do in fact make such a claim. Our ultimate purpose is to assist those who negotiate, draft, and interpret international commercial contracts, by identifying the delocalized norms which they encounter, and thus to put the *lex mercatoria* into a useful perspective.

The book is the result of a genuine collaborative. The original concept of the book and most if its initial research, however, were developed by Mr. Draetta. We express our sincere appreciation to Dennis J. McElwee, a third year student at the University of Denver College of Law for his research assistance, and to Diana Eggleston and Janell Smith of the Promus Companies Law Department for their research, editorial and organizational assistance.

I. THE NOTION OF INTERNATIONAL BUSINESS CONTRACTS

Chapter 1. International Contracts and the Lex Mercatoria

This chapter will discuss briefly the features of international contracts by which they are distinguished from domestic contracts. It also will introduce the lex mercatoria as it is currently debated, discussing its origins, its content, its relationship with international uniform laws and domestic laws, such as the U.S. Uniform Commercial Code, and the extent of its use.

1.1 International Contracts[1]

Although we are neutral as to the theoretical legal existence of the lex mercatoria, there is little doubt that international contracts can be distinguished from wholly domestic contracts in several important ways. First, the obvious factors of culture, language, and distance result in an international contractual relationship being more complex than a purely domestic one. Since parties have a greater degree of insecurity, they have developed the types of extra-judicial and, indeed, extra legem devices that will be discussed later. Second, international contracts tend to involve larger amounts of money and tend to be of a longer duration than domestic contracts. They are more likely than domestic contracts to be "relational" in nature.[2] Third, and most importantly for our purposes, the international contractual relationship is regarded differently than the wholly domestic relationship by legislators and judges with respect to the selection of the governing law.

It generally is recognized that parties to an international contract enjoy a wide range of freedom as to the choice of law applicable to their contract. For example, this principle is recognized in both mu-

---

1. Although some have argued effectively that "transnational" is more accurate, we use the term "international" contracts to refer simply to contracts the parties to which are located in different national jurisdictions.

2. *See* § 6.2 *infra.*

3

nicipal[3] and international[4] law. In particular, parties to an international contract may submit it to a law having no connection with any of the elements of their contractual relationship,[5] or even to more than one law.[6]

When parties from different countries undertake an international business transaction, however, choosing the governing law often proves to be a sensitive issue. One does not wish to appear distrustful, but few would submit to "rules of the game" with which they are un-

---

3. As opposed to purely domestic contracts, which must be submitted to local law. *See, e.g.*, G. Delaume, TRANSNATIONAL CONTRACTS § 1.01 (1989); V. Nanda & D. Pansius, LITIGATION OF INTERNATIONAL ISSUES in U.S. COURTS § 7.03 (1986); Delaume, *What is an International Contract? An American and Gallic Dilemma*, 28 INT'L & COMP. L.Q. 258–279 (1979); Van Heck, *Signification et limites du principe de l'autonomie de la volonté dans les contrats internationaux*, 1957 REVUE DE DROIT INTERNATIONAL ET DROIT COMPARÉ 81 (1957); Giuliano, *La loi applicable aux contrats: problèmes choisis*, RECUEIL DE L'ACADEMIE DE DROIT INTERNATIONAL DE LA HAYE, tome 158, p. 199.

4. It is contained, for example, in the "European Community Convention on the Law Applicable to Contractual Obligations," opened for signature June 19, 1980, 23 O. J. Eur. Comm. (No. L266) I (1980), Arts. 1 (1) & 3 (3), and now in force in all EC member states.

5. To illustrate: a subcontract between a French and a U.S. company on one side and an Italian company on the other side, relating to the construction of a campus at Riyadh University in Saudi Arabia, contained the following choice-of-law clause, which was subsequently enforced by an ICC arbitral tribunal: "Because the parties hereto have been unable to agree that the laws of either France, United States of America or Italy should govern, the parties have decided by mutual agreement that the subcontract shall be governed and construed in accordance with the laws of Switzerland."

6. *See* "Convention on the Law Applicable to Contractual Obligations," Art. 3 (1). This technique of submitting an international contract to more than one law is called *dépecage*, a French word that means "cutting into pieces." On *dépecage*, see G. Delaume, TRANSNATIONAL CONTRACTS § 1.04 (1989); E. Rabel, THE CONFLICT OF LAWS — A COMPARATIVE STUDY 380–390 (1947).

familiar.[7] The eventual outcome of an international business transaction may, however, well depend on the choice of law. As one observer has aptly stated, "a common foundation of mutual understanding among merchants is essential to a viable commercial practice across national borders."[8] An equal footing between parties is often sought.[9] Different legal systems may have divergent, if not contradictory, legal rules that hamper the flow of international commerce and investment.[10] Furthermore, national laws may change overnight to the disadvantage of the contracting parties.[11]

Consequently, negotiators of international contracts (beginning with the "state contracts," i.e., contracts between a national state and a foreign private party) began to "delocalize" choice-of-law clauses by using various formulae intended to avoid the application of a specific national law to their contractual relationship. These formulae made reference to "general common principles," "principles of equity," "principles of good faith and good will," "principles of international law," "international trade usages as applied by the ICC Arbitral Tribunal," and similar expressions meant to constitute an alternative to the submission of the contract to a domestic law.[12]

This practice was inconsistent with the traditional conflict of laws approach, which was predicated on the need for any international contract to be submitted to a national law. Comparative commentators

---

7. *See* Letter to Horatio G. Spafford (March 17, 1814), quoted in Bartletts Familiar Quotations 389 (15th ed. 1980).

8. Stoecker, *The Lex Mercatoria: To What Extent Does It Really Exist?* 7 J. Int'l Arb. 106 (1990).

9. *See* Lando, *The Lex Mercatoria in International Commercial Arbitration*, 34 Int'l & Comp. L.Q. 747, 748 (1985).

10. *See* Stoecker, *The Lex Mercatoria: To What Extent Does It Really Exist?* 7 J. Int'l Arb. 101 (1990).

11. *See* Mustill, *The New Lex Mercatoria: The First Twenty-Five Years*, 4 Arb. Int'l 99 No. 46 (1988).

12. *See generally* Lalive, *Contracts Between a State or a State Agency and a Foreign Company*, 18 Int'l & Comp. L.Q. 987 (1969); Giardina, *State Contracts: National vs. International Law*, Ital. Y.B. Int'l L. 147 (1980/ 1981); McNair, *The General Principle of Law Recognized by Civilized Nations*, 1957 Brit. Y.B. Int'l L. 1 (1957).

took two approaches to this development. Some developed the concept of "self regulatory contracts" (in French: *contrats sans loi*; in Italian: *contratti senza legge*; in German: *rechtsordnunglose Verträge*), asserting a contract could be submitted only to its own provisions, autonomous of any law.[13] Other commentators maintained that the reference to international trade usages meant only their incorporation into national laws applicable to international contracts. These must be identified by traditional conflict of laws provisions. The latter approach, of course, frustrates the clear intention of parties that adopt de-localized dispute settlement provisions to remove their relationship from the provisions of municipal law.

The real issues in this connection are:

1. Whether parties to an international contract may submit it to a legal system other than a national law; and

---

13. *See generally* Reimann, Zur Lehre vom "Rechtsordnunglosen" Vertrag (1970); Schmitthoff, *The Law of International Trade, its Growth, Formulation and Operation*, The Sources of International Trade 3 (1964); Bourquin, *Arbitration and Economic Development Agreements*, 1960 Bus. Law. 860 (1960). The concept of a self-regulatory contract was thoroughly criticized in the Aramco vs. Saudi Arabia arbitral award, 1963 Revue Critique de Droit International Prive 272 (1963): "[I]t is obvious that no contract exists *in vacuo*. . . . [It] is necessarily related to some positive law which gives legal effects to the reciprocal and concordant modifications of intent made by the parties. The contract cannot even be conceived, without a system of law under which it is created." For more critiques, *see* Mann, *The Proper Law of Contracts Concluded by International Persons*, 1959 Brit. Y.B. Int'l L. 34 (1959); Peyrefitte, *Le problème du contrat dit "sans loi"*, 1965 Recueil Dalloz Sirey 119 (1965). The practice of international contracts shows that a "self-governing" clause often is accompanied by a traditional choice of law provision. *See, e.g.*, Art. 122, "General Conditions for Construction Contracts in use with the Electricity Corporation, an agency of the Kingdom of Saudi Arabia," which reads as follows: "The provisions of this contract shall form a self-contained source of law for the interpretation of this Contract. All disputes, differences, etc. shall be settled on the basis of the Contract, considering also the will of the parties concerned. The proper law shall be the law of the Kingdom of Saudi Arabia". The reference to the Saudi law most probably is limited to its public order provisions.

2. Whether international trade practices and usages constitute such a legal system.

1.2 The Concept of the Lex Mercatoria

It is widely acknowledged that international business customs and practices have contributed significantly to the development of business law.[14] Questions remain, however, as to when and how an international business practice or custom actually becomes law, whether that "law" is truly independent of the many countries' laws penetrated by international business transactions, and how that law is then applied to international business?

The concept of independent business practices rising to the level of international private business law has been termed the lex mercatoria or law merchant.[15] It has been described as "an expression of the in-

---

14. *See generally* Trakman, THE LAW MERCHANT: THE EVOLUTION OF COMMERCIAL LAW (1983).

15. *Id.* at 8, quoting G. Malynes, LEX MERCATORIA (3d ed. 1986). The notion of lex mercatoria was first developed in continental Europe and particularly in France in the early 1960s. Its recognized father is Professor Berthold Goldman. *See* Goldman, *Frontières du droit et lex mercatoria*, 1964 ARCHIVES DE LA PHILOSOPHIE DU DROIT 177 (1964); Berthold Goldman, *La lex mercatoria dans les contrats et l'arbitrage internationaux*, 1979 CLUNET 475 (1979). Much discussion of the lex mercatoria is contained in the collection of studies in honour of Professor Goldman, entitled LE DROIT DES RELATIONS ECONOMIQUES INTERNATIONALES, ETUDES OFFERTS A BERTHOLD GOLDMAN (Paris 1982), as well as in COLLOQUE DE BALE SUR LA LOI REGISSANT LES OBLIGATIONS CONTRACTUELS (Basle & Frankfurt 1983). The roots of the concept can be found in P. Jessup, TRANSNATIONAL LAW (1956), who refers to natural law; W. Jenks, THE PROPER LAW OF INTERNATIONAL ORGANIZATIONS 150 (1962); McNair, *The General Principles of Law Recognized by Civilized Nations*, 1957 BRIT. Y.B. INT'L L. 1 (1957); Verdross, *Die Sicherung von Ausländischen Privatrechten aus Abkommen zur Wirtschaftlichen Entwicklung mit Schiedklauseln*, 18 ZEITSCHRIFT FÜR AUSL. ÖF. RECHT UND VOLKERRECHT 635 (1957–1958), who already saw the lex mercatoria as a complete and autonomous legal system; Kahn, LA VENTE COMMERCIALE INTERNATIONALE 37 (1961), who described the passage from contractual law to positive law. *See also* Berman, *The*

creasing uniformity of commercial laws in the major jurisdictions";[16] "general principles and customary rules";[17] "rules . . . common to all or most of the States . . . and if not ascertainable . . . [those] . . . most appropriate and equitable;"[18] "uniform rules accepted in all countries;"[19] . . . "contract practices, understandings, regulations, and decisions [which] constitute a body of customary law which is the foundation on which national and international commercial legislation has been and continues to be built;"[20] and "[a]n international body of law founded on commercial understandings and contract practices."[21]

Opponents of the concept have described it as "principia mercatoria," a collection of general principles having no independent legal effect, similar to the Emperor's clothes, which had no existence whatsoever.[22] It also has been described as a "mythical view of a transnational law of state contracts whose sources are elsewhere."[23]

Law of International Commercial Transactions (Lex Mercatoria), 2 EMORY J. INT'L DISP. RES. 235, 237 (1988); David-Popescu, NEW DIRECTIONS IN INTERNTIONAL TRADE (UNIDROIT) (1977).

16. P. WOOD, LAW AND PRACTICE OF INTERNATIONAL FINANCE 1–34 (1981).

17. Stoecker, *The Lex Mercatoria: To What Extent Does It Really Exist?* 7 J. INT'L ARB. 105 (1990).

18. *Id.*

19. *Id.* at 106.

20. Berman, *The Law of International Commercial Transactions (Lex Mercatoria)*, 2 EMORY J. INT'L DISP. RES. 235, 237 (1988).

21. *Id.*

22. Highet, *The Enigma of the Lex Mercatoria*, 63 TUL. L. J. 613, 616 (1989).

23. Delaume, *Comparative Analysis as a Basis of Law in State Contracts: The Myth of the Lex Mercatoria*, 63 TUL. L. J. 575, 611 (1989). For other strong opposition to the notion of lex mercatoria, *see* Mann, *England Rejects "Delocalized" Contracts and Arbitration*, 33 INT'L & COMP. L.Q. 196, 197 (1984); Lagarde, *Approach critique à la lex mercatoria*, LE DROIT DES RELATIONS ECONOMIQUES INTERNATIONALES, ETUDES OFFERTS A BERTHOLD GOLDMAN 146 (1982); A. Boggiano, INTERNATIONAL STANDARD CONTRACTS: THE PRICE OF FAIRNESS 13–23 (1991), who, however, refers only to standard contracts and forms that undoubtedly could

Given the importance to business of building long-term relationships, how then are legitimate disputes decided and how often is a specific national law, rather than an international principle possibly belonging to the lex mercatoria, used to control an international transaction? Two surveys have been conducted in an attempt to answer these questions.

The first, designed by Leon E. Trakman and limited to the crude oil industry, was directed to 33 in-house legal counsel employed by companies engaged primarily in the international oil markets.[24] Fifteen responded to questions regarding the percentage of contracts since 1974 that led to disputes over contract performance. Only 12 percent of the contracts during this period resulted in disputes. Of these, seventy-six percent were settled informally between the parties, 9 percent were settled through arbitration, and 13 percent through litigation.[25] Litigation in domestic jurisdictions was preferred only where the tribunal was considered favorable to both parties and where the law applied was "commercially acceptable."[26] Respondents who favored arbitration said that it was less expensive and generally reflected actual business practice instead of the construction of such practice by the judiciary. The contract references to international agreements, such as the Uniform Law of International Sales, and the rules of trade and legal associations were seen as expressing faith in the growth of international usage as a means of resolving conflicts. Both international usage and the preference for arbitrators from the business world echo the presence of a developing lex mercatoria.

The second survey, conducted by Matti Kurkela, dealt with international practices regarding the use of documentary credits. More than

---

not constitute principles of lex mercatoria themselves but only evidence their existence. On this last point, *see* U. Draetta, Il Diritto dei Contratti Internazionali. La Formazione Dei Contratti 109–113 (1984).

24. These companies were so identified by Oil and Gas International Yearbook (1978/1979) and The Financial Times. *See* L. Trakman, The Law Merchant: The Evolution of Commercial Law 120 (1983).

25. *Id.* at 53.

26. *Id.* at 57.

200 questionnaires were sent to international banks.[27] Although only 21 answers were received, they represented 15 different countries and almost every continent.[28] This survey shows that only a few banks agree expressly on the applicable law for any relationship. Agreements on the place of jurisdiction or means of settling disputes are very rare. The Uniform Customs and Practices for Documentary Credits (UCP)[29] are referred to without exception. When required, most banks seem to lean toward the law of the place of payment.[30] Most preferred negotiation and arbitration as a means to resolve disputes. "The great majority found courts of law inexperienced and slow."[31]

The preference for arbitration, the lack of specificity with regard to choice of law, and the consistent use of international documents for reference support a call for an international lex mercatoria. It has been suggested that "[t]he documentary letter of credit is so completely identical with the UCP that it may be said to belong to an autonomous legal system and that its doctrine is the first manifestation of a lex mercatoria, an international commercial law distinct from any national system."[32]

1.3 Early Origins of the Lex Mercatoria

Many of the observations noted above are thought to have resulted in the formation of early merchant courts in medieval Europe. It has been postulated that the lex mercatoria of the Middle Ages was produced by merchants faced with inadequate laws supplied by their principals.[33] Merchant business customs have been evolving since the

---

27. *See* M. Kurkela, Letters of Credit Under International Trade Law: U.C.C., UCP and Law Merchant 7 (1985).

28. *Id.* at 489.

29. *Id.* at 2.

30. *Id.* at 314.

31. *Id.* at 315.

32. *Id.* at 15 and 332.

33. *See* Stoecker, *The Lex Mercatoria: To What Extent Does It Really Exist?* 7 J. Int'l Arb. 102 (1990).

"Lex Rhodia" of the Mediterranean in the third century B.C.[34] Cicero (106–43 B.C.) has been quoted by U.S. courts as having said that certain business practices were "in a great measure, not the law of a single country only, but of the commercial world."[35]

Early merchant law was laden with concepts of "equity" or *ex aequo et bono*. The Consuls of Bologna called for judgments "following what they believe is fair."[36] The Venice Council decreed that custom was to govern, and good conscience was secondary. Courts at Aquilia required consideration of the simple truth as "usage and equity of merchants demanded."[37] "Justice embodied a standard which transcended strict legal rules as it adapted to the dynamics of trade relationships."[38]

The speed of adjudication was likewise important to the early law merchant.[39] Justice was said to be rapid. For example, in some cases it was to be administered in the interim between the arrival and departure of a ship. The statutes of Bresica (1313), the Leges Genuenses (1403–1407), and the statute Calimalae of Florence (1302) instructed judges to adopt summary procedures.[40] Similar instructions were found for early French, German, and English merchant tribunals.[41]

Individuals with merchant experience were chosen as judges.[42] Merchant juries were used by Lord Mansfield in England after 1856.[43] Merchant courts dedicated to specific areas of commerce evolved. The English Court of the Staple was responsible for hearing matters re-

---

34. *See* L. Trakman, THE LAW MERCHANT: THE EVOLUTION OF COMMERCIAL LAW 8 (1983).

35. *Id.* at 28, quoting Swift vs. Tyson, 41 U.S. 1, 18 (1842).

36. *See* L. Trakman, THE LAW MERCHANT: THE EVOLUTION OF COMMERICAL LAW 12 (1983).

37. *Id.*

38. *Id.*

39. *Id.*

40. *Id.* at 13.

41. *Id.* at 14.

42. *Id.* at 15.

43. *Id.* at 28. *See also* Williams, *Book Review*, 97 HARV. L. REV. 1495, 1499 (1984).

garding the importation of certain commodities. It held exclusive jurisdiction over disputes involving tin, leather, and woodfells and was headed by merchant leaders of the community.[44] The mandatory law of the forum was secondary to the customary law of the international regime.[45]

In its original form, the medieval law merchant did not withstand vast changes in economics or politics. As trade expanded, trade conditions changed continuously. Different customs were encountered due to the greater diversity of trading communities.[46] The Great Fairs of Champagne, for example, developed practices different from those elsewhere. Royal ordinances likewise changed merchant practices.[47] Lack of impartiality also became a problem. For example, the merchants of Antwerp refused to submit to the law of London because of discrimination against them.[48] Under English law, a uniform law merchant was undermined by the Carta Mercatoria, which required disputes to be resolved in accordance with the customs of the market town where the contract was made.[49]

The medieval law merchant was transformed to blend with local influences and local rules of procedure.[50] Chief Justice Coke was attributed with limiting the scope of the lex mercatoria in England. He proclaimed that the law merchant was a part of English law, which eventually subjected the law merchant to national legal controls and common law judges.[51] Merchant courts in their various forms were subsequently abolished or assimilated into the common law system.[52] As a result, merchant rules grew less flexible and pleadings more

---

44. *See* L. Trakman, THE LAW MERCHANT: THE EVOLUTION OF COMMERCIAL LAW 16 (1983).
45. *Id.* at 17.
46. *Id.* at 19.
47. *Id.*
48. *Id.* at 20.
49. *Id.* at 21.
50. *Id.* at 24.
51. *Id.* at 26.
52. *Id.*

formal and time-consuming. Custom had to comply with rules of positive law.[53]

1.4 Contents of the Current Lex Mercatoria

The new law merchant is comprised of several elements, including public international law, uniform laws, general principles of law recognized by commercial nations, rules of international organizations, customs and usages, standard form contracts, and reports of arbitral awards.[54] The applicability of a number of these elements has been disputed.

The inclusion of public international law as a source of the law merchant has been criticized both because it does not necessarily reflect the understanding of the international trading community and because public international law generally governs relations among states, not among private parties.[55] Public international law, however, has been applied to contracts between governments and private parties.[56] Provisions of the 1969 Vienna Convention on the Law of Trea-

---

53. *Id.* at 35.

54. *See* Lando, *The Lex Mercatoria in International Commercial Arbitration*, 34 INT'L & COMP. L. Q. 749–51 (1985).

55. *See* Stoecker, *The Lex Mercatoria: To What Extent Does It Really Exist?* 7 J. INT'L ARB. 120 (1990). *See also* McNair, *The General Principles of Law Recognized by Civilized Nations*, 1957 BRIT. Y.B. INT'L L. 1, 6 (1957), stating that "[the lex mercatoria] is not public international law, but shares with public international law a common source of recruitment and inspiration, namely the general principles of law recognized by civilized nations."

56. *See* Lando, *The Lex Mercatoria in International Commercial Arbitration*, 34 INT'L & COMP. L. Q. 749 (1985). *See also* Texaco vs. Libya Arbitration, 4 Y. B. COMM. ARB. 181 (1979), which recognized that, under a new concept, contracts between states and foreign private persons could be "internationalized," in the sense of being subjected to public international law. The arbitrator adopted this concept and held that under certain conditions, "contracts between States and private persons come within the ambit of a particular and new branch of international law: the international law of contracts." Also, in the famous *Aramco* case, *Saudi Arabia vs. Aramco*, 27 INT'L L. REP. 117 (1967),

ties reflect the common practice of legal systems and therefore are suitable for international contracts.[57] Also, the World Bank Convention of 18 March 1965, the Convention on the Settlement of Investment Disputes Between States and Nationals of Other States, which established an International Centre for Settlement of International Disputes, refers to general international law principles.[58] In all these cases, however, it is not public international law as such that is a source of the lex mercatoria. Rather, the lex mercatoria shares with public international law certain common general principles of law or customary clauses. For example, the two share the concepts of pacta sunt servanda, rebus sic stantibus, and the prohibition of undue enrichment.

International uniform laws also have contributed to the international lex mercatoria. These include, for example, the 1966 Convention of the International Sale of Goods, revised in 1980, the 1988 Convention on the Carriage of Goods by Sea, the 1956 Convention on the Contract for the International Carriage of Goods by Road, the 1930 Uniform Law for Bills of Exchange and Promissory Notes, and the 1929 Convention for the Unification of Certain Rules Relating to International Carriage by Air, revised in 1955. International uniform laws, however, are not themselves part of the lex mercatoria. Once approved by the member states, they become part of the respective national

---

the arbitrators decided to apply the international law to the contract. In favor of applying international law to "state contracts," *see, e.g.,* Jennings, *State Contracts in International Law,* 1961 Brit. Y. B. Int'l L. 161 (1961); Weil, *Problèmes relatifs aux contrats passés entre un état et un particulier,* Recueil des Cours de L'Académie de Droit International de la Haye, III, 101 (1969). As to the ICC arbitration practice, in ICC Case No. 3493, SPP Middle East Ltd. vs. Arab Republic of Egypt, 9 Y.B. Comm. Arb. (1984), the arbitrators found that the reference to Egyptian law included in the contract "must be construed as to include such principles of international law as may be applicable and . . . the national laws of Egypt can be relied upon only in as much as they do not contravene said principles."

57. U.N. Doc. A/CONF. 39/27, at 289 (1969), 1155 U.N.T.S. 331.

58. *See generally* Brower, *Jurisdiction Over Foreign Sovereigns: Litigation vs. Arbitration,* 17 Int'l Law. 681 (1983); Delaume, *ICSID Arbitration and the Courts,* 77 Am. J. Int'l L. 784 (1983).

laws. The existence of a uniform international law is evidence of certain international trade usages, to the point that a consensus on them can be reached among states through an international treaty.

General principles of law and international trade usages typically find their way into the lex mercatoria. Arbitrators have been known to make use of the International Encyclopedia of Comparative Law.[59] Rules, recommendations, and codes of conduct emanating from International Organizations are employed also.[60] When related to contracts, these measures may serve to define good faith and fair dealing.[61] Customs and usages, including "INCOTERMS," the Uniform Customs and Practices of Documentary Credits, and force majeure and hardship clauses drafted by the ICC, likewise provide guidance to arbitrators and are included.[62] The international use of standard form contracts and the reporting of arbitral awards are also elements of the international lex mercatoria.[63] Of course, neither standard form contracts nor ICC documents can be considered as a codification of the lex mercatoria, because in the community of merchants there is no codifying authority; rather, such forms and documents constitute evidence of the existence of a certain number of sufficiently consolidated international trade usages.

Inclusion of "general principles of law, rules of international organizations, customs and usage, and standard form contracts have been criticized as having no effect unless commonly accepted by the trading community."[64] Admittedly, trading communities can be diverse. For example, New York banking practices and international banking practices differ with regard to the requirement of a "full set" of bills

---

59. *See* Lando, *The Lex Mercatoria in International Commercial Arbitration*, 34 INT'L & COMP. L. Q. 750 (1985), quoting ICC Award No. 4505/84 (unpublished).

60. *Id.* at 747, 750.

61. *Id.*

62. *Id.*

63. *Id* at 751. *But see* A. Boggiano, INTERNATIONAL STANDARD CONTRACTS: THE PRICE OF FAIRNESS (1991) 13–23 (denying that standard contacts are part of the lex mercatoria).

64. *See* Lando, *The Lex Mercatoria in International Commercial Arbitration*, 34 INT'L & COMP. L. Q. 751 (1985).

of lading in cost, insurance, and freight (c.i.f.) contracts.[65] Likewise, in the context of present national diversities, the trade practices generally used in U.S.-Chinese business may differ from some methods employed in transactions between Brazil and Lebanon.

It has been postulated that diverse trade practices have produced the concept of a "micro" lex mercatoria, which has no point of contact with the "classical" version of the law merchant.[66] We question why it is necessary to make such distinctions. In reality, each transaction may be based on both a "macro" and "micro" set of principles. Among others, U.S.-Chinese contracts and Brazilian-Lebanese transactions would have in common such "internationally recognized" concepts as the primacy of contractual terms, the invalidity of fraud, the requirement of good-faith dealings, the requirement to mitigate losses, and terminology agreed upon by such commonly used references as INCOTERMS.[67] "Micro" lex mercatoria may be determined by an arbitrator to be those practices unique to each national group that, through their repetitive use, should have been known by both parties.

The use of arbitral awards as a basis for formulating a lex mercatoria also has been criticized. The basis for this criticism is the fact that so few awards are actually publicized.[68] In addition, motives for nondisclosure might include the desire of businesses to maintain confidentiality and the protection of trade secrets. In the absence of more publication, decisions by arbitral tribunals will differ even given the same set of facts.[69] The reporting of arbitral awards, however, seems to be growing, and their significance in establishing the contents of the lex mercatoria will be discussed below.[70]

---

65. *See* Williams, *Book Review*, 97 Harv. L. Rev. 1495, 1506 (1984).

66. *See* Mustill, *The New Lex Mercatoria: The First Twenty-Five Years*, 4 Arb. Int'l 93, 94 No. 46 (1988).

67. *Id.*

68. *See* Stoecker, *The Lex Mercatoria: To What Extent Does It Really Exist?* 7 J. Int'l Arb. 121 (1990).

69. *Id.*

70. *See* § 1.6.A *infra*.

1.5 The Lex Mercatoria and Codifications: Relationship to the Vienna Convention and the United States Uniform Commercial Code

It has been postulated that the Vienna Sales Convention does not compete with but complements the lex mercatoria.[71] The Convention provides that parties may choose other legal principles to govern a transaction.[72] It also states that "[t]he parties are considered, unless otherwise agreed, to have impliedly made applicable a usage of which the parties know or ought to have known and which in international trade is widely known to and regularly observed by" parties involved in the particular type of trade.[73] Consequently, international business usages and terms, part of the lex mercatoria, are given great weight in applying the Vienna Convention.

Many other international conventions, especially in the area of arbitration, refer to international trade usages and expressly contemplate that parties to a contract may submit it to rules of law other than a national law.[74] Also, the Uniform Commercial Code (U.C.C.) has

---

71. *See* Audit, *The Vienna Sales Convention and the Lex Mercatoria*, LEX MERCATORIA AND ARBITRATION 139 (T. Carbonneau, Ed. 1990).

72. *See* "United Nations Convention on Contracts for the International Sale of Goods," (1980) Art. 6, 52 Fed. Reg. 6262 (March 2, 1987) [hereinafter U.N. Sales Convention], For a commentary, *see* J. Honnold, UNIFORM LAW FOR INTERNATIONAL SALES UNDER THE 1980 UNITED NATIONS CONVENTION (1982).

73. U.N. Sales Convention, Art. 9 (2).

74. Article VII (1) of the Geneva Convention on International Commercial Arbitration, dated April 21, 1961, requests that arbitrators take trade usages into account in all cases. Some authors have expressed the opinion that such usages should prevail over a conflicting national law. Fouchard, L'ARBITRAGE COMMERCIAL INTERNATIONAL 340 (1965); Benjamin, *The European Convention on International Commercial Arbitration*, 1961 BRIT. Y.B. INT'L L. 478, 492 (1961). Article 42 (1) of the World Bank Convention of 18th March 1965 (Convention on the Settlement of Investment Disputes between States and Nationals of Other States) refers to "rules of law as may be agreed by the parties." It also may be worth mentioning Article 33 (3) of the UNCITRAL arbitration

recognized the law merchant as "supplementing" its provisions. Section 1-103 of the Uniform Commercial Code, entitled "Supplementary General Principles of Law Applicable," specifically includes the law merchant as supplementing its provisions. Supplementation of the U.C.C. is permitted unless a principle is "displaced by the particular provision of the Code itself."[75] Section 1-205 also gives recognition to "course of dealing" and "usage of trade." Express contractual terms, as would be expected, control both course of dealing and usage of trade.

While upholding "usage of trade" would seem to support concepts of the lex mercatoria,[76] Official Comment No. 5 to Section 1-205 contains an important clarification in this regard. The authors state that a usage of trade need be neither "universal" nor "ancient nor immemorial." "[F]ull recognition is thus available for new usages and for usages currently observed by the great majority of descent dealers," regardless of descent. Trade codes likewise may be considered according to this comment.[77] This is contrary to the British outlook expressed in 1873 by Judge Blackburn. In *Crouch v. Credit Foncier of England*, Judge Blackburn held that a custom had to be truly "ancient" in its origins and consistently practiced in order to be admitted into law.[78] It appears that the U.C.C. in this respect is a bit closer to the intent of the medieval law merchant than British law.

The connection between the law merchant and the Uniform Commercial Code is more than supplementary or casual. Official Comment

---

rules, which allows the arbitrators not to apply any national law; Article 13 (4) and (5) of the ICC arbitration rules; as well as the ICC recommendation to the arbitrators to apply "general principles of law and international customary rules and trade usages" when the parties expressed the intention that no national law should be applicable to the contract.

75. U.C.C. § 1-205 (1987).

76. *See* L.Trakman, THE LAW MERCHANT: THE EVOLUTION of COMMERICAL LAW 33 (1983).

77. U.C.C. § 1-205, Official Comment No. 5, reprinted in SELECTED COMMERCIAL STATUTES 49, 50 (West 1989).

78. *See* L. Trakman, THE LAW MERCHANT: THE EVOLUTION of COMMERICAL LAW 147 (1983).

No. 3 to U.C.C. Section 1-105 elaborates extensively on the relationship of the U.C.C. to the law merchant. This discussion arises in the context of applying the U.C.C. to disputes where one state has enacted it and the other has not. The comment appears as follows:

> Thus a conflict of laws decision refusing to apply a purely local statute or rule of law to a particular multi-state transaction may not be valid precedent for refusal to apply the Code in an analogous situation. Application of the Code in such circumstances may be justified by its comprehensiveness, by the policy of uniformity, *and by the fact that it is in large part a reformulation and restatement of the law merchant and of the understanding of a business community which transcends state and even national boundaries.* In particular, where a transaction is governed in large part by the Code, application of another law to some detail of performance because of an accident of geography may violate the commercial understanding of the parties.[79]

It is reasonable to assume that the authors of the U.C.C. looked upon it as an early crystalization of the law merchant, while acknowledging that the lex mercatoria would continue to develop and in doing so "supplement" the Code. Consequently, once uniform laws have been codified and adopted by a state, it is no longer necessary to resort to the lex mercatoria to find a solution. This has led one commentator to correctly observe that uniform laws are part of the lex mercatoria when they have not been adopted by states.[80]

1.6 Further Evidence of the Use of the Law Merchant

A. Arbitral Decisions

In addition to the repeated use of such items as the UCP, evidence of the current status and use of the law merchant in international contracts may be found in two locations: arbitral decisions and the statutes that recognize them. Since most arbitral decisions are not

---

79. U.C.C. § 1-105, Official Comment No. 3, reprinted in SELECTED COMMERCIAL STATUTES 32 (West 1989) (emphasis added).

80. *See* Stoecker, *The Lex Mercatoria: To What Extent Does It Really Exist?* 7 J. INT'L ARB. 120 (1990).

published, their use to formulate law presents certain problems. It is understandable that in the highly competitive modern commercial world it would be detrimental for a business to disclose its transactional failures to its competition. Most awards also remain unpublished due to the fact that parties generally accept the arbitrators' decision and it is usually unnecessary for a party to seek enforcement of an award.[81] However, a number of published decisions provide confirmation for applicability of an international law merchant. It must be observed, in this respect, that according to the existing international arbitration conventions — the New York Convention of June 10, 1958 and the Geneva Convention of April 21, 1961 — the national courts must enforce arbitral awards rendered in accordance with the lex mercatoria. This is because the lex mercatoria cannot exercise any control on the rules applied by the arbitrators to the merit of the dispute.

In *Sapphire International Petroleums Ltd. v. National Iranian Oil Company*,[82] the arbitrator adopted lex mercatoria as the applicable law instead of national law. The arbitrator's decision was based on the inapplicability of state law, which could be altered by the state and is "often unknown or badly known to one of the contracting parties."[83] However, in another case, *Soc. Fougerolle v. Banque de Proche Orient*, where the arbitrators decided the dispute according to principles generally applicable in international commerce, rather than a particular state law, commentators have suggested that the true foundation of the award was difficult to ascertain and may not have been the lex mercatoria.[84] This award was attacked in France, where the attack was rejected by the Cour de Cassation.

In the dispute involving *Pabalk Ticaret v. Ugilor/Norsolor*, the arbitrators directly applied the lex mercatoria instead of choosing between

---

81. *See* Lew, *The Autonomy of International Arbitration, Reality and Fact,* Fin. Times, Feb. 16, 1989, § 1, at 10.

82. 13 Int'l & Comp. L.Q. 1011 (1969). *See* M. Kurkela, Letters of Credit Under International Trade Law: U.C.C., UCP and Law Merchant 14, 331 (1985).

83. *Id.* at 14.

84. Mustill, *The New Lex Mercatoria: The First Twenty-Five Years,* 4 Arb. Int'l 99, No. 46, at 106 (1988).

two national laws.[85] This decision was appealed in both Austria and France. In Austria, the appeal was based on the contention that arbitrators had entered on matters beyond the scope of what they were entrusted with and that the award violated mandatory provisions of law. Austrian courts held that an award resulting from an unauthorized application of equity was not an award outside of the powers of the arbitrators, and that the application of equity did not contradict any Austrian laws. In France, the Cour de Cassation upheld the award. Some authors have pointed out that the decision of the appellate courts was only a recognition of a court's limited power to assail the reasoning of an arbitral tribunal, and not an endorsement of the law merchant.[86]

An agreement involving oil exploration was the subject of a dispute in *Deutsche Schachtbau und Tiefbohrgesellschaft abH and the Government of Ras Al Khaisal*, in which the arbitrators held that internationally accepted principles were simply dicta.[87] However, when enforcement of the award was sought in England, it was appealed. The basis for the appeal was that it was contrary to public policy to enforce a judgment based on uncertain principles. The appeal was denied on the ground that the decision of the arbitrators was governed by Swiss law, the losers did not challenge the award in Switzerland, and they did not contradict the contention that awards based on general principles were acceptable under ICC rules of arbitration.

Another pertinent decision is that of *Sola Tiles, Inc. v. Iran*.[88] In this case, an individual who had business interests in Iran assigned a power of attorney to an individual within Iran. Due to political circumstances, the document was stamped and signed by the Iranian consul in San Francisco. The Iranian government argued that the assignment was invalid. The documents did not fulfill the formal re-

---

85. For a discussion, *see id.*

86. *Id.*

87. *Id. See* a summary of the decision in 14 Y.B. COMM. ARB. 111 (1989).

88. For a discussion, *see* Noecker, *Estoppel: What's the Government's Word Worth? — An Analysis of German Law, Common Law Jurisdictions, and of the Practice of International Arbitral Tribunals*, 24 INT'L LAW. 409, 436 (1990).

quirements of Iranian law, which stipulated that the document be authorized within Iran. The tribunal held that it would be inequitable to deem the assignment invalid due to the fact that it was signed by an official of the Iranian government, and that the government of Iran was responsible for circumstances that prevented the claimant from fulfilling the formal requirements.[89]

In *Mechema Ltd. (England) vs. S.A. Mines, Minéraux et Mtaux (Belgium)*,[90] the arbitrators reached the following decision:

> Having established that the character of the contract and the place where it has its effect, necessarily exclude an obligatory application of either Belgian or English law, it is for the above-mentioned reasons that the arbitrators will abide by the *lex mercatoria* in the exercise of their power as *amiable compositeurs.*

In this case the fact that the arbitrators were allowed to decide as amiable compositeurs, i.e., according to what they considered just and equitable, made it easier for them to disregard the application of a national law.

In ICC Arbitration Case No. 3540, between a French contractor and its Yugoslav subcontractor,[91] the arbitrators decided to apply the lex mercatoria, within certain limits, i.e., they felt it necessary to examine "whether the solution contained in the award, based on the *lex mercatoria* and the application of the maxim *pacta sunt servanda*, leaving aside the international public policy would be fundamentally different from that resulting from national law."

A decision by the Arbitral Tribunal of the Netherlands Oils, Fats and Oilseeds Trade Association, of June 29, 1980 flatly stated that "in cases like this, only the terms and conditions used by the parties and customary in trade are decisive, and these terms have to be interpreted according to the meaning they usually have in the trade circles concerned."[92]

---

89. *Id.*
90. Award of November 3, 1977, published in 7 Y. B. COMM. ARB. 77, 79 (1982).
91. 7 Y.B. COMM. ARB. 124, 129 (1982).
92. 7 Y.B. COMM. ARB. 145 (1981).

In the famous ad hoc arbitration, *B.P. vs. Libya*,[93] the Swedish arbitrator, Judge Gunner Lagergren, made a fine distinction between international law and general principles of law, and decided to apply the latter to the contract in the absence of principles common to the law of Libya and international law.

The arbitrator Dupuy also applied the lex mercatoria in the case *Texaco and Calasiatic vs. Libya*.[94] Many ICC arbitral awards have expressly referred to the lex mercatoria.[95] Even some national courts have occasionally expressly recognized the application of the lex mercatoria to international contracts.[96]

In the light of the thousands of international arbitrations that are held annually,[97] the above discussion involving a small number of cases may seem inconclusive on the application of the lex mercatoria in international arbitrations. It has been contended, however, that only about 25 published cases involved the law merchant.[98] Although there is evidence that some unreported awards also relied upon the lex mercatoria,[99] it is impossible to discover how many awards did so. The Court of Arbitration of the International Chamber of Commerce

---

93. 5 Y.B. Comm. Arb. 143, 150 (1980).

94. 1977 Clunet 363 (1977).

95. *See, e.g.*, ICC Case No. 1641/69, 1974 Clunet 888 (1974); ICC Case No. 1675/69, 1974 Clunet 895 (1974); ICC Case No. 1512/71, 1974 Clunet 905 (1974); ICC Case No. 2375/75, 1976 Clunet 973 (1976); ICC Case No. 1434/75, 1976 Clunet 978, 987 (1976); ICC Cases No. 2745 and 2762/77, 1978 Clunet 999 (1978); ICC Case No. 2879/78, 1979 Clunet 989, 996 (1979).

96. Judgment of February 8, 1982, Corte Cass. (Italy), published in 1982 Rivista di Diritto Internazionale Privato e Processuale 829 (1982) (strongly criticized by Mann, *England Rejects "Delocalized" Contracts and Arbitration*, 33 Int'l & Comp. L.Q., 196 (1984).)

97. *See* Mustill, *The New Lex Mercatoria: The First Twenty-Five Years*, 4 Arb. Int'l 99, No. 46, at 115 (1988).

98. *Id.*

99. *Id.* at 116.

estimates that no more than 10 percent of ICC awards need to be enforced and that for larger cases this percentage is even lower.[100]

Those opposed to the concept of the law merchant often rely on the findings in *Klockner v. Cameroon*, where an award was annulled because the arbitrators "had reached their decision, allegedly based on international law, without having established as a matter of priority the content of the host state's law."[101] Some support also is found in the decision rendered in *Liberian Eastern Timber Corp. v. Republic of Liberia*, where the tribunal held that the ICSID Convention requires that in the absence of any express law chosen by the parties, the law of the contracting state is paramount within its own territory but is subjected to control by international law.[102]

B. State Practice

The problem of enforcing arbitral awards based on international principles instead of on state law is addressed in a number of national statutes. The liberty of the parties and arbitrators to decide their own rules, including use of lex mercatoria, depends on national laws,[103] although international arbitration conventions prevent a review of the merits of the arbitral awards by national courts. The French decree of May 12, 1981 added new provisions on arbitration to the Code of Civil Procedure. These provisions give recognition to French and foreign awards based specifically on the lex mercatoria.[104] In Germany,

---

100. *See* Lew, *The Autonomy of International Arbitration, Reality and Fact*, FIN. TIMES, Feb. 16, 1989, § 1, at 10.

101. For a discussion, *see* Delaume, *Comparative Analysis as a Basis of Law in State Contracts: The Myth of the Lex Mercatoria*, 63 TUL. L.J. 592 (1989).

102. For a discussion, *see id.*

103. *See* Stoecker, *The Lex Mercatoria: To What Extent Does It Really Exist?* 7 J. INT'L ARB. 115 (1990).

104. *See* Lando, *The Lex Mercatoria in International Commercial Arbitration*, 34 INT'L & COMP. L. Q., 757 (1985). *See also* Fouchard, *L'arbitrage international en France après le decret du 12 mai 1981*, 1982 CLUNET 374 (1982). Many French authors see in this new provision (Art. 1497 of the Code of Civil Procedure) a statutory consecration of the lex mercatoria. See also footnote 119 on page 29.

awards may be set aside only if they violate a strong principle of German public policy. It is not sufficient that an award merely violates mandatory provisions of German Law.[105]

Although the English Court of Appeal has rejected the concept of "delocalized arbitration,"[106] the United Kingdom adheres to the Convention on the Settlement of Investment Disputes between States and Nationals of Other States.[107] Parties to a contract are entitled to agree on non-national law such as the lex mercatoria under the terms of this agreement. Under the Arbitration Act of 1979, parties also may agree in writing to exclude the right to bring questions of law before British courts.[108]

The United States Supreme Court has stated that the interpretation of law by arbitrators normally is not subject to review by the courts unless there has been manifest disregard for the law. A manifest disregard has been described as occurring when arbitrators correctly understand and state the law but subsequently disregard it.[109] Lebanese rules were changed in 1983 to emulate the French. These likewise give maximum credence to decisions based on international trade principles such as the lex mercatoria.[110]

Following a challenge to decisions rendered by the Iran/U.S. Claims Tribunal, Dutch law was changed to recognize the validity of international awards that do not "manifestly" exceed the limits of the Dutch legal system. The Iran/U.S. Claims Tribunal was exempted from all other Dutch arbitration laws except the registration of awards with the Hague District Court.[111] In Switzerland, Article 24 of the Swiss Arbi-

---

105. *See* Lando, *The Lex Mercatoria in International Commercial Arbitration*, 34 INT'L & COMP. L. Q., at 757 (1985).

106. *See* Stoecker, *The Lex Mercatoria: To What Extent Does It Really Exist?* 7 J. INT'L ARB. 116 (1990).

107. *See* Lando, *The Lex Mercatoria in International Commercial Arbitration*, 34 INT'L & COMP. L. Q. 758 (1985).

108. *Id.*

109. *Id.*

110. *See* Ziade, *Lebanon: International Arbitration Provisions of the Code of Civil Procedure*, 27 I. L. M. 1022, 1025 (1988).

111. *See* Hermann, *An Arbitrators $1 bn Dream*, FIN. TIMES, Dec. 8, 1983, § II, at 27.

tration Concordat provides that in lieu of agreement by the parties, the arbitral tribunal may decide the rules of procedure.[112]

Canadian arbitration laws were modified in 1985.[113] If the parties do not reach an agreement as to which law will apply, arbitrators are not bound to follow the appropriate national provisions on conflict of laws. They are free to determine the rules they consider best, including the lex mercatoria.[114]

Although there has been much disagreement over the applicability of the lex mercatoria in recent arbitration decisions, it is increasingly obvious that national laws regarding arbitration are being opened to accommodate a wider variety of international concepts. Greater freedom on the part of arbitrators to select laws they deem appropriate is a common feature of many of these new rules. Although it may be argued that some of these statutes do not mention the lex mercatoria by name, it is difficult to dispute the fact that they allow its application and enforcement.

1.7 Conclusion

It is not the purpose of this book to take a position as to the legal nature of the lex mercatoria, but to describe the internationally accepted trade usages in the limited area of contract "pathology" that have acquired a degree of autonomy. In the preceding paragraphs, the emerging notion of the lex mercatoria has been described, primarily with respect to the opinions of scholars and the arbitral decisions making reference to it. Since the lex mercatoria resembles the common law in that it develops over time and by accretion, more forceful argument as to its true legal nature can be made after more enquiries are made as to its actual content.

A few concluding remarks are in order. First, the lex mercatoria in its strict sense can only be customary in nature, i.e., the product of

---

112. *See* Stoecker, *The Lex Mercatoria: To What Extent Does It Really Exist?* 7 J. Int'l Arb. 116 (1990).

113. *See* Noecker, *The New Legislation on Arbitration in Canada*, 22 Int'l Law. 829 (1988).

114. *Id.* at 833.

usages consolidated within a nonstructured community, such as the community of merchants. Similarly, rules of customary international law are the product of another nonstructured community, that of nation-states. The lex mercatoria cannot be statutory or codified because there is no legislating or codifying body in the community of merchants comparable to what happens in the community of states. Once reduced to statutory provisions, the various international trade usages become part of national laws and cease to constitute lex mercatoria.

Since the lex mercatoria is customary in nature, its development is similar to the development of international law, primitive law, and the common law. The concept of the lex mercatoria was developed by civil law scholars, and its harshest critics seem to be scholars from a common law background. This provides an interesting paradox. Civil lawyers, who are used to law being created by authority, by legislation, and in a dramatic way, tend to view the legal nature of the lex mercatoria with favor. Common lawyers, who are accustomed to law being developed by accretion and by the users of law as opposed to students of it, often have rejected the development of the lex mercatoria. It is hard to explain this paradox. Perhaps it is because the relatively amorphous nature of common law *rules* requires that common legal *systems* be more formal as to the way law is made. The relative security in which civil law rules exist may, on the other hand, permit civil lawyers to be more substantive and subjective as to the creation of law. Or perhaps it is merely due to Britain's geography and the relatively unimportant role international trade plays in the U.S. economy.

Second, it cannot be denied that the critics of the lex mercatoria "have landed some powerful blows."[115] Two criticisms are the most general. The first is definitional: the lex mercatoria has been defined in various ways,[116] and none of the definitions is very helpful; for example, if the entire lex mercatoria consists of principles that are

---

115. *See* Mustill, *The New Lex Mercatoria: The First Twenty-Five Years*, 4 ARB. INT'L 99, No. 5, at 100 (1988).

116. *See* Stoecker, *The Lex Mercatoria: To What Extent Does It Really Exist?* 7 J. INT'L ARB. 105, 106 (1990).

common to all (major) legal systems, one logically may inquire as to its utility. Why make reference to a national law when national law contains the same principles? If the lex is "the rules of the game of international trade,"[117] where are these rules collected? If they are not collected and publicized, then how does the lex simplify international business disputes? Also, critics of the lex mercatoria find definitions circular and vague, since they assume the lex is whatever law applies, which could include national law. If the lex is simply international commercial practice, its critics believe it to be least useful when it is most needed, when diverse cultures clash or when commercial practice is in the process of change.

The second general criticism concerns the substance of the lex mercatoria. To the extent that it consists of general principles, found in all or almost all jurisdictions, the lex mercatoria appears to be superfluous. In any case, general principles are rarely determinative of the actual cases. It is the interpretation and application of these principles that assume significance in the resolution of disputes. Since the lex is rarely invoked, and even more rarely is clearly interpreted (and reported), its critics find it difficult to see how it can bring more certainty and fairness (in the sense of realization of reasonable expectations) to international business transactions.

Finally, even the most enthusiastic supporters of the lex mercatoria do not and cannot claim that it can be used to resolve many international business disputes without reference to some other body of law. The principles of the lex mercatoria only cover certain areas of contract law. Other areas, such as contractual capacity, must always be governed by national law. In addition, regulatory and public policy matters such as tax, antitrust, and environmental questions always must be examined under the lex fori. In other words, while the lex mercatoria may eventually be the "better" law for international business contracts, there always will be "otherwise applicable laws,"[118] generally those of the lex fori or lex loci actus. In this respect, it may be observed that the lex may be as useful for what it excludes as for what it includes. Its content is similar to the general principles of all major

---

117. *See id.*, citing Langen.
118. RESTATEMENT (SECOND) OF CONTRACTS § 188 (1971).

legal systems, but it may exclude certain unique exceptions and re-strictions on these principles found in certain national legal systems.[119] Perhaps, in its way, the lex is most significant in adding something of substance — by subtraction — to the law of international business.

---

119. Upholding a lower court enforcement of an arbitral award in which the arbitrator applied the *lex mercatoria* to an international contract which did not contain a choice-of-law provision, the *Cour de Cassation* had held that the *lex mercatoria* is law (*régles de droit*). The arbitrator would have exceeded his mandate had he applied equity or *principia*. Cassation civile 1, October 22, 1991, n1354 PRF, Compañia Valenciana de Cementos Portland S.A. v. Sté. Primary Coal Inc., REVUE DE JURIS-PRUDENCE DU DROIT DES AFFAIRES, 1/92 n. 107. The judgment of the *Cour d'Appel* and a comment by Goldman are found in 1990 CLUNET 430–442 (1990). These judgments are consistent with the relatively secure position both the lex mercatoria and the concept of the "international contract" enjoy in French law.

II. BREACH OF CONTRACT AND REMEDIES IN INTERNATIONAL TRADE PRACTICE

Chapter 2. Breach of Contract and Entitlement to Damages

2.1 General

The main pathological aspect of international business contracts is the breach of one of the parties' obligations.[1] With respect to monetary obligations, breach consists of a failure or delay in making the payments due. With respect to non-monetary obligations, breach is non-performance, delayed or interrupted performance, or performance differing from that contractually agreed.

The general principles governing liability for breach of international business contracts are derived from similar principles in municipal legal systems, principally those of the United States and the major Western European trading countries. Their modification by international trade practice, however, has produced some of the new lex mercatoria in the area. This chapter will discuss the main difference between the common law and civil concepts of breach — the requirement of fault — and will examine how each system introduces flexibility. The fault requirement in the lex mercatoria and international trade practice will be examined.

A fundamental distinction between the common law and civil law concepts of breach of contract, and consequent entitlement to damages, is the requirement of fault of the party committing a breach in the civil law, and its absence in the common law.[2] The fault distinction is a result of different conceptions of the contractual relationship, since English common law was developed by merchants, and continental civil law was developed by priests. The aphorism reflects the importance of the concept that the common law was developed as a

---

1. "Breach" is a common law term, and it contains some common law connotations. It is, however, "more flexible" than "non-performance." *See* 2 K. Zweigert & H. Kötz, AN INTRODUCTION TO COMPARATIVE LAW 179 (2d ed. 1987). It is regularly used by comparativists writing in English; and it is not used here in its more restrictive common law sense, but rather to connote both civil law and common law unexcused non-performance.

2. "'Fault' in law generally means either willful wrongdoing or negligence, i.e., a failure to take reasonable care." P. Atiyah, AN INTRODUCTION TO THE LAW OF CONTRACT 184 (3d ed. 1981).

historical process to solve practical problems.[3] The great codes of continental Europe, on the other hand, were written by scholars and are reflections of the philosophical and moral precepts of the time they were written.[4] Thus, the civil law frequently is described as being more moral and philosophical than the common law.[5] In the civil law concept of contract, a party promises to do or not to do something and if the party fails to keep the promise, the party can be forced by a court to "conform to his promise."[6] Liability only attaches to a party who can be blamed for behaving otherwise than as agreed in a contract. Fault is thus essential to the civil lawyer for the availability of contractual remedies.[7]

Fault plays a very different role in the common law conception of contract. In common law countries, contract liability has a more objective nature, and no assessment of a degree of fault is needed to ascertain the existence of a breach of contract. Thus, in principle, the requirement that a contract be performed in accordance with its terms is absolute, and the absence of fault is not a defense to an action for

---

3. "More than any other legal system now in force, English law demands a study of its historical origins. . . . Some legal systems are more consciously tied to their past than others . . . and none more than England." 2 K. Zweigert & H. Kötz, AN INTRODUCTION TO COMPARATIVE LAW 188 (2d ed. 1987).

4. "[T]he Code civil is founded on the creed of the Enlightenment and the law of reason that social life can be put into a rational order if only the rules of law are restructured according to a comprehensive plan." *Id.* at 88.

5 "French contract law is both more 'moral' and more dogmatic; English contract law is both more 'economic' and more pragmatic." CONTRACT LAW TODAY: ANGLO-FRENCH COMPARISONS 386 (D. Harris & D. Tallon, eds. 1989).

6. *Id.* at 174.

7. See Nicholas, *Introduction to the French Law of Contract* in CONTRACT LAW TODAY: ANGLO-FRENCH COMPARISONS 18 (D. Harris & D. Tallon, eds. 1989); A. Von Mehren & J. Gordley, THE CIVIL LAW SYSTEM 1106 (2d ed. 1977). Article 276 of the German Bürgerliches Gesetzbuch (BGB) states simply that "A debtor is responsible, unless otherwise provided, for wilful default and negligence." See N. Horn, H. Kötz, and T. Leser, GERMAN PRIVATE AND COMMERCIAL LAW 112–114 (1982). The concept of fault is normally part of a discussion of the availability of remedies in

breach of contract.[8] Common law systems thus treat all contract obligations as guarantee obligations, i.e., guarantees of a given result, failing which a contract is breached.[9]

To the extent that fault is relevant to the breach of common law contractual obligations at all, it is relevant substantively, and not only with respect to remedies. The very notion of contract in the common law is tied not to performance but to remedies for the failure of performance.[10] The ultimate common law statement in this respect was made by Justice Holmes, who described the promises made by contracting parties as risks undertaken, denying the existence of any duty to perform a contract. For Holmes, every bilateral contract gives each party the option of performance or the payment of damages in lieu of performance.[11]

---

the civil law. G. Treitel, REMEDIES FOR BREACH OF CONTRACT: A COMPARATIVE ACCOUNT 8 (1988).

8. "In relation to a claim for damages for breach of contract, it is, in general, immaterial why the defendant failed to fulfill his obligations and certainly no defense to plead that he had done his best." Raineri v. Miles, [19810 A. C. 1050, 1086]. "Failure or refusal to perform a contractual promise when performance has fallen due is *prima facie* a breach." G. Treitel, THE LAW OF CONTRACT (7th ed. 1987); "Any failure to perform a contractual duty which has become absolute constitutes a breach." CORBIN ON CONTRACTS § 12-1 (2d ed. 1963); "When performance of a duty under a contract is due, any non-performance is a breach." RESTATEMENT (SECOND) OF CONTRACTS § 260(2) (1981); "The (party) who fails in any respect to perform when performance is due has not only failed to earn a discharge but has also become liable for breach of contract. This is true even if the defect is insubstantial, even if it is neither willful nor negligent, and even if the (party) is unaware of it." FARNSWORTH ON CONTRACTS § 8.8 (1990).

9. 2 K. Zweigert & H. Kötz, AN INTRODUCTION TO COMPARATIVE LAW 193 (2d ed. 1987).

10. "A contract is a promise or set of promises for the breach of which the law gives a remedy. . . ." RESTATEMENT (SECOND) OF CONTRACTS § 1 (1981). Linzer, *On the Amorality of Contract Remedies — Efficiency, Equity, and the Second Restatement*, 81 COLUM. L. REV. 111 (1981).

11. O. Holmes, THE COMMON LAW, Lecture VIII (1881). "The duty to keep a contract at common law means a prediction that you must pay damages if you do not keep it, — and nothing else. If you commit a tort,

In actuality, however, the inflexible general fault concepts of both the common law and the civil law countries have never been as absolute as they are stated in principle, and have been much ameliorated theoretically and practically.[12] In the common law countries, the absolute nature of contract performance has been softened by the use of implied terms, reliance theories, and, in the United States, by imposition of liability in tort for deliberate breach of contract. In civil law countries, strict liability is introduced by the concepts of obligations of guarantee (in French: *obligations de garantie*),[13] and more importantly for international agreements, the distinction between contracts that emphasize the manner of performance (in French: *obligations de moyens*),[14] and contracts that specify a given result (in French: *obligations de résultat*). Both systems excuse performance for the events of impossibility, changed circumstances, and mistakes. These different

---

you are liable to pay a compensatory sum. If you commit a contract, you are liable to pay a compensatory sum unless the promised event comes to pass, and that is all the difference. But such a mode of looking at the matter stinks in the nostrils of those who think it advantageous to get as much ethics into the law as they can." Holmes, *The Path of the Law*, 10 HARV. L. REV. 457, 462 (1897). Holmes's extreme positivism has been the subject of frequent attack and "has never been universally accepted." Linzer, *On the Amorality of Contract Remedies — Efficiency, Equity, and the Second Restatement*, 81 COLUM. L. REV. 111 (1981). *See, e.g.,* P. Atiyah, ESSAYS ON CONTRACT, 57–72 (1986); H. Hart, THE CONCEPT OF LAW 39 (1961).

12. CONTRACT LAW TODAY: ANGLO-FRENCH COMPARISONS 18 (D. Harris & D. Tallon, eds. 1989); " . . . the practical differences between the two types of systems are much less significant than their apparently conflicting theories might suggest." G Treitel, REMEDIES FOR BREACH OF CONTRACT 7 (1988); " . . . the gradual weakening of the principle of fault has brought German law closer to other legal systems, which do not require fault but allow a possibility of exculpation." N. Horn, H. Kötz, & H. Leser, GERMAN PRIVATE AND COMMERCIAL LAW 114 (1982).

13. CONTRACT LAW TODAY: ANGLO-FRENCH COMPARISONS 18 (D. Harris & D. Tallon, eds. 1989).

14. Farnsworth translates *obligation de moyens* as "obligation to appropriate means." Farnsworth, *On Trying to Keep One's Promises: The Duty of Best Efforts in Contract Law*, 46 U. PITT. L. REV. 4 (1984).

types of contracts or obligations result in different allocations of the burden of establishing entitlement to damages.

2.2 The Common Law Concepts Regarding Entitlement to Damages

There have always been exceptions to the strict liability approach of the common law toward contract performance, and there are a number of ways the concept of obligations having a less rigorous and more tenuous content is introduced. The most important inclusion of fault in contract performance is perhaps the inclusion of judicially implied terms.[15] Implied terms that introduce an element of fault to determine liability include implied covenants of good faith,[16] implied obligations of cooperation,[17] and implied covenants against prevention of performance.[18] The English doctrine of fundamental breach, "now abandoned,"[19] introduced an element of fault with respect to the enforcement of exemption clauses.[20] The choice of remedy frequently

---

15. " . . . where English law resorts to the device of the implied term, French law is likely to have recourse to a rule." CONTRACT LAW TODAY: ANGLO-FRENCH COMPARISONS 18 (D. Harris & D. Tallon, eds. 1989).

16. "Every contract imposes on each party a duty of good faith and fair dealing in its performance and enforcement." RESTATEMENT (SECOND) OF CONTRACTS § 231 (1981). *See* FARNSWORTH ON CONTRACTS §§ 7.17–7.17b. In Mallozzi v. Carapelli, [1975] 1 LLOYD'S REP. 229, an English court found that a contract for the sale of grain that provided that its parties were to agree a port of discharge while the ship was en route required the parties to at least negotiate in good faith to agree the port. "Implied contractual obligations may coexist with express provisions which seemingly negate them where common expectations or the relationship of the parties as structured by the contract so dictate." Wakefield v. Northern Telecom, Inc., 769 F.2d 109 (1985).

17. CHITTY ON CONTRACTS § 849 (26th ed. 1989).

18. *Id.* § 850.

19. CONTRACT LAW TODAY: ANGLO-FRENCH COMPARISONS 389 (D. Harris & D. Tallon, eds. 1989). *See* Photo Production Ltd. v. Securicor Transport Ltd., [1980] A. C. 827.

20. CHITTY ON CONTRACTS § 883 et seq. (26th ed. 1989).

contains a fault element.[21] Much has been written on the merger or blurring of the line between contract and tort.[22] Conceptually, the introduction of tort concepts into contract law by, for example, allowing punitive damages for breach of contract, introduces an element of the fault concept.[23]

The closest equivalent to the civil law distinction of *obligations de résultat* and *obligations de moyens*, however, are those obligations where an obligee undertakes only to do what is "reasonable," or to exercise "due diligence," or to apply "best efforts."[24] The term "best efforts" is an American one. Such obligations are called "best endeavours" in England.[25]

Best-efforts obligations normally arise by the express agreement of parties to a contract[26] or, occasionally, a precontractual document such

---

21. Fault plays a role in reliance theories of recovery and in the duty to mitigate damages. *See* § 3.2 *infra.*

22. Atiyah describes the idea of the merger of contract and tort as having become "pretty trite," noting that it is "increasingly evident in the case law of modern times. . . ." P. Atiyah, Essays on Contract 8 (1986). In the civil law, of course, contract and tort both are included in the law of obligation. Sometimes it is not evident from court decisions under which theory a judgment is rendered. Contract Law Today: Anglo-French Comparisons 17 (D. Harris & D. Tallon, eds. 1989).

23. G. Treitel, Remedies for Breach of Contract: A Comparative Account 78–79 (1988). Treitel describes the common law concept of the unavailability of punitive damages for breach of contract as having been "considerably eroded."

24. "Our common law counterpart of the French obligation to appropriate means is, of course, the duty of best efforts." Farnsworth, *On Trying to Keep One's Promises: The Duty of Best Efforts in Contract Law*, 46 U. Pitt. L. Rev. 4 (1984).

25. *See generally* Yarcoe-Cocks, *Best Endeavours*, 1986 Law Soc. Gaz. 1992 (1986).

26. Farnsworth, *On Trying to Keep One's Promises: the Duty of Best Efforts in Contract Law*, 46 U. Pitt. L. Rev. 1, 4 (1984).

as a letter of intent.[27] Sometimes, however, best-efforts obligations more closely resemble French *obligations de moyens* in that they are implied by courts irrespective of the language of a written agreement.[28] The resemblance to the civil law *obligation de moyens* is clearest in situations involving professionals where courts impose a best-efforts standard to reduce a standard of performance expressed in a contract.[29] The imposition of best-efforts obligations to impose a standard not expressly agreed in a contract occurs most frequently in cases involving distribution agreements, franchise agreements, and other exclusive dealing contracts,[30] and percentage leases.[31]

Although there has been much common law judicial discussion of the good-faith standard, there has been little treatment of the best-efforts standard.[32] Judicial pronouncements with respect to best-efforts obligations often treat them as imposing the same duties as good-faith

---

27. Thompson v. Liquichemica of America Inc., 481 F. Supp. 365 (S.D.N.Y. 1979).

28. Zilg v. Prentice-Hall, 717 F.2d 671 (2d Cir. 1983). *See generally* FARNSWORTH ON CONTRACTS § 7.17 (1990).

29. *Id.* and cases cited. In English law, contracts for the services of professionals impose "duties of care." G. Treitel, THE LAW OF CONTRACTS 644 (7th ed. 1987) and cases cited. At least one English case has drawn the same distinction between a contract of sale and a contract for services as is drawn in German law. Young & Marten Ltd., v. McManus Childs Ltd., [1969] 1 A. C. 454.

30. *See* Wood v. Lucy, Lady Duff-Gordon, 222 N.Y. 88, 118 N.E. 214 (1917).

31. FARNSWORTH ON CONTRACTS § 7.17 (1990). *See* Stoddard v. Illinois Improvement & Ballast Co., 275 Ill. 199, 113 N.E. 913 (1916); Seggebruch v. Stosor, 309 Ill. App. 385, 33 N.E.2d 159 (1941).

32. "I ask myself, could anything be less specific or more uncertain? There is absolutely no criterion by which best endeavours and practicability are to be judged." Bower v. Bantam Invs. Ltd., [1972] 3 All E.R. 349, 355. "No coherent analysis of best efforts obligations has been undertaken." Goetz & Scott, *Principles of Relational Contracts*, 67 VA. L. REV. 1089, 1111 (1981).

obligations.[33] Indeed, they sometimes confuse the two concepts altogether.[34]

Best-efforts obligations differ from those of good faith with respect to the degree of effort undertaken by a party. An obligation to use best efforts requires that parties be diligent in pursuit of a result.[35] The best-efforts standard is thus more exacting than the good-faith standard.[36] It appears to have a Golden Rule aspect; a party's best efforts are those the party would undertake on the party's own behalf unless the efforts relate to professional skills not possessed by the other party, in which case best efforts are those that a prudent person

---

33. The court in Channel Home Centers v. Grossman, 795 F.2d 291 (3d Cir. 1986), cited Thompson v. Liquichemica, Inc., 481 F. Supp. 361 (S.D.N.Y. 1979), as standing for the proposition that parties may agree to negotiate in good faith even though the case itself concerned a best-efforts clause.

34. Farnsworth, *On Trying to Keep One's Promises: The Duty of Best Efforts in Contract Law*, 46 U. PITT. L. REV. 1, 8 (1984).

35. *Id.* FARNSWORTH ON CONTRACTS § 7.17; "We think the 'best endeavors' means what the words say; they do not mean second-best efforts endeavors." Sheffield Dist. Ry. Co. v. Great Central Ry. Co., 27 T.L.R. 451 (1911); "Perhaps the words 'best endeavors' in a statute or contract mean something different from doing all that can reasonably be expected — although I cannot think what the difference might be." Overseas Buyers Ltd. v. Grandadex S.A., [1980] 2 Lloyd's Rep 608; "I can feel no doubt that, in the absence of any context indicating to the contrary, this should be understood to mean that the purchaser is to do 'all he reasonably can' to ensure that the planning permission is granted. If it were refused by the local Planning Authority, and if an appeal to the Secretary of State would have a reasonable chance of success, it could not, in my opinion, be said that he had 'used his best endeavors' to obtain the planning permission if he failed to appeal." IBM United Kingdom Ltd. v. Rockware Glass Ltd., [1980] F.S.R. 335; "Best endeavors are something less than efforts which go beyond the bounds of reason, but are considerably more than casual and intermittent activities." Pips (Leisure Production) Ltd. v. Walton, [1980] 43 P.C.R. 415.

36. " . . . it is clear that the duty of best efforts is more onerous than that of good faith." FARNSWORTH ON CONTRACTS § 7.17. *But see* Triple-A Baseball Club Assocs. v. Northeastern Baseball, 832 F.2d 214 (1st Cir. 1987).

in the same situation would use.[37] In *Bloor v. Falstaff Brewing Corp.*,[38] for example, a case involving an express agreement to use "best efforts to promote a high volume of sales"[39] of a brand of beer, the court had no difficulty in finding that a blatant policy of promoting a competing brand at the expense of the "best-efforts" brand did not meet the standard imposed by the best-efforts duty.[40] In *Grossman v. Lowell*,[41] a party to a contract for the purchase of real estate that contained a financing contingency and an obligation of the purchaser to use "best efforts" to obtain a mortgage within 60 days, was found to have failed to fulfill the best-efforts duty by making but three telephone calls and one mortgage application.

2.3 The Civil Law Concepts Regarding Entitlement to Damages

The distinction between *obligations de moyens and obligations de résultat* in civil law countries is conceptually more important than the relatively rarely applied best-efforts duty in common law countries.[42] For civil lawyers, the distinction provides a basis of analysis of contractual obligations and a method to allocate the burden of proof.

---

37. 2 FARNSWORTH ON CONTRACTS § 7.17b (1990); Farnsworth, *On Trying to Keep One's Promises: The Duty of Best Efforts in Contract Law*, 46 U. PITT. L. REV. 1, 9 (1984).

38. 601 F.2d 609 (2d Cir. 1979).

39. 601 F.2d 609, 610.

40. "[The agreement] did not require Falstaff to spend itself into bankruptcy to promote the sale of Ballentine products, it did prevent the application to them of [the defendant's] philosophy of emphasizing profit uber (sic) alles without fair consideration of the effect on Ballentines's volume." 601 F.2d 609, 614. *Bloor* involved an egregious instance of ignoring the duty of best efforts. "Unfortunately, a best efforts obligation . . . inherently implies a serious monitoring problem." Goetz & Scott, *Principles of Relational Contracts*, 67 VA. L. REV. 1089, 1115 (1981).

41. 703 F. Supp. 282 (S.D.N.Y. 1989).

42. In French law, the *obligation de moyens* sometimes is called the *obligation de prudence et diligence*. The *obligation de résultat* sometimes is called the *obligation determinée*.

Although the distinction originated in France, and is particularly well established French law,[43] it is present in the law of Italy,[44] Holland,[45] Belgium,[46] and Germany[47] as well. A similar concept seems to exist in Islamic Law.[48]

In its essence, the distinction serves to provide a simple formula for the allocation of the burden of proof to establish entitlement to damages in case of breach of contract. With respect to an *obligation de moyens*, a performing party must undertake a certain course of action according to standards of diligence. An *obligation de moyens*, however, does not oblige a performing party to guarantee that its course of action ultimately will achieve a given result.

The classification of obligations as those of *moyens* or *résultat* is a question of law. Scholars and courts in civil law countries frequently classify as *obligations de moyens* the Roman law obligations of *facere*,

---

43. The distinction was illustrated for the first time in France by Demogue, TRAITÉ DES OBLIGATIONS EN GENERAL 1237 (1927), and then adopted by the French Cassation Court (e.g., judgments of the Cour de Cassation of June 27, 1939 and May 27, 1940, 1941 Recueil Dalloz 53 (1941)) as well as many other French scholars such as, Thomas, *La distinction des obligations de moyens et des obligations de résultat*, 1937 REVUE CRITIQUE DE LEGISLATION ET DE JURISPRUDENCE 636 (1937); Frossard, LA DISTINCTION DES OBLIGATIONS DE MOYENS ET DES OBLIGATIONS DE RÉSULTAT (1965); Viney, TRAITÉ DE DROIT CIVIL, VOL. IV — LES OBLIGATIONS, LA RESPONSIBILITÉ, CONDITIONS 626–665 (1980).

44. *See* the in-depth analysis by Mengoni, *Obbligazioni di risultato e obbligazioni di mezzi*, 1954 RIVISTA DI DIRITTO COMMERCIALE 185–209, 280–320, 365–396 (1954).

45. *See* 1 Hartkamp, VERBINDENISSENRECHT 184 (1988).

46. *See* De Page, TRAITÉ ELEMENTAIRE DE DROIT CIVIL BELGE 198 (1975).

47. In German law, the distinction between *obligations de moyens* and *obligations de résultat* does not exist in general terms. A concept that is very close is that of the *Dienstvertrag* (BGB §§ 611–630), pursuant to which only an activity is required, as opposed to the *Werkvertrag* (BGB §§ 631–651) and the *Kaufvertrag*, pursuant to which a result is required. Witt & Bopp, *Best Efforts, Reasonable Care: considerations de droit allemand*, 1988 INT'L BUS. L. J. 1035 (1988).

48. Saleh, *Remedies for Breach of Contract under Islamic and Arab Laws*, 4 ARAB L. Q. 269 (1989).

i.e., obligations imposing a duty to do something, and classify as *obligations de résultat* the Roman law obligations of *dare*, i.e., obligations imposing a duty to give something. *Obligations de moyens* are breached by faulty performance. A party commits a breach by not applying the necessary degree of care and diligence in discharging the party's obligation. A breach is not committed if, in spite of having applied diligent efforts, the expected result does not materialize due to external obstacles beyond the reasonable control of an obligee.

Like the common law best-efforts duty,[49] *obligations de moyens* often are identified as the obligations of individual practitioners of professions, such as doctors, lawyers, and teachers. Such *obligations de moyens* are discharged by, respectively, adopting the most appropriate diagnostic tools, applying the most effective advocacy of the interests of the client, and using the most advanced teaching standards. Professionals are not liable for lack of improvement of the health of a patient, a judgment against a client, or the academic failure of a student.

In almost all civil law countries, the required standard of diligence, as to the *obligations de moyens*, varies depending on whether or not the obligee is expected to be a professional with respect to the obligation undertaken. In the first case, the standard is to perform in accordance with the state of the art. In other cases it is to discharge obligations according to normal standards of diligence, i.e., the standard of the *diligens paterfamilias* without any particularly specialized expertise.[50]

In *obligations de résultat*, on the other hand, the end result a creditor wants to achieve constitutes the content of the obligation. A debtor commits itself to produce a result as such, and the mere failure of achieving it constitutes a breach of the obligation, entitling the creditor to reimbursement of damages, irrespective of the degree of dili-

---

49. FARNSWORTH ON CONTRACTS §7.17 (1990).

50. The diligens pater familias or *bon père de famille* is the equivalent of the common law "reasonable man." References to the "diligens pater familias", or *bon père de famille* appear in many provisions of the code Napoléon, notably in Article 1137 (in connection with the obligations of the custodian). This provision has provided the base for the elaboration of the notion of *obligations de moyens* in civil law countries. *See generally* B. Nicholas, FRENCH LAW OF CONTRACT 49 (1982).

gence applied by the debtor. Payment obligations are typical examples of *obligations de résultat*.

In most municipal laws, the only limitation to the liability for breach of an *obligation de résultat* is force majeure, an extraordinary and non-foreseeable event beyond the control of the obligee that determines the objective impossibility of discharging an obligation.[51]

The main practical consequence of the distinction between *obligations de moyens* and *obligations de résultat* is the allocation of the burden of proof of breach of contract.[52] The creditor of an *obligations de moyens* must prove that a debtor has not applied diligence. The mere absence of an expected result is sufficient to entitle the creditor of an *obligation de résultat* to damages. The debtor must prove the existence of a force majeure condition.

The classification of obligations would seem to a common lawyer to be a question of fact, but this is not so. In French law, it is a question of law over which the cour de cassation exercises control.[53] The classification of a particular obligation depends on the nature of a contract, and seems to deal with party expectation. If an obligation reasonably can be expected to be performed in similar situations, it is an *obligation de résultat*.[54] The distinction is "far from precise," and the jurisprudence "offers no clear principle."[55] Though sometimes criticized because it is not expressly contemplated as such in any statutory provision, the distinction between *obligations de résultat* and *obligations de moyens* can be considered as established in most civil law systems.[56]

---

51. *See, e.g.*, Art. 1148 of the French Code Civil. The Italian and German civil codes do not expressly mention force majeure, but include corresponding concepts, such as the impossibility of performing due to causes outside the control of the obligee (e.g., Arts. 1218 and 1256 of the Italian Codice Civile).

52. G. Treitel, REMEDIES FOR BREACH OF CONTRACT: A COMPARATIVE ACCOUNT 10 (1988).

53. B. Nicholas, FRENCH LAW OF CONTRACT 52 (1982).

54. *Id.*

55. *Id.*

56. In public international law, the distinction has a different meaning. *Obligations de résultat* are those that impose on a state the duty to achieve

2.4 The Practice of International Business Contracts

The civil law approach to the necessity of fault is more articulated than that of the common law, and it provides a useful framework for the consideration of the breach of international contracts. The distinction between *obligations de moyens* and *obligations de résultat* is widely accepted and understood by the drafters and interpreters of international contracts, although its practical application is slightly different in an international setting than in a purely domestic one.

As in domestic contracts governed by a civil law system, when an *obligation de moyens* deriving from an international contract is breached, the damaged party, in order to establish its entitlement to damages, must prove that the breach is the fault of the obligee. In other words, the existence of a cause-to-effect relationship between the behavior of the obligee and the breach of the obligation is a prerequisite for the further identification of the amount of the actual damages to which the other party is entitled. For *obligations de résultat*, on the other hand, the mere lack of the promised result determines the obligee's liability in the presence of an actual damage suffered by the other party. No investigation as to whether the breach of the obligation is attributable to the fault of the obligee is necessary to establish entitlement to damages.

Typical *obligations de résultat* in international trade practice are those that characterize the main performance of the contractor in international construction contracts. Such obligations generally are discharged through the achievement of a given result, the completion of the works. The "turn-key contract,"[57] often used in international con-

---

a given result, leaving it free to adopt the internal measures it deems fit, while *obligations de moyens* are those compelling a state to a given course of action without leaving any discretion to it as to how such an obligation should be discharged. *See* Combacau, *Obligations de résultat et obligations de comportement: Quelques questions et pas de response*, MELANGES OFFERTS A PAUL REUTER — LE DROIT INTERNATIONAL: UNITÉ ET DIVERSITÉ 181 (1981).

57. The term "turn-key contract" is translated as *contrat clef en mains* in French, *contratto chiavi in mano* in Italian, and *Vertrag zur schlüsselfertigen Übergabe* in German.

struction projects, demonstrates the recognition of the *obligation de résultat* concept. In a turn-key contract, a contractor discharges its obligation by delivering a facility ready to operate, even a manufacturing facility capable of producing an agreed level of production (in French: *contrats "produits-en-main"*).[58]

Many obligations of members of a consortium or a joint-venture, constituted among co-contractors to perform an international construction contract, are *obligations de résultat*, to the extent they are instrumental in the discharge of the obligations undertaken toward the final customer, or "owner."[59]

Similarly, the duties under a de-localized international sales contract are *obligations de résultat*. In international contracts of sale, breach of an obligation is established without the need for investigating the degree of diligence or the fault of an obligee. This conclusion can be derived from Article 25 of the Vienna Convention on the International Sale of Goods.[60] The concept of "fundamental breach" in the

---

58. Brabant, Le Contrat International de Construction 197 (1981). "l'entrepreneur assumera une *obligation de résultat* par example, si les specifications techniques fixent des performances a attendre ou des normes de qualité. To comply with certain standards of quality" ("the contractor will undertake an *obligation de résultat*, for example, if the technical specifications establish certain standards of quality to be met"); Stokes, International Construction Contracts 84 (1978).

59. Dubisson, Les Groupements D'Enterprises pour les Marchés Internationaux 43 (1985); Baptista & D. Barthez, Les Associations D'Enterprises (Joint Ventures) dans le Commerce International 49 (1989).

60. "Convention relating to a Uniform Law on the International Sale of Goods," July 1, 1964, 834 U.N.T.S. 107, Art. 25. [hereinafter Vienna Convention]. "The [Uniform Law on the International Sale of Goods and the Vienna Convention] more closely resemble common law than civil law systems." G. Treitel, Remedies for Breach of Contract 23 (1988). The Vienna Convention does not mention fault, does not distinguish between guarantee and other obligations, and does not deal with *obligations de moyens*. *Id.* Article 25 of the Vienna Convention is as follows: "A breach of contract committed by one of the parties is fundamental if it results in such detriment to the other party as substantially to deprive him of what he is entitled to expect under the contract, unless the party in breach did not foresee and a reasonable person of the same kind in

Vienna Convention is broader than that of common law countries, and seems to mean unexcused failure of performance. It is independent of the fault of an obligee. Although the reference to the foreseeability of the resulting damage to the non-breaching party mitigates the requirement of "fundamental breach" standard, it still can be maintained that the Vienna Convention considers the obligations of the seller as *obligations de résultat* because foreseeability of damage is not related to fault so much as reasonability.

Under Article 25, a breach is fundamental if it substantially deprives a party of that which the party is entitled to expect under the contract, unless the party in breach could not have foreseen such a result. This definition originally was proposed as Article 23 of the Convention. In the official commentary on the Draft Convention,[61] where the breach is fundamental, the breaching party must prove that "he had no reason to foresee" that damage resulting from the breach. It is important to note that in Official Comment to proposed Article 23 (now Article 25), the time at which a party in breach should have foreseen the consequences of a breach is not specified and the decision on which time to apply foreseeability is "left to the tribunal." However in the section regarding damages, Article 74, foreseeability of consequential damages is fixed at the time of the conclusion of the contract, defined in Article 23 as when acceptance becomes effective. The definition of fundamental breach in Article 25 appears to employ the "relational" concept of contract, allowing for changes in expectations that would not be foreseeable until well after the offer has been accepted. The damages section, however, fixes foreseeable damages

---

the same circumstances would not have foreseen such a result." For commentary on this provision, *see* Bianca & Bonell, COMMENTARY ON THE INTERNATIONAL SALES LAW — THE 1980 VIENNA SALES CONVENTION 205 (1987); J. Honnold, UNIFORM LAW FOR INTERNATIONAL SALES (1982). For analysis of other aspects of the Vienna Convention, *see* Blodgett, *The U.N. Convention on the Sale of Goods and the "Battle of the Forms"* 18 COLO. LAW. 421 (1989) and Murray, *An Essay on the Formation of Contracts and Related Matters Under the United Nations Convention on Contracts for the International Sale of Goods*, 8 J. L. & COMM. 11 (1988).

61. Commentary on the Draft Convention on Contracts for the International Sale of Goods, Prepared by the Secretariat, U. N. Doc. A/CONF. 97/5, 14 March 1979, Art. 23, Commentary No. 4.

at the time of effective acceptance. When taken together, these two clauses indicate that the full consequences of a fundamental breach "known as the foreseeable" to the breaching party sometime after conclusion of the contract may not be recoverable as damages by the non-breaching party.

The drafters of the Uniform Commercial Code likewise rejected the "tacit agreement" test for the recovery of consequential damages as explicitly stated in Official Comment No. 2 to Section 2-715, and hold the defendant liable for "any loss resulting from general or particular requirements and needs for which the seller *at the time of contracting* had reason to know."[62]

Article 25 of the Vienna Convention is said to make it possible to deal with "situations in which a trivial deviation from the contract produces surprisingly serious consequences."[63] Professor Honnold interprets Article 25 as stating that a "minor deviation [such as a one day delay] might not constitute a fundamental breach if the buyer's special need for prompt shipment arose only after the seller dispatched the goods,"[64] and notes that the Convention's departure from the test of foreseeability at the time of the making of the contract has been extensively criticized.[65]

The inverse of this scenario is interesting to ponder. May one of the parties avoid, cancel, or terminate a contract for a minor breach under the Vienna Convention? The Convention appears to go further than the U.C.C. in restricting the right to "avoid" the contract for a minor breach.[66] Where the problem is one of "delaying" performance, however, the Convention contains a notice requirement or *Nachfrist* (as adopted from German law). After the waiting party has notified the delaying party that performance must be made within a specified reasonable period, and the delaying party has not performed, the no-

---

62. U.C.C. § 2-715 (2).

63. See J. Honnold, Uniform Law for International Sales Under The 1980 United Nations Convention 212 (1987).

64. *Id.* at 213.

65. *Id.* n.3.

66. *See* Honnold, *The New Uniform Law for International Sales and the UCC: A Comparison*, 18 Int'l Lawyer 21, 27 (1984), quoting CISG Arts. 25, 49, and 64.

tifying party may avoid the contract without regard to the materiality of the breach.[67]

Some of the cases decided by the Arbitration Court of the International Chamber of Commerce of Paris provide additional support in determining when an obligation deriving from an international contract is an *obligation de moyens* or an *obligation de résultat*. For example, in a 1984 case,[68] the International Chamber of Commerce Court of Arbitration established that a buyer's obligation to issue a letter of credit in favor of a seller is an *obligation de résultat*.

The areas where *obligations de résultat* can be found in international trade practice are sufficiently wide that it can be posited that unless an obligation is clearly characterized by the way it is worded as an *obligation de moyens*, in international trade practice it is an *obligation de résultat*. In this respect, international trade practice has been more heavily influenced by the common law notion of objective liability for breach of contract, rather than by the recourse to subjective criteria of fault and diligence that characterize the civil law systems. Indeed, most of the obligations deriving from international contracts concerning mineral exploitation, supply of oil, gas, or other raw materials, distribution of goods can be classified as *obligations de résultat* because the concepts of diligence and fault generally do not come into consideration.

It is evident that the area of risk of an obligee is rather wide in international contracts providing for *obligations de résultat*. There is an effective presumption of the existence of a cause-to-effect relationship between the behavior of an obligee and the breach of its obligation, so that liability for breach is triggered by the mere failure to achieve a promised result. It is thus understandable that contractual limitations or exclusions of liability frequently are negotiated to limit such risk and to provide for a different risk allocation.[69] In the ab-

---

67. *Id.* at 27–28, quoting CISG Arts. 47 (1), 49 (1) (b), 63 (1), and 64 (1) (b).

68. ICC Arbitration Court Award No. 4338 of 1984, 1985 Clunet 983 (1985). In this case, a buyer had issued a letter of credit not duly confirmed by the bank. The court stated that the buyer committed a breach, even if the delay in confirming the letter was attributable to the fault of the bank.

69. *See* Chapter 4 *infra*.

sence of an agreement providing for a different risk allocation, liability for breach of international contracts normally is not affected by fault or diligence on the part of an obligee.

Obligations de moyens do, however, exist in international trade practice. Since the new lex mercatoria is largely customary law, the creation of exceptions is subject to party autonomy, and *obligations de moyens* thus are created by contract. They can be identified as such by the language of international contracts. The following survey of the most common *obligations de moyens* in international trade practice emphasizes the private creation of less than absolute performance obligations.

Obligations "to cooperate"[70] frequently are encountered in international contracts. They are found most frequently in the precontractual phase of a transaction, where parties often agree to comply with standards of good faith during the forthcoming negotiations. Obligations to cooperate, which are *obligations de moyens*, are found in most letters of intent with respect to conducting the negotiations, handling confidential information supplied by one of the parties, entertaining parallel negotiations, and interrupting discussions.[71]

After a contract is executed, the wording of some contractual obligations may reveal their nature as *obligations de moyens*. This is particularly true when expressions such as "to do all one's best" or "to make the best efforts" are used.[72] It is obviously incorrect to believe that obligations so characterized are deprived of any legal con-

---

70. For a survey of such obligations, *see* Morin, *Le devoir de cooperation dans les contrats internationaux. Droit et pratique*, 1980 DROIT ET PRATIQUE DU COMMERCE INTERNATIONAL 9 (1980); M. Fontaine, DROIT DES CONTRATS INTERNATIONAUX — ANALYSE ET REDACTION DE CLAUSES 91 (1989).

71. *See generally* R. Lake & U. Draetta, LETTERS OF INTENT AND OTHER PRECONTRACTUAL DOCUMENTS 126 (1989). Many examples of letters of intent are contained in Fontaine, *Les lettres d'intention dans la négotiation des contrats internationaux*, 3 DROIT ET PRATIQUE DU COMMERCE INTERNATIONAL 73 (1977).

72. Express best-efforts obligations frequently are undertaken in international contracts. *See generally "Best Efforts," "Reasonable Care," "Due Diligence," and Industry Standards in International Agreements*, 1988 INT'L BUS. L. J. 983 (1988); *"Best Efforts" Clauses in Contracts Entered into*

text, so that their inclusion in the contract bears no legal consequence. These obligations imply the use of a certain degree of diligence on the part of the obligee, who will be held liable for damages if the other party can produce evidence to the effect that due diligence was not used.[73]

"Best-efforts" clauses are used in a great variety of situations in international agreements. Some of the most frequently encountered situations where best efforts obligations are undertaken include:

1. The obtaining of approvals and authorizations from government authorities or from other third parties, required for an agreement to enter into force or for a transaction contemplated by a contract to close;[74]

2. Contract adaptation, i.e., the effort to cooperate in finding acceptable contract modifications when unexpected intervening force majeure or hardship circumstances change the bases of the transaction originally contemplated by the parties;[75]

---

by Romanian Foreign Trade Organisations, 1988 INT'L BUS. L. J. 1043 (1988).

73. *See* M. Fontaine, DROIT DES CONTRATS INTERNATIONAUX — ANALYSE ET REDACTION DES CLAUSES 106–124 (1989), especially at 121: "le debiteur s'engage a valoriser aux mieux ses competences dans l'accomplissement de la prestation promise. La formule est cependant exigeante: ce sont ses meilleurs efforts que le debiteur doit fournir." [The obligee shall exercise its competency in the discharge of its duties. The formulation requires, therefore that the obligee exercise its best efforts.] And, with reference to due diligence obligations: "Il n'est plus question de se referer a la competence specifique de debiteur; on exige de lui qu'il adopte la conduite generalement attendue d'un debiteur diligent placé dans les memes circonstances." [It is no longer a question of referring to a specific competence of the obligee; the obligee is required to perform generally as a diligent party in the same circumstance.]

74. ICC Arbitral Decision No. 3987, (1983) CLUNET 943 (1983) (with comments by Derain) deals expressly with a dispute concerning the legal implications of a clause providing for a best-efforts obligation to obtain some required governmental authorizations.

75. *See* the examples cited in M. Fontaine, DROIT DES CONTRATS INTERNATIONAUX — ANALYSE ET REDACTION DES CLAUSES 103 (1989). For the discussion of force majeure and hardship clauses, *see* Chapter 5 *infra*.

3. Cooperation between the parties for the removal of a force majeure situation;[76]

4. The supply to the other party of necessary or useful data and information or of necessary or useful technical assistance to facilitate performance by the other party.

5. "Cold comfort" undertakings to the lending institution, issued by the parent company of a subsidiary receiving a loan.[77]

6. The satisfaction of conditions precedent to the entry into force of an agreement.

7. The exploitation of an exclusive or non-exclusive territory in an international distributorship or international franchise agreement.[78]

Also, *obligations de moyens* can be found in cooperation agreements (consortia, joint-ventures) among participants to a public tender for international construction projects (where, as mentioned before, the inter-company obligations most frequently are characterized as *obligations de résultat*). These include obligations pertaining to the leader (in French: *chef de file*) of the group of the companies selected to represent the group to the final customer and to coordinate the work of the various participating companies.[79]

Other *obligations de moyens* contained in international construction contracts are those of engineers and other technical consultants to an owner[80] and some of the non-monetary obligations of an owner. The

---

76. *Id.*

77. Ralph B. Lake & U. Draetta, LETTERS OF INTENT AND OTHER PRE-CONTRACTUAL DOCUMENTS 13–14, 33–35, 141 (1989); 2 P. Wood, LAW AND PRACTICE OF INTERNATIONAL FINANCE § 13.05 (1983).

78. *See generally* 1 INTERNATIONAL AGENCY AND DISTRIBUTION AGREEMENTS § 11.8.1 (T. Clasen, ed. 1991); M. Abell, THE INTERNATIONAL FRANCHISE OPTION (1990), and the sample contracts contained in each.

79. In some cases, the leader is replaced by a "steering committee" having the same functions. *See* Baptista & D. Barthez, LES ASSOCIATIONS D'ENTERPRISES (JOINT-VENTURES) DANS LE COMMERCE INTERNATIONAL 55–63 (1986); Dubisson, LES GROUPEMENTS D'ENTERPRISES POUR LES MARCHES INTERNATIONAUX 97–114 (1985).

80. The Guide for International Engineering Contracts, drafted by the Economic Commission for Europe of the United Nations (Geneva, 1983)

latter include obligations to coordinate the works of the various co-contractors and not to interfere with their activities, and obligations to perform tests to facilitate acceptance of the works. An owner is liable for the breach of such *obligations de moyens* only if the owner does not apply the necessary degree of diligence in discharging them.[81]

Some *obligations de moyens* now have become part of international trade usages as consistently applied by international commercial arbitral

expressly qualifies as *obligations de moyens* the obligations of the engineer. Similarly, the Fédération Internationale des Ingenieurs Conseils (FIDIC) contract model entitled "International General Rules of Agreement between Client and Consulting Engineer for Design and Supervision of Construction of Works", ed. 1979, at clause 2.3.1 provides that "the Consulting Engineer shall exercise all reasonable skill, care and diligence . . . and shall carry out all his responsibilities in accordance with recognized professional standards. The Consulting Engineer shall in all professional matters act as faithful adviser to the Client and, in so far as any of his duties are discretionary, act fairly as between the Client and third parties." This wording, and particularly the reference to the "care and diligence," is significant for the qualification of the obligations of the engineer as *obligations de moyens*. Two important ICC arbitration decisions discuss the role of the engineer in international construction contracts: ICC Award No. 3790 of January 20, 1983, 1983 CLUNET 910 (1983), 1984 INT'L CONSTR. L. REV. 372 (1984), 1986 YRBK COMM. ARB. 119 (1986); ICC Award No. 4416, 1985 CLUNET 969 (1985), 1985 INT'L CONSTR. L. Rev. 67 (1985). *See also* D. Wallace, THE INTERNATIONAL CIVIL ENGINEERING CONTRACT 23 (1974); Cottam, *The Powers of the Engineer*, 1986 INT'L CONSTR. L. REV. 149 (1986); Mortimer-Hawkins, *FIDIC — An Engineer's View of the Engineer's Role*, 1984 INT'L CONSTR. L. REV. 4 (1984); Crivellaro, *Appalti internazionali: il ruolo dell' "engineer,"* 1987 DIRITTO DEL COMMERCIO INTERNATIONALE 207 (1987).

81. M. Fontaine, DROIT DES CONTRATS INTERNATIONAUX — ANALYSE ET REDACTION DES CLAUSES 93–95 (1989); Mayeur, *Les obligations de l'acheteur dans les ventes internationales d'ensembles industriels*, 1986 INT'L BUS. L.J. 747 (1986). This author specifies, however, (at 751) that other obligations of the owner are, on the contrary, undoubtedly *obligations de résultat*. This is the case, obviously, of the obligation to pay the contract price, but also of some other non-monetary obligations, such as those of providing the land or an adequate project to the contractor.

tribunals, which enforce them even if they are not expressly provided for in international contracts.[82] Examples of these obligations are:

1. The obligation of both parties to an international contract not to cause undue harm to the other party. The International Chamber of Commerce Court of Arbitration has reduced the amount of damages otherwise due to a party that violated such an obligation by not cooperating with the other party in facilitating the discharge of the obligations of the latter;[83]

2. The obligation of either party to inform the other party of any circumstance likely to affect performance of the contract. This obligation has been enforced by the International Chamber of Commerce Court of Arbitration against a buyer that did not inform a seller of the unavailability of foreign currency to make payments,[84] and against a prime contractor that did not timely inform its subcontractor of the failure of an owner to make payments in a situation where the payments to subcontractors were subject to a "pay when paid" clause;[85]

3. The obligations of the damaged party to mitigate the amount of damages due;[86]

4. The obligation of parties in litigation not to behave in a manner that had the effect of widening the scope of the dispute between them. This obligation has been enforced by the International Chamber of Commerce Arbitration Court against a party that

---

82. For further details, *see* Jarvin, *L'obligation de coopérer en bonne foi; examples d'application au plan de l'arbitrage international*, Report made at the seminar entitled "L'arbitrage commercial international — Apport de la jurisprudence arbitrale" held by the International Chamber of Commerce in Paris on April 7–8, 1986.

83. *See* the ICC arbitration cases (unpublished) quoted by Jarvin, *supra* note 82.

84. ICC Arbitration Case No. 3093/3100, 1979 CLUNET 951 (1979).

85. The ICC award is dated 1985 and is not published.

86. This obligation is discussed in more detail in § 3.4C *infra*. *See generally* the survey of the subject in 1987 INT'L BUS. L. J. 347–405 (1987).

drew down a performance bond as a reaction to an arbitration request from the other party, without the existence of any real situation of risk or urgency;[87]

5. The obligations of the litigating parties to cooperate in good faith during discovery proceedings.[88]

It should be emphasized again that liability for breach of all such internationalized *obligations de moyens* requires the existence of fault — in this case the lack of diligence — of an obligee. It is not a given result to which the other party is entitled, but a given behavior in accordance with standards of correctness, good faith, and diligence. The breach of an internationalized *obligation de moyens*, and the consequent liability for damages, is the result of behavior not consistent with such standards. Proof of noncompliance lies with the party asserting a breach.

---

87. ICC Arbitration Case No. 3896, 1983 CLUNET 914 (1983).
88. ICC Arbitration Case No. 1434, 1976 CLUNET 982 (1976).

Chapter 3. The Quantification of Damages

3.1 General

In the preceding chapter, the concept of entitlement to damages was discussed. Specifically, the fault concept was addressed, and it was suggested that international trade practice is influenced more by the civil law fault concept than by that of the common law. In the texts of international contracts and by extension in the new lex mercatoria there are cases in which entitlement to damages arises upon the establishment that an obligor has not applied a given degree of care in discharging its obligations under a contract, as opposed to cases where the entitlement to damages is the automatic consequence of the mere objective failure of an obligor to deliver a required result.

In this chapter, the next step — the quantification of damages — will be discussed. First, we will study how the common law and civil law systems address the issue. This analysis will constitute the background for the discussion regarding the quantification of reimbursable damages in the practice of international business contracts. There are three general possible consequences of a contract breach: enforced performance, termination, and substitutional relief. The latter, for which we will use the common law terminology — reimbursement of monetary damages — is the most pertinent to international contracts.

Termination can be usefully seen as a form of self-protection, and it will be dealt with in that context.[1] A number of comparative analyses have noted the apparent common law and civil law differences of approach with respect to enforced performance.[2] Civil codes emphasize performance, to the extent that enforced performance[3] is usually

---

1. *See* § 4.7 *infra.*

2. G. Treitel, REMEDIES FOR BREACH OF CONTRACT: A COMPARATIVE ACCOUNT 43–74 (1988); CONTRACT LAW TODAY: ANGLO-FRENCH COMPARISONS 263–270 (D. Harris & D. Tallon, eds. 1989); 2 K. Zweigert & H. Kötz, AN INTRODUCTION TO COMPARATIVE LAW 157–176 (2d ed. 1987); Dawson, *Specific Performance in France and Germany,* 57 MICH L. REV. 495 (1959); Szladits, *The Concept of Specific Performance in Comparative Law,* 4 AM. J. COMP. L. 208 (1955).

3. "By enforced performance is meant, in its broadest sense, a process whereby the creditor obtains as nearly as possible the actual subject matter

expressed as the primary remedy. Damages are available only if enforced performance is unavailable.[4] The common law, on the other hand, emphasizes damages, and enforced performance as an exceptional remedy, is always discretionary.[5] The difference of approach, however, is not actually as significant in practice as in theory. First, enforced performance is usually impractical. Businesspeople prefer termination and a claim for damages to enforced performance.[6] This preference is due partly to the difficulty of executing decrees for enforced performance, but primarily due to the dynamic nature of commerce. Businesses cannot wait for the machinery of justice to enforce promises.[7] The practical difficulties of enforcement are accentuated when parties to a contract are in different countries.

Second, as in many other areas of contract law, the practical differences between the common and civil law approaches are not as

---

of his bargain, as opposed to compensation in money for failing to obtain it." G. Treitel, REMEDIES FOR BREACH OF CONTRACT: A COMPARATIVE ACCOUNT 43 (1988). Included in the conceptual heading of enforced performance are the common law concept of specific performance, the civil law concepts of enforcement of "guarantee" liability (*Gewährleistung* in German; *garantie* in French), obligations to bring about a situation that would have existed had there been no breach (*Naturherstellung* in German; *exécution en natur* in French), and various doctrines of permissible "self-help." As to the latter, *see* Hillman, *Contract Modification and "Self-Help" Specific Performance: A Reaction to Professor Narasimhan*, 75 CORNELL L. REV. 62 (1989).

4. CONTRACT LAW TODAY: ANGLO-FRENCH COMPARISONS 245, 265 (D. Harris & D. Tallon, eds. 1989); G. Treitel, REMEDIES FOR BREACH OF CONTRACT: A COMPARATIVE ACCOUNT 44 (1988).

5. FARNSWORTH ON CONTRACTS §§ 12.4, 12.5 (1990).

6. This does not seem to have been the view of the drafters of the German Civil Code, who erroneously thought that disappointed creditors would always prefer performance to damages. 2 K. Zweigert and H. Kötz, AN INTRODUCTION TO COMPARATIVE LAW 161 (2d ed. 1987).

7. "Active participants in commerce and their legal advisors who are familiar with the practical problems of coercing action usually choose to supply their needs elsewhere and proceed with business — subject to compensation for damages after the cumbersome processes of litigation have taken their course." J. HONNOLD, UNIFORM LAW FOR INTERNATIONAL SALES 302 (1982).

great as they seem in theory.[8] While the civil law appears to view enforced performance as the primary remedy, in practice actions for damages are the norm.[9]

Enforced performance thus is not usually an element of international contract disputes or contemplated in international trade practice. Nevertheless, the difference in approach is so fundamental that some commentators have despaired at international efforts at uniformity.[10] It is perhaps for this reason that the drafters of the 1980 Vienna Convention did not address the issue. The Vienna Convention adopts the civil law approach with "delicate adjustments and compromises."[11] This approach provides enforced performance even in situations where an injured party could have made a substitute contract.[12] Enforced performance is not available where a creditor has already sought a remedy "inconsistent" with enforced performance,[13] or in the case of delivery of nonconforming goods, where the delivery of such goods constitutes a fundamental breach.[14] More importantly, the broad ability to enforce is "considerably restricted" by Article 28 of the Convention,[15] which

---

8. "There is evidence that in practice the systems converge to some extent, that the types of contract which are specifically enforced in both systems share common characteristics." CONTRACT LAW TODAY: ANGLO-FRENCH COMPARISONS 245 (D. Harris & D. Tallon, eds. 1989) *See also* G. Treitel, REMEDIES FOR BREACH OF CONTRACT: A COMPARATIVE ACCOUNT 47, 75 (1988).

9. " . . . French law generally admits the issuance of judgments for performance in kind but enforces them in a very grudging manner." 2 K. Zweigert & H. Kötz, AN INTRODUCTION TO COMPARATIVE LAW 165 (2d ed. 1987). *See also* N. Horn, H. Kötz, & H. Leser, GERMAN PRIVATE AND COMMERCIAL LAW 110–111 (1982).

10. 2 K. Zweigert & H. Kötz, AN INTRODUCTION TO COMPARATIVE LAW 174 (2d ed. 1987).

11. J. Honnold, UNIFORM LAW FOR INTERNATIONAL SALES 299 (1982).

12. "U.N. Convention on Contracts for the International Sale of Goods", Art. 46 [hereinafter Vienna Convention].

13. Vienna Convention, Art. 49(1).

14. Vienna Convention, Art. 49(2). *See* Chapter 2 *supra*, notes 60, 61, and accompanying text.

15. *See* G. Treitel, REMEDIES FOR BREACH OF CONTRACT: A COMPARATIVE ACCOUNT 74 (1988).

provides that a court is not obliged to order enforced performance unless the remedy is available under its municipal law. Thus, common law courts have the ability to apply considerable restrictions on the availability of specific performance of contracts made pursuant to the Convention.

Although the common and civil law conceptual frameworks regarding damages are quite different, they share several important elements. First, although the terminology is different and sometimes contradictory, both systems seek to place a damaged party in the same position the party would have been in had no loss been suffered, while at the same time preventing recovery in excess of the loss suffered.[16] Second, both systems permit recovery of money for injury to the conceptually familiar expectation, reliance, and restitutionary interests.[17] Third, both systems are reluctant to award damages that a damaged party could have avoided or that a damaged party caused.[18]

---

16. G. Treitel, REMEDIES FOR BREACH OF CONTRACT: A COMPARATIVE ACCOUNT 76–82, 89 (1988); B. Nicholas, FRENCH LAW OF CONTRACT 219 (1982); N. Horn, H. Kötz, & H. Leser, GERMAN PRIVATE AND COMMERCIAL LAW 110 (1982).

17. *See generally* G. Treitel, REMEDIES FOR BREACH OF CONTRACT: A COMPARATIVE ACCOUNT 82–105 (1988). Theoretical wrestling with these concepts and the relationship between them has primarily occupied the attention of common law writers and judges. The civil law is more flexible, and civil law courts normally do not discuss the bases for damage awards. The French Code Civil does not expressly refer to theoretical bases of recovery. Section 307 of the German Bürgerliches Gesetzbuch (BGB), however, identifies the reliance interest, and BGB § 346 identifies the restitution interest. Dickson, *The Law of Restitution in the Federal Republic of Germany: A Comparison with English Law*, 36 INT'L & COMP. L. O. 751 (1987). The usual measure of recovery in German law is for injury to the expectation interest (*Schadenersatz wegen Nichterfüllung*).

18. "Mitigation" is a common law term and is an important element in the determination of damage in the common law. A "duty" to mitigate damages does not exist in French law, but the practice of French judges is to take the conduct of the injured party into account when damages are awarded. CONTRACT LAW TODAY: ANGLO-FRENCH COMPARISONS 384 (D. Harris & D. Tallon, eds. 1989); B. Nicholas, FRENCH LAW OF CONTRACT

Finally, both systems seek to limit damages in a way that prohibits recovery for injuries that are too remote. It is this last concept with which international contract practice is most concerned. The main difficulty for international lawyers is not predicting limitations when litigation arises, but seeking to exclude categories of damages during a contract negotiation that will be understood by both parties and enforced by a court or arbitral body should disputes arise.

3.2 Common Law Principles

A. General

An English court has noted that "the assessment of damages is not an exact science."[19] It is, in fact, one of the areas the determination of which common law judges have the most discretion. English and U.S. legal theorists have identified the same general interests, an injury to which may be the basis for the recovery of damages for a contract breach. These are:

1. The expectation interest, which is the value of the breaching party's promise. Damages awarded for the expectation interest seek to place a non-breaching party in the same position the party would have been in had no breach occurred. This includes lost profits;[20]

2. The reliance interest, which compensates the non-breaching party for expenses incurred in the expectation that an obligation be discharged.[21] Damages awarded for the reliance interest seek to

---

226 (1982). The German principle of *Vorteilsausgleichung* "covers much the same ground" as the common law principle of mitigation. G. Treitel, REMEDIES FOR BREACH OF CONTRACT: A COMPARATIVE ACCOUNT 186 (1988).

19. The Heron II, Koufos v. Czarnikow, Ltd., [1969] 1 A.C. 350, 425.

20. McGREGOR ON DAMAGES § 52 (15th ed. 1988); FARNSWORTH ON CONTRACTS §§ 12.1, 12.4 (1990).

21. Fuller & Perdue, *The Reliance Interest in Contract Damages*, 46 YALE L. J. 52 (1936); 47 YALE L. J. 373 (1936); P. Atiyah, *Fuller and the Theory of Contract*, in ESSAYS ON CONTRACT 73 (1986); Slawson, *The Role of Reliance in Contract Damage*, 76 CORNELL L. REV. 197 (1990).

place a non-breaching party in the same position the party would have been in had there been no contract; and

3. The restitution interest, which compensates a non-breaching party for benefits conferred upon a breaching party.[22]

The common law determination of damages is related to the fault concept discussed in Chapter 1. Since liability for breach of contract is theoretically strict, damages are awarded without regard to the conduct of the breaching party.[23] Thus, there are no awards of "punitive" (the usual U.S. term) or "exemplary" (the usual English term) damages for breach of contract.[24]

---

22. *See generally* Lord Goff & G. Jones, LAW OF RESTITUTION (3rd ed. 1986); 2 CHITTY ON CONTRACTS §§ 2031–2153 (26th ed 1989); FARNSWORTH ON CONTRACTS § 12.16 (1990); G. Palmer, THE LAW OF RESTITUTION (1978). "When awarded independently, it is usually to deprive the defendant of an unjust enrichment in cases where no breach of contract has occurred, e.g. where the contract was void for mistake or was terminated for frustration." CONTRACT LAW TODAY: ANGLO-FRENCH COMPARISONS 248 (D. Harris & D. Tallon, eds. 1989). Unlike U.S. courts, English courts have never been troubled by combining restitution and expectation awards. G. Treitel, REMEDIES FOR BREACH OF CONTRACT: A COMPARATIVE ACCOUNT 98 (1988).

23. FARNSWORTH ON CONTRACTS § 12.8 (1990). Fault, however, plays a role in the civil law in the determination of the amount of damages. G. Treitel, REMEDIES FOR BREACH OF CONTRACT: A COMPARATIVE ACCOUNT 144–148 (1988).

24. Such damages are awarded regularly for tort actions in the United States, and have been awarded for contract actions that have a tort element of some kind. FARNSWORTH ON CONTRACTS § 12.8 (1990). In English law, this type of damages is highly exceptional even in tort cases. MCGREGOR ON DAMAGES §§ 406–423 (15th ed. 1988). The concept of punitive damages is primarily one of the common law, despite the relevance of fault as a necessary condition of liability in civil law systems. Even common law judgments in tort can encounter difficulties in recognition and enforcement in civil law countries. Beucher & Sandage, *United States Punitive Damage Awards in German Courts: The Evolving German Position on Service and Enforcement*, 23 VAND. J. TRANS. L. 967 (1991); Schütze, *Recognition and Enforcement of Punitive Damage Awards in Germany*, 11 U. PA. J. INT'L L. 581 (1990).

All legal systems place limitations on the extent to which damages may be recovered. There is, however, disparity within and among common and civil law systems as to the extent of these limitations. These limitations are of primary concern to the drafters of international contracts.

1. English Law

Of the systems surveyed, English law makes the greatest effort to treat the assessment of damages in a formal, coherent manner. The English approach is more formal,[25] and English judges have attempted to impose a logical construct on the assessment of contract damages.[26]

Limitations on damage assessment in English law center around the notions of causation and foreseeability.[27] Causation is the cause-to-effect relationship between the breach and the damages incurred. It is conceptually more important in both the civil and common law of

---

25. *See generally* P. Atiyah & R. Summers, FORM AND SUBSTANCE IN ANGLO-AMERICAN LAW (1987). Atiyah and Summers describe "formal" and "substantive" conceptions of law as having to do with attitudes toward rules. Quoting Pound and Llewellyn, they posit that "[t]here is widespread evidence that a great many American judges and theorists have held to, and continue to hold to, a conception of a rule as a mere guideline." *Id.* at 88. "By contrast, we believe that nearly all English lawyers and judges adhere to a narrower and more formal conception of what a rule is. . . . They . . . have a conception of a rule in which the rule is highly mandatory and in which the rationales, principles, and policies underlying or involved in the rule are viewed as something distinct from the rule itself . . ." *Id.* at 89.

26. *Id.* at 84. "The British cases, unlike U.S. cases, reflect a formal approach to contract damages." Murphey, *Consequential Damages in Contracts for the International Sale of Goods and the Legacy of Hadley,* 23 GEO. WASH. J. INT'L L. & ECON. 415, 442 (1989).

27. The two concepts often are confused by both English and U.S. judges as being part of a larger concept of "remoteness." *See generally* G. Treitel, REMEDIES FOR BREACH OF CONTRACT: A COMPARATIVE ACCOUNT 153–155 (1988). McGREGOR ON DAMAGES Ch. 6 (15th ed. 1988). The English case that identifies the dual nature of "remoteness" most clearly is Monarch S.S. Co. v. Karlshamns Oljefabriker, [1949] A.C. 196.

tort. In contract law, the limitation requires that recoverable losses be a "direct" result of a contract breach. Its significance arises in situations involving the intervening acts of the non-breaching party and third parties, and events.[28]

The criterion of foreseeability mitigates the consequence of applying the criterion of causation too rigidly, so that *all* damages caused by the breach would be reimbursable. As stated in the 1854 seminal case of *Hadley v. Baxendale*,[29] damages that are a consequence of a breach, but are too remote, are not recoverable. Recoverable damages are only those that are reasonably within the contemplation of both parties when making the contract.

The *Hadley* principle was subsequently redefined by the U.K. Court of Appeal in the 1949 case *Victoria Laundry (Windsor) v. Newman Industries Limited*.[30] Here, the court introduced the criterion of "reasonable foreseeability" as a test to evaluate the degree of liability for breach of contract. The court observed that the requisite foreseeability of the damages refers not only to the foreseeability that can be expected from any reasonable person who is aware of the "ordinary course of the events," but also to that which can be expected from people in possession of particular and specific knowledge. The difficulty of creating a formal structure for the assessment of damages is illustrated by the contradictory and inconsistent application of these general principles to specific cases.

First, considerable confusion exists as to the application of the theoretical bases of recovery; the relationship between interests is neither settled nor clear. To a greater extent than their more flexible civil law counterparts, common law courts continue to concern themselves with

---

28. MᴄGʀᴇɢᴏʀ ᴏɴ Dᴀᴍᴀɢᴇs §§ 233–241 (15th ed. 1988).

29. (1854) 9 Exch. 341: "Where two parties have made a contract which one of them has broken, the damages which the other ought to receive in respect of such breach should be such as may be fairly and reasonably supposed to have been in contemplation of both parties, at the time when they made the contract, as the probable result of its breach." The rule of *Hadley v. Baxendale* is sometimes thought to be one of the few English legal imports from France; the English court referred to articles 1149 to 1151 of the *code civil*.

30. (1949) 2 K.B. 528 (C.A.).

questions of overlaps and classification. The basic rule that the expectation and reliance interests are mutually exclusive, for example, has not always been followed.[31]

Second, decisions following *Victoria Laundry* have introduced some new terminology and alternatively emphasized either foreseeability of damages or that damages be a direct consequence of the breach, as if the two criteria were mutually exclusive.[32] Other decisions have strongly criticized the criteria followed by *Victoria Laundry*, with particular reference to the notion of "reasonable foreseeability," and have proposed alternative criteria; in particular, the narrower criterion of "with the contemplation of the parties."[33] Finally, the imprecision of rules relating to damages creates more judicial discretion than in other areas of contract law.[34]

---

31. The English courts came to opposite conclusions respectively in two 1957 cases: Cullinane v. British "Rema" Manufacturing Co., [1954] 1 Q.B. 292, and Andrews v. Hopkinson, [1957], 1 Q. B. 229. *See generally* G. Treitel, REMEDIES FOR BREACH OF CONTRACT: A COMPARATIVE ACCOUNT 96–97 (1988).

32. *See* the much discussed cases *Re Polemis*, [1921] 3 K. B. 560 (C. A.) and Overseas/Tankslup (U.K.) v. Morts Docks and Engineering Co. (the Wagon Mound), (1961) A. C. 388 (P. C.). *See generally* Wilson, *Un arrêt important en matière de causalité: Wagon Mound*, 1962 REVUE INTERNATIONALE DE DROIT COMPARÉ 575 (1962).

33. *See*, in particular, Czarnikow v. Koufos, (1969) 1 A. C. 350; Parsons v. Uttley Ingham & Co., (1978) Q. B. 791 (C. A.). *See generally* McGREGOR ON DAMAGES §§ 247–264 (15th ed. 1988). "Even with respect to problems which are inherently difficult to force into a framework of formal rules — such as the foreseeability principle of *Hadley v. Baxendale* — English courts still try to formulate the law in terms of specific formal rules and most English judges try (if, as some may think, rather futilely) to apply these rules formally." P. Atiyah & R. Summers, FORM AND SUBSTANCE IN ANGLO-AMERICAN LAW 84 (1987).

34. "The power of the court to choose between the various possible methods of assessment obviously gives it a very considerable discretion as to the size of the ultimate award." G. Treitel, REMEDIES FOR BREACH OF CONTRACT: A COMPARATIVE ACCOUNT 174 (1988). "For their part, English courts sometimes use the foreseeability test to relieve business of only marginal viability from excessive burdens of liability." CONTRACT LAW TODAY: ANGLO-FRENCH COMPARISONS 292 (D. Harris & D. Tallon, eds. 1989).

The term "consequential damages" is widely used in international private contracts. It is properly used in English law in contrast to "normal damages" to differentiate between losses which all non-breaching parties would suffer and losses which are peculiar to the non-breaching party in question.[35] In this context lost profits are a consequential loss in English law.[36] With respect to exclusion clauses, however, the expression has been interpreted to refer to damages outside the limitation of *Hadley v. Baxendale* (i.e., to losses which are less direct and more remote.)[37] This latter meaning is frequently used in the United States and in international practice.

2. United States Law

United States law occupies a via media between the more subjective approach of civil law courts and theorists and the more restrictive, formal approach of English law. United States judges have struggled with the same difficulties of assessing damages as their English common law counterparts. The same theoretical bases of recovery exist in both common law systems but the terminology varies. Despite the Herculean efforts of some U.S. contract theorists, damages in the United States are, if anything, less capable of formal determination than in England. The trend in U.S. assessment of damages has been to compensate the non-breaching party more liberally.[38]

The term "consequential damages,"[39] or "consequentials,"[40] is used in the United States with great imprecision to refer to several types of

---

35. McGregor on Damages § 26 (15th ed. 1988).

36. *Id.*

37. *See* the 1978 case Croudace Construction Ltd. v. Cawood's Concrete Products Ltd., [1978] 2 Lloyd's Rep. 55.

38. Murphey, *Consequential Damages in Contracts for the International Sale of Goods and the Legacy of Hadley*, 23 Geo. Wash. J. Int'l L. & Econ. 415, 422 (1989).

39. "The term *consequential* is traditional . . ." Farnsworth on Contracts § 12.9 (1990).

40. "This lawyer's colloquialism should be discouraged in formal legal writing." B. Garner, A Dictionary of Modern Legal Usage 143 (1987).

relatively remote damages. An influential publicist, Professor Treitel, identifies three common law senses of the term.[41] First, it can refer to damages that are too remote to be recoverable.[42] Many lawyers use the term to connote losses that may be recoverable in some situations, but not in a particular one. In this sense, the term often is used in exclusion clauses in both domestic and international contracts. Second, it refers "simply to the loss or gain which a party suffers in consequence of not receiving the thing contracted for."[43] Third, the term refers to injury or damage to person or property (other than the object of the contract).[44]

The concept of "consequential damages" is specifically contemplated by Sections 2-715(2) and 2-719(3) of the U.S. Uniform Commercial Code.[45] However, in spite of this definition, use of the term involves

---

41. G. Treitel, Remedies for Breach of Contract: A Comparative Account 87 (1988).

42. *See, e.g.*, Georgia Code § 20-1406.

43. G. Treitel, Remedies for Breach of Contract: A Comparative Account 87 (1988).

44. "Consequential damages of this kind are not confined to physical harm; they may for example include amounts which a buyer of goods has to pay to a sub-buyer by reason of the seller's failure to deliver in accordance with the contract." G. Treitel, Remedies for Breach of Contract: A Comparative Account 87 (1988). " . . . consequential damages do not arise within the scope of the immediate buyer/seller transaction, but rather stem from losses incurred by the nonbreaching party in its dealings, often with third parties, which were a proximate result of the breach, and which were reasonably foreseeable by the breaching party at the time of contracting." Petroleo Brasileiro, S. A., Petrobas, v. Ameropan Oil Corp., 372 F. Supp. 503, 508 (E.D.N.Y. 1974).

45. U.C.C. § 2-715 (2): "Consequential damages resulting from the Seller's breach include: (a) any loss resulting from general or particular requirements and needs of which the Seller at the time of contracting had reason to know and which could not reasonably be prevented by cover or otherwise; (b) injury to person or property proximately resulting from any breach or warranty." U.C.C. § 2-719 (3): "Consequential damages may be limited or excluded unless the limitation is unconscionable. Limitation of consequential damages for injury to the person in the case of consumer goods is prima facie unconscionable but limitation of damages where the loss is commercial is not."

so many uncertainties that many have proposed that it be dropped.[46] The distinction between "direct," "incidental," and "consequential" damages is a question of fact, and U.S. case law is neither clear nor consistent.[47]

As in England, the question of consequential damages frequently arises in the context of clauses that attempt to exclude them. The Uniform Commercial Code provides that an exclusion of consequential damages is ineffective when it is "unconscionable."[48] United States courts have found it difficult to recognize the existence of "unconscionability" in contractual relationships between knowledgeable parties.[49]

---

46. CORBIN ON CONTRACTS § 1011 (2d ed. 1963) observes that any damage is in a certain way "consequential," and proposes more orthodox alternatives such as "special damages" or "indirect damages." Corbin also is wary of damage assessments based on the "natural consequences" of the breach. "This term renders no service whatever in the process of reaching a decision; it is probably the most commonly used verbal justification of decisions already arrived at." *Id.*

47. "The precise demarcation between direct and consequential damages is a question of fact, and the commercial context in which a contract is made is of substantial importance in determining whether particular items of damages will fall into one category or the other." American Electric Power Co. v. Westinghouse Electric Corp., 418 F. Supp. 435, 459 (S.D.N.Y. 1976).

48. There is no definition of the word "unconscionable in the U. C. C.. Comment 1 to § 2-302 U.C.C. gives "only the most general guidance" that an unconscionable clause is so one-sided as to lead to the conclusion that the parties really did not want it. The purpose of the statutory provision is the "prevention of oppression and unfair surprise . . . and not of disturbance of allocation of risks because of superior bargaining power." "The commentary then gives a series of examples based on pre-Code cases, confirming the reader's suspicion that the term is undefinable." FARNSWORTH ON CONTRACTS § 4.28 (1990). *See also Article Two Warranties in Commercial Transactions*, 64 CORNELL L. REV. 30, 215 (1978); *The Enforceability of Contractual Clauses Excluding Sellers from Liability for Consequential Damages under Section 2-719 of the Uniform Commercial Code*, 58 WASH. U. L. Q. 317 (1980).

49. Such difficulties are evident, for example, in a number of cases decided in favor of Westinghouse Electric Co., where the contractual exclusion

Knowledgeable parties, of course, are likely to be just those who are parties to international contracts. As a result, the possibility of conventionally excluding liability for consequential damages from a practical point of view is rather wide. The extent of such exclusion is still unclear, however, in those cases where a warranty obligation is, for example, limited to an obligation to "repair or replace" defective products.

If such an obligation is breached, some courts have upheld exclusions of consequential damages. Others have held that a party breaching an obligation to "repair or replace" may not obtain limited liability for consequential damages.[50]

From the perspective of the negotiator and drafter of international contracts, neither English law nor U.S. law offers the definite criteria

---

of consequential damages has been enforced: Potomac Electric Power Co. v. Westinghouse Electric Co., 385 F. Supp. 572, 579 (D.D.C. 1974); K & C Inc. v. Westinghouse Electric Co., 263 A.2d 390, 393 (Pa. Supp. Ct. 1970); Royal Indemnity Co. v. Westinghouse Electric Co., 385 Fed. Supp. 520, 524–525. In the last case, the court stated: "Since limitation of consequential damages where the loss is commercial is not prima facie unconscionable, plaintiff must raise genuine factual issues, the determination of which are germane to the claim of unconscionability. This was not a purchase of a passenger ticket, a coffee percolator, a washing machine or an automobile. This was not a take-it or leave-it transaction. It was one that involved the manufacture and installation of an item at a price in excess of 10,000,000 dollars with many details that were to be hammered out by knowledgeable parties. It involved two industrial giants of the nation, and the terms of the agreement were the subject of extensive negotiations over a three-year period." "It makes little sense in the context of two large, legally sophisticated companies to invoke . . . the unconscionability doctrine." Continental Airlines v. Goodyear Tire & Rubber Co., 819 F.2d 1519, 1527 (9th Cir. 1987).

50. *See* U.C.C. § 2-719 (1)(b) and compare the conflicting decisions in the cases American Electric Power Co. v. Westinghouse, 418 F. Supp. 435 (S.D.N.Y. 1976), with comment in CORBIN ON CONTRACTS § 1472 (1962) (in the sense of the limitation of the liability); Soo Line R.R. Co. v. Fruehauf Corp., 547 F.2d 1315 (8th Cir. 1977); Fargo Machine and Tool Co. v. Kearney and Trecker Corp., 428 F. Supp. 364 (E.D. Mich. 1977) (in the sense of unlimited liability).

for the identification of the reimbursable damages businesspersons seek. Courts seem to decide on common sense and equity considerations applied on a case-by-case basis, rather than on a systematic approach to the issue.

3.3 Civil Law Principles

The unpredictability associated with the assessment of damages is no less pronounced in civil law systems. These systems suffer from so many uncertainties that some commentators have concluded that the courts decide questions of damages simply based on what they perceive to be equitable and then dress up their decisions with "legal" reasoning.[51]

A fundamental difference between the assessment of damages in England and in France or Italy is that damages questions in the former are questions of law,[52] while the determination of damages in France and Italy are questions of fact to be decided by a trial judge.[53] This difference gives French and Italian judges broad powers to award damages based on intuition and justice over which the cour de cassation has "only a formal control."[54] It also accounts for the theoretical outpourings of common law judges and publicists and the relative paucity of same in civil law countries. Civil law awards of damages

---

51. The observation is made by Morello, *Profili comparatistici*, in RISARCIMENTO DEL DANNO CONTRATTUALE ED EXTRA-CONTRATUALLE 176 (G. Visintini, ed. 1984).

52. English courts characterize remoteness questions as "substantive" and assessment (quantification) issues as procedural. G. Delaume, TRANS-NATIONAL CONTRACTS § 4.05 (1989), noting the case of D'Almeida Araujo LDA v. Sir Frederick Becker & Co., Ltd., [1952] 2 Q.B. 329; 2 All E.R. 288, in which an English court determined an issue of foreseeability issue under the proper law of the contract (that of Portugal) but assessed damages under the lex fori (that of England). Similarly, U.S. courts consider how damages are measured as a question of law, but consider the amount of damages as a question of fact.

53. CONTRACT LAW TODAY: ANGLO-FRENCH COMPARISONS 292 (D. Harris & D. Tallon, eds. 1989); *But see* note 47 *supra*.

54. *Id.*, at 274.

are not accompanied by discursive explanations, and their theoretical basis thus is difficult to determine.

Article 1151 of the French Code Civil states that the damages that are reimbursable as a consequence of a contract breach are those that are the direct and immediate consequence of the breach itself.[55] Article 1150 establishes the additional requirement of foreseeability at the time the obligation was undertaken.[56] Although the rules are expressed with the typical clarity of the Code Civil, French courts have widened or restricted the area of reimbursable damages, applying fairness, equity, and other criteria that seem appropriate from case to case.[57]

A similar situation exists in Italy. The Italian rules concerning the quantification of reimbursable damages are contained in Articles 1223 and 1225 of the Italian Codice Civile. Article 1223 confines reimbursable damages to those that are the "direct and immediate" consequence of a breach.[58] Such a statutory provision assumes that the issue as to

---

55. C.C. 1151: "Even where the non-performance of the agreement is due to the *dol* of the debtor, damages in respect of the actual loss suffered by the creditor and the gain of which he has been deprived should include only what is the immediate and direct consequence of the non-performance." [Translated in B. Nicholas, French Law of Contract 223 (1982).]

56. C.C. 1150: "When the non-performance of the obligation is not due to the *dol* of the debtor, he is liable only for such damage as was foreseen or as one could have foreseen at the time of the contract." [Translated in B. Nicholas, French Law of Contract 223 (1982).]

57. *See generally* H. Mazeaud & L. Mazeaud, 2 Traité Théorique et Pratique de la Responsabilité Civil Délictuelle et Contractuelle 781 (1970). "The criterion for determining what damage is direct is, predictably, elusive." B. Nicholas, French Law of Contract 224 (1982). French courts have lessened the subjective criterion set down in the C.C. 1150, and apply more objective criterion based on risk assumption. Contract Law Today: Anglo-French Comparisons 293 (D. Harris & D. Tallon, eds. 1989).

58. Cod. Civ. 1223: "Measure of Damages. The measure of damages arising from non-performance or delay shall include the loss sustained by the creditor and the lost profits insofar as they are a direct and immediate consequence of the non-performance or delay." [Translated in M. Beltramo, G. Longo, & J. Merryman, The Italian Civil Code 323 (1969).]

whether an obligee is liable for damages based on objective or subjective considerations of the type discussed in the preceding chapter has been addressed previously and entitlement to damages has been established. Article 1225 of the Code further limits reimbursable damages to those that could be foreseen by the obligee at the time the obligation was undertaken.[59]

It would appear, as in French law, that these provisions offer sufficiently rational and simple criteria to determine the amount of the reimbursable damages. However, this is not the case. First, Italian scholars have engaged in some rather obscure semantic disputes that have not contributed to a clarification of the issue.[60] Second, Article 1223 has been the subject of conflicting interpretations, which have added to the confusion.[61] For example, according to some commentators, even "indirect" damages are reimbursable under certain circumstances. As a result, some courts have broadened the scope of damages accordingly, awarding indirect damages when they believe that such an award is equitable.[62]

German law rejects the requirement of foreseeability and limits damages primarily by the requirement that there be an adequate causal

---

59. Cod. Civ., Art. 1225: "Foreseeability of Damages. If the non-performance or delay is not caused by the fraud or malice of the debtor, compensation is limited to the damages that could have been foreseen at the time the obligation arose." [Translated in M. Beltramo, G. Longo, & J. Merryman, THE ITALIAN CIVIL CODE 323 (1969).]

60. Many Italian scholars have complained of these obscurities. *See, e.g.*, Realmonte, IL PROBLEMA DEL RAPPORTO DI CAUSALITÁ NEL RISARCIMENTO DEL DANNO 79 (1967).

61. The full range of these conflicting interpretations is reported by Cassottana, *Osservazioni sul rapporto di consequenzialitá immediata e diretta di cui all'art. 1223 cod. civ.*, 1984 ANNALI GENOVA 298 (1984).

62. Corte di Cassazione Judgement of January 26, 1980, n. 643, 1980 REPERTORIO GIUSTIZIA CIVILE 3 (1980); Corte di Cassazione Judgement of January 21, 1980, n. 476, 1980 GIURISPRUDENZA ITALIANA, I, 549 (1980); Corte di Cassazione Judgement of June 19, 1979, n. 3684, 1974 REPERTORIO GIUSTIZIA CIVILE 39 (1979). An interesting survey on the subject is made by Visintini, *Il criterio legislativo delle consequenze dirette e immediate*, in RISARCIMENTO DEL DANNO CONTRATTUALE ED EXTRA-CONTRATTUALE 9 (1984).

connection (*adäquater Kausalzusammenhang*) between breach and loss.[63] In practice and in the view of commentators, however, the German legal limitation device is very similar to those of the common law countries; both being based on a reasonability test.[64] The same subjectivity and lack of predictability has been noted in German damage assessment as in those of other countries.[65]

3.4 The Practice of International Business Contracts

International trade practices with respect to damages have evolved in an attempt to accommodate the civil and common law traditions while at the same time affording the parties as much discipline, uniformity, and certainty as possible. For many international contracts, the issue is simply left for resolution by the proper or chosen law of the contract. For the negotiators and drafters of such contracts, the most important issues become those related to jurisdiction and conflicts of law. The negotiators and drafters of many other international contracts, however, repeatedly have adopted concepts and formulae related to contract damages that cannot be clearly connected to any specific municipal legal system. These have acquired the autonomous, international nature that characterizes elements of the new lex mercatoria.

A. "Consequential Damages"

The clearest example of such a "de-localized" or "de-nationalized" contract provision is the frequent use of the term "consequential damages" in international contracts. Although the term generally is found in clauses that exclude liability for "consequential damages," in some cases it is used in clauses that provide just the opposite (i.e., that such damages are to be included).

---

63. N. Horn, H. Kötz, & H. Leser, GERMAN PRIVATE AND COMMERCIAL LAW 111 (1982).

64. G. Treitel, REMEDIES FOR BREACH OF CONTRACT: A COMPARATIVE ACCOUNT 162–166 (1988).

65. *See* Carbone, IL FATTO DANNOSO NELLA RESPONSABILITÁ CIVILE 31, 282 (1969).

One logically could assume that since the U.S. legal system contains the only statutory reference to the term "consequential damages," parties to international contracts who refer to "consequential damages" intend to adopt the U.S. definition (unclear as it is) as previously described. Such an assumption would be incorrect, however, since reference to "consequential damages" often is made in international contracts that are submitted to laws other than that of the United States or other common law jurisdictions.

Indeed, the term frequently is used in international contracts in which the parties choose a civil law jurisdiction where the whole concept of "consequential damages" is totally foreign. One might conclude that when parties to such a contract refer to "consequential damages," they actually intend to mean the civil law concept of "indirect damages."[66] The use of the expression "consequential damages" in such event would simply be terminological imprecision, sometimes mitigated by the fact that reference often is made indiscriminately to "consequential or indirect damages." This conclusion should not be accepted either. The concept of "consequential damages" in common law systems, and of "indirect damages" in civil law systems, are very different. In U.S. law, "consequential damages" form part of the expectation interest and normally are reimbursable unless specifically excluded. In civil law systems, however, "indirect" damages are reimbursable only if a contract expressly so provides. Furthermore, one of the most important items of damages, the loss of profit, is included in the expectation interest, a "consequential" loss under U.S. law, while in civil law jurisdictions, lost profits are direct and not indirect losses.

The fact is that parties to international contracts frequently refer to "consequential damages" without much caring whether U.S. law is applicable to the contract, and in fact without much consideration of the municipal law applicable to the contract. They thus appear to adopt a notion of "consequential damages" that, while undoubtedly having its roots in U.S. law (as is often the case in the area of international

---

66. C.C. 1151 and Cod. Civ. 1223 relate to the damage limitation mechanism of causation. Consequential loss relates to foreseeability. "The distinction between direct and indirect damage is . . . easy to illustrate, but much harder to define." G. Treitel, Remedies for Breach of Contract: A Comparative Account 167 (1988).

trade usages), has acquired a significant degree of autonomy and de-localization.

The use of the term "consequential damages" together with the term "indirect damages" can be explained on the basis that the latter term has undergone a similar evolution. The two terms are used jointly not because they have the same or comparable meanings in the law systems from which they respectively originate, but because the concepts of both "consequential damages" and "indirect damages" have acquired a common meaning in international trade usage through an evolutionary process that has made them autonomous from their municipal systems of origin. Evidence of this evolution can be found without difficulty. First, there is a widespread assumption by negotiating parties and dispute resolving tribunals that parties to international business contracts have similar professional and international expertise. International trade is one of the last refuges of the principle of caveat emptor, and there are no international rules aimed at protecting a "weak" party against a stronger one.[67] This assumption of knowledgeability has been affirmed repeatedly by the jurisprudence of the Court of Arbitration of the International Chamber of Commerce.[68] As a consequence, an exclusion clause that deals with liability for

---

67. Rules related to the U.S. concept of "unconscionability" designed to protect a weaker party are common in many municipal legal systems. Articles 1341 and 1342 of the Italian Civil Code require a specific signature in signing of acceptance by the party to which "leonine" conditions are imposed in standard contract forms. A survey of similar rules in various national laws, aimed at protecting the weaker party, is contained in Bonell, LE REGOLE OGGETTIVE DEL COMMERCIO INTERNAZIONALE 138–151 (1976). It is interesting to note that some of these laws specifically exclude international contracts from the scope of application of such protecting statutory provisions. This is the case of the English Unfair Contract Terms Act of 1977 (§ 26.1) and Sale of Goods Act of 1893 (§ 5 of the 1973 Amendment Act). The German *Allgemeine Geschäftsbedingungengesetz* (AGBG) in many cases applies to both commercial and consumer contracts governed by German law, but is inapplicable to contracts for which the proper law determined by conflicts rules or chosen by the parties is that of a foreign jurisdiction.

68. ICC Arbitration Cases No. 1990, 1974 CLUNET 897 (1974); No. 1512, 1974 CLUNET 905 (1974); No. 2438, 1976 CLUNET 969 (1976); No. 2291,

"consequential damages" is never limited by the U.S. concept of "unconscionability."

Secondly, in an attempt to overcome the uncertainties and contradictions of the various municipal laws with respect to the determination of "direct" or "indirect" damages in the civil law, or foreseeable, unforeseeable, or "consequential" in the common law, the negotiators and drafters of international contracts normally provide detailed lists of items of damages that are defined as "consequential." Such detailed lists of items of "consequential" damages are typical in clauses aimed at excluding liability for them. Loss of profit is almost invariably part of such lists, as are damages deriving from claims from the final users of the goods or services, the supply of which are the object of international contracts.[69]

1976 CLUNET 989 (1976); No. 3130, 1981 CLUNET 932 (1981); No. 3380, 1981 CLUNET 928 (1981).

69. Many clauses widely adopted in the international trade practice contain the express exclusion of consequential damages and a detailed list thereof. A contract for the supply of a nuclear plant for the production of electrical energy recites as follows: "In no event, whether as a result of breach of contract, tort liability (including negligence), strict liability or otherwise, and whether arising before or after commercial operation of the Plant, shall contractor be liable for damages caused by reason of unavailability of the Plant, Plant shutdowns or service interruptions (including loss of anticipated profits, loss of use of revenue, inventory or use charges, cost of purchased or replacement power, cost of capital, or claims of customers), or other special, incidental, or consequential damages of any nature." An international contract for the supply of locomotives includes the following clause: "In no event shall the Seller (including its subcontractors) be liable for any indirect or consequential damages, including, but not limited to, damages for losses of revenue, cost of capital, claims of customers for service interruptions or failure of supply, and costs and expenses incurred in connection with labor overhead, transportation or substitute facility or supply sources." A contract for the sales of gas turbines for the production of electrical energy contains the following clause: "Notwithstanding any other provisions of this Contract (including indemnity), the Contractor shall not be liable to the Client for indirect damages caused to the Client such as loss of production, loss of profit, loss of orders, claims of customers of the Client, down-time costs, cost of replacement power or consequential

While the exclusion of consequential damages is the norm, some international contracts expressly provide that "consequential" damages are reimbursable. A third type of international contract does not address the issue.

Some of the widely accepted models of international contracts, such as the Fédération Internationale des Ingénieurs-Conseils (FIDIC) forms for Electrical and Mechanical Works,[70] contain a clear exclusion of consequential damages, while other forms are less clear in this respect.[71] The conclusion probably can be drawn that in the practice of international business contracts the exclusion of consequential damages is not a presumed norm. On the contrary, when such an exclusion is not expressly agreed, the non-performing party is liable for consequential damages. Many international contracts overcome difficulties as to the identification of the specific items of damage comprised within the concept of consequential damages by providing a detailed list of the items of damages to be deemed "consequential." Failing such an express contract provision, the identification of reimbursable damages is as difficult in international trade practice as it is in the various municipal laws.

---

damages of any nature." It is evident that the concern of the drafters of the above-mentioned clauses is to cover all possible damages likely to be of similar nature: *consequential, indirect, special, incidental*. To overcome any problem of definition, though, the drafters have spelled out clearly the damages they intended in fact to exclude.

70. Clause 42.1 of the FIDIC (Fédération Internationale des Ingénieurs-Conseils) Conditions of Contract for Electrical and Mechanical Works (3d ed. 1987), recites as follows: "Neither party shall be liable to the other for any loss of profit, loss of use, loss of production, loss of contracts or for any other indirect or consequential damage that may be suffered by the other, except (a) as expressly provided in Clause 27, and (b) those provisions of these Conditions whereby the Contractor is expressly entitled to receive profit." Clause 27, to which Clause 42.1 refers, contemplates the payment of liquidated damages for late delivery.

71. The FIDIC Conditions of Contract for Works of Civil Engineering Construction (4th ed. 1987), are rather ambiguous as to whether or not the liability for consequential damages is excluded. In lieu of any express limitation of liability, Clause 20 of such conditions provides for a rather obscure risk allocation between the contractor and the employer.

A statutory term of reference exists, however, at least for those international contracts that are the subject of treaties establishing uniform legislation, as is the case in the Vienna Convention for the International Sale of Goods. Articles 74 and 77 of the Convention adopt the principle that damages for breach of a contract governed by the Convention must be foreseeable and unavoidable. The Convention does not particularly stress causation as a damage-limiting concept because its drafters believed the notion of foreseeability was sufficient.[72] Furthermore, the Vienna Convention (contrary to many civil law countries)[73] does not provide that foreseeability is inoperative as a limitation when there has been willful misconduct by the party in breach. The effect is a strict regime of foreseeability as a limitation of loss.[74]

---

72. "Damages for breach of contract by one party consist in a sum equal to the loss, including loss of profit, suffered by the other party *as a consequence of the breach*. Such damages may not exceed the loss which the party in breach *foresaw or ought to have foreseen* at the time of the conclusion of the contract, in the light of the facts and matters of which he then knew or ought to have known, as a possible consequence of the breach of contract." Vienna Convention, Art. 74 (emphasis added). Article 74 only refers to damages incurred "as a consequence of the breach;" the requisite that the damages must be the "immediate and direct" consequence of the breach, as contemplated, among others, by French and Italian law, is not emphasized. Furthermore, it has to be observed that the requisites of the causation and the foreseeability do not coincide, to the extent the cause-to-effect relationship must be identified as of the moment when the damage occurs, while the foreseeability of the damage must be evaluated as of the time of conclusion of contract. *See generally* Bianca-Bonell, Commentary on the International Sales Law — The 1980 Vienna Convention 538 (1987); J. Honnold, Uniform law for International Sales §§ 403–408 (1982). Murphey, *Consequential Damages in Contracts for the International Sale of Goods and the Legacy of Hadley,* 23 Geo. Wash. J. Int'l L. & Econ. 415 (1989); Comment, *Measuring Damages Under the UNCISOG,* 50 Ohio St. L. Rev. 737 (1987).

73. *See, e.g.,* Art. 1225 of the Italian Civil Code.

74. *See* Bianca-Bonell, Commentary on the International Sales Law — The 1980 Vienna Convention 538 (1987).

For international contracts not governed by international conventions establishing uniform legislation, the basic rules in the area of liability for damages can be drawn from international arbitrations. As in the Vienna Convention, the concept of foreseeability is the principal criterion for the limitation of damages. A recent award of the International Center for the Settlement of Investment Disputes (ICSID) arbitral tribunal, in the case *Amco v. Republic of Indonesia*,[75] establishes some general legal principles in this area. "According to the rules and principles common to the most important legal systems the damages which are reimbursable for breach of contract are only those which are direct and foreseeable. The requisite of the direct nature of the damages is nothing but a consequence of the need for a cause-to-effect relationship between the breach and the damage. The requisite of the foreseeability is contemplated practically everywhere."[76]

The arbitral tribunal of the International Chamber of Commerce seems to have adopted some generally accepted rules in the area of liability for damages as well. First, there is little doubt that a non-performing party is liable both for the entire damnum emergens (direct out-of-pocket damage) and for the lucrum cessans (loss of profit).[77] The view of many businesspeople that liability for damages does not extend to loss of profit, is somewhat inherently limited to the value of the contract or a percentage thereof, is incorrect. The quantification of damages, particularly the determination of lost profits, is made by the ICC arbitral practice by considering the *cours ordinaire des choses et ce qui était prévisible* (the ordinary course of things, as well as what was foreseeable).[78]

---

75. The award, dated Nov. 10, 1984, is published in 1987 CLUNET 145 (1987).

76. Translation from French.

77. *See* ICC Award No. 1526, 1974 CLUNET 918 (1974). Often, the ICC arbitrators also share the tendency of municipal law judges to evaluate damages on an equitable basis in the absence of more objective criteria. *See* ICC Award No. 2216, 1975 CLUNET 920 (1975). *See also* the ICSID arbitral tribunal award of 4–9 February 1988, Societé Quest Africaine des Bétons Industriels v. Républic de Senegal, 117 CLUNET 201 (1990).

78. This was expressly stated in ICC Award No. 1526. *See also* ICC Award No. 2404, 1976 CLUNET 995 (1976). Worthy of particular mention is the ICC Award No. 21398, 1975 CLUNET 929 (1975), where the arbitrators

The criterion of foreseeability, which is expressed in both common and civil law systems, thus is recognized as a limit to the liability for damages in the practice of international business contracts.

B. *Interest and Currency Fluctuations*

Another trend emerging from international arbitration concerns the interest element of damage assessment. The accrual of interest often is recognized only from the date of an arbitration request.[79] Arbitrators tend to set the interest rate according to equity when they must decide ex aequo et bono.[80] Otherwise, they are inclined to adopt the rate applicable in the country of the creditor.[81] On this subject it is particularly interesting to note the practice of the U.S./Iran Claims Tribunal, where interest payments have been awarded at "varying rates."[82] Of particular interest are the *Sylvania* and *McCollough* cases. In the *Sylvania* case, the arbitrator Böckstiegel considered a 12 percent per year interest rate applicable. Böckstiegel derived such a rate from the returns on investment of the plaintiff, even if such plaintiff had in fact incurred higher financial costs. In *McCollough*, the arbiter Virally found an annual simple rate of interest rate of 10 percent per year to be a "fair rate of interest."[83]

---

applied liquidated damages not expressly agreed upon by the parties. The arbitrators found that a liquidated damages clause corresponded to the international trade usages and applied it as in international norm.

79. ICC Award No. 2745/2762, 1978 Clunet 990 (1977).

80. ICC Award No. 2879, 1979 Clunet 989 (1979); ICC award No. 3226, 1980 Clunet 959 (1980).

81. ICC Award No. 2375, 1976 Clunet 973 (1976); ICC award No. 3093/ 3100, 1980 Clunet 951 (1980).

82. The Iran-United States Claims Tribunal 1981–1983 34 (R. Lillich, ed. 1984).

83. For further details on these cases, *see* Wetter, *Interest as an Element of Damages in the Arbitral Process*, 1986 Int'l Financial L. Rev. 20 (1986). Wetter's analysis deals with the different approaches to the interest as an element of damages followed by the three chambers in which the U.S.-Iran Claims Tribunal was divided, under the chairmanships of Böckstiegel, Virally, and Brower, respectively.

If the currency in which a payment is to be made under a contract, the breach of which is the subject of an international arbitration, is different from the currency of the creditor, devaluation losses generally are awarded as an element of damages. Neither municipal law nor arbitral practice in this respect is settled, particularly as to the issue of whether currency devaluation damages and interest can be cumulatively charged to a breaching party.[84]

---

84. *See generally id.*; F. Mann, THE LEGAL ASPECT OF MONEY 286–289 (1982). The following ICC arbitrations awarded damages based on currency devaluations and interest from the date payments were due, assessing them cumulatively: ICC Awards No. 2745 and 2762, 1978 CLUNET 999 (1978); ICC Award No. 2879, 1979 CLUNET 991 (1979). *See also* Derain's comment to ICC Award No. 2142, 1974 CLUNET 902 (1974), where two other unpublished ICC awards are quoted as an expression of a general principle that the devaluation of the currency in which payments were due is to be assessed from the date payments were due, and is to be included as an additional item of damage to interest for late payment. This principle is well established in Italian law, (Court of Cassation Decision No. 5670 of November 30, 1978, 1979 Giurusprudenza Commerciale, I, 526 (1979); and in Swiss law, Engel, TRAITÉ DES OBLIGATIONS EN DROIT SUISSE 469 (1973). In the common law countries, the analysis is framed in terms of when the exchange rate for a breach of contract is fixed, the alternatives being at the time of the breach or the time a judgment is rendered. English courts traditionally rendered damage awards in pounds sterling at the conversion rate on the day a breach occurred. MCGREGOR ON DAMAGES §§ 332–335 (15th ed. 1988). Since the important case of Miliangos v. George Frank (Textiles), [1976] A. C. 443, however, English courts calculate awards for breach of contract in sterling on the day of the judgment, thus shifting the exchange risk to the party in breach. The courts of New Zealand have followed the Miliangos case. *See* Naylor & Sons Ltd. v. New Zealand Cooperative Wool Marketing Ass'n Ltd., [1981] 1 N.Z.L.R. 361 (C.A.); Volk v. Hirstlens (NZ) Ltd., [1987] 1 N.Z.L.R. 385 (HC). See Black, *Damages for Foreign Exchange Losses in Contract Actions*, 1991 N.Z. REC. L. REV. 189 (1991). The general U.S. rule is the same as the English rule prior to the *Miliangos* case, but U.S. courts distinguish between the two exchange alternatives based on conflicts of law principles — the place of performance of the contract in question, the governing law of the contract, and the country in which a cause of action arises. Generally, if a contract requires payment in a foreign currency in the United States, the exchange rate at the time of a

C. Mitigation

Mitigation is an obligation that is part of international trade usages, as well as a part of both the common law and the civil law.[85] It is mentioned in many arbitral decisions,[86] and the concept is included in Article 77 of the Vienna Convention.[87] The approach of the Vienna Convention is consistent with that of the Uniform Commercial Code.[88]

---

breach is applied. If, however, a contract requires payment abroad in foreign currency, the exchange rate at the time a judgment is rendered is applied. *See generally* CORBIN ON CONTRACTS § 1005 (2d ed. 1963). Similar conclusions can be drawn from international sales contracts, based on the 1980 Vienna Convention.

85. *See* note 18 *supra,* and accompanying text.

86. The obligation by the damaged party to mitigate the damages incurred is expressly enforced as a general principle of international trade law by the following ICC awards: No. 2142, 1974 CLUNET 892 (1974); No. 2103, 1974 CLUNET 902 (1974); Nos. 2216, 2139, and 2478, 1975 CLUNET 917, 925, 929 (1975); No. 2404, 1976 CLUNET 995 (1976); No. 3344, 1982 CLUNET 978 (1982).

87. "A party who relies on a breach of contract must take such measures as are reasonable in the circumstances to mitigate the loss, including loss of profit, resulting from the breach. If he fails to take such measures, the party in breach may claim a reduction in the damages in the amount by which the loss should have been mitigated".

88. *See* U.C.C. § 2-706.

Chapter 4. Contractual Exclusions and Limitations of Liability

4.1 General

The special nature of international contracts frequently causes the parties to create an autonomous, "closed" agreement. For this reason, most international contracts contain agreed limitations and exclusions of liability that are negotiated by the parties. Some of these limitations and exclusions, which characterize the new lex mercatoria, are so frequently encountered that they have become the expectations of international lawyers. This chapter discusses the more important contractual exclusions and limitations of liability from the international perspective.

A theme of this book is that the civil law distinction between *obligations de moyens* and *obligations de résultat* provides a useful context to consider the "pathological" aspects of international contracts. The distinction can be used to analyze contractual exclusion and limitation of the liability for damages. Some contractual exclusion and limitation of liability clauses preclude entitlement to damages altogether; others affect only the amount.

Force majeure clauses are typical examples of the first type of situation. Such clauses have the effect of relieving an obligee from any liability for non-performance, not only with respect to *obligations de moyens* (because a force majeure situation leaves no room for fault or negligence), but also with respect to *obligations de résultat*. Other examples of total exclusions are contractual provisions that condition entitlement to damages on the existence of a certain degree of fault, e.g. willful misconduct or gross negligence. Such clauses obviously are applicable only to *obligations de moyens* because the degree of diligence by an obligee in performance is only relevant with respect to them.

The second type of clause that limits liability assumes that a breach of contract entitles a damaged party to damages, but limits the amount. For example, such clauses may establish a ceiling above which damages are no longer due or a time limit after which no claim for damages may be made. Liquidated damages clauses clearly belong in this category of contractual limitation of liability.

The following paragraphs examine the most typical clauses excluding or limiting liability in international business contracts.[1] We must, however, emphasize that the clauses discussed here must always be distinguished from those whose purpose is to limit the content of an obligation itself. For example, as the term is used here, disclaimer clauses do not include clauses that provide that the obligation of an architect or engineer in an international construction contract is only to re-do defective drawings, with the exclusion of any additional liability. Also not included are clauses that limit the responsibility of an equipment supplier, under an international sales contract, to repair or replace defective parts. Although these clauses sometimes are referred to as "limiting" liability, they really only define the scope of an obligation, beyond which there is no breach of contract at all.

Similarly, we will not consider "hold harmless" clauses. Although they may have the same effect as a contractual disclaimer of liability, their nature is different. Through a hold harmless clause, a party is entitled to recourse against another party to recover damages the first party owes or had to pay to a third party. These contractual indemnity clauses frequently are used, for example, to provide for the indemnification of a purchaser (in an international sales contract) or the licensee (in an international license agreement) against possible claims of third parties alleging violation of industrial property rights in connection with the products sold or manufactured under license. "Hold harmless" clauses do not imply a disclaimer of liability toward a third party. They do, however, represent a form of risk allocation; similar to disclaimer clauses, they produce a shifting of the risk of payment of damages from one party to another.[2]

---

1. The usual English terms for the provisions discussed in this chapter are "exemption clause" and "exclusion clause." In the United States, these often are called "disclaimer clauses" and "limitation clauses."

2. A number of examples of "hold harmless" clauses are included in THE HOLD HARMLESS AGREEMENT (National Underwriter Company, Georgia Chapter, ed. 1977). *See also* Adams-Brownsword, *Contractual Indemnity Clauses*, 1982 J. BUS. L. 200–209 (1982).

4.2 Force Majeure Clauses in International Trade Practice

The concept of force majeure, an event excluding liability for damages, has evolved progressively in international trade practice by assuming many original and autonomous features distinct from similar legal concepts. This evolution has been so conspicuous that it was mainly around the concept of force majeure (together with the related concept of *hardship*)[3] that the theory of the new international lex mercatoria originated.[4] The solutions to problems caused by the effect of time on the performance of contracts offered by municipal laws lag well behind the developments introduced with respect to international business contracts.

It must be remembered that international contracts are generally long-term, relational contracts. Municipal systems, in dealing with force majeure issues, were traditionally confronted with contracts, such as sales contracts, where the performance of both parties occurred immediately or over a relatively short period. For this reason, the negotiators and drafters of international contracts have developed private solutions, better articulated than those offered by municipal laws, to the problems created by the effect of time.

The concept of force majeure is an accepted principle of public international law.[5] The approach of municipal legal systems to the

---

3. § 6.5 *infra*.

4. Goldman, *La lex mercatoria dans les contrats et l'arbitrage internationaux: réalité et perspectives*, 1979 CLUNET 488 (1979), includes force majeure clauses among the first items in his list of the content of the new international lex mercatoria. On the relationship between force majeure clauses and lex mercatoria, *see also* Kahn, *Force majeure et contrats internationaux de longue durée*, 1975 CLUNET 474–485 (1975), M. Fontaine, DROIT DES CONTRATS INTERNATIONAUX 234 (1989); Van Ommeslaghe, *Les clauses de force majeure et d'imprévision (hardship) dans les contrats internationaux*, ICC Document No. 460/233; and 1980 REVUE DE DROIT INTERNATIONAL ET DE DROIT COMPARÉ 15 (1980).

5. "Vienna Convention on the Law of Treaties," ART. 61; S. Rosenne, BREACH OF TREATY 70–72 (1984); Giuliano-Scovazzi-Treves, 1 DIRITTO

problem of impossibility of performance varies from country to country. Roman law conceived it as vis major,[6] i.e., as an unforeseeable and inevitable event, outside the control of an obligee, which makes it absolutely impossible to discharge an obligation. Based on that concept, some Romanistic legal systems, such as those of France[7] and Belgium,[8] have expressly adopted civil code provisions by which the concept of force majeure operates independent of party agreement. The Italian[9] and German[10] legal systems have adopted the similar concept of impossibility of performance due to causes beyond the control of an obligee.

INTERNAZIONALE 609–610 (1983); T. Elias, THE MODERN LAW OF TREATIES 128–134 (1974).

6. De Medio, *Caso fortuito e forza maggiore nel diritto romano*, 1908 BOLLETTINO ISTITUTO DI DIRITTO ROMANO 157 (1908).

7. "There is no occasion for damages where, in consequence of *force majeure* or *cas fortuit* the debtor has been prevented from conveying or doing that to which he was obliged or has done that what he was debarred from doing." Code Civil, Art. 1148. The terms force majeure and *cas fortuit* have the same meaning in French law. *See generally* B. Nicholas, FRENCH LAW OF CONTRACT 193–204 (1982); Weill-Terre, DROIT CIVIL — LES OBLIGATIONS 474 (1980); Nicolas, *Force Majeure and Frustration*, 27 AM. J. COMP. L. 231 (1979); Tunc, *Force Majeure et absence de faute en matière contractuelle*, 1945 REVUE TRIMESTRELLE DE DROIT CIVIL 244 (1945); Smith, *Impossibility of Performance as Excuse in French Law: The Doctrine of Force Majeure*, 45 YALE L. J. 452 (1936).

8. De Page, 2 TRAITÉ ELEMENTAIRE DE DROIT CIVIL BELGE 542–599 (3d ed. 1964).

9. Arts. 1176, 1218, and 1256 of the Italian Civil Code, commented by De Lorenzi, CLASSIFICAZIONI DOGMATICHE E REGOLE OPERAZIONALI IN TEMA DI RESPONSABILITA CONTRATTUALE (1981).

10. § 306 BGB. N. Horn, H. Kötz, & H. Leser, GERMAN PRIVATE AND COMMERCIAL LAW 96–101 (1982); 1 Larenz, LEHRBUCH DES SCHULDRECHTS 250–265 (1979); 1 Esser, SCHULDRECHT § 33 (1970); Dawson, *Judicial Revision of Frustrated Contracts: Germany*, 63 B. U. L. REV., 1039 (1987).

The concept of force majeure is not a part of common law systems.[11] Consistent with the common law approach of strict liability for breach, the traditional common law rule was that conditions rendering performance impossible that occurred after the execution of a contract did not excuse performance because the parties could have provided for such matters in their contract.[12] Modern developments have much eroded this rule, however, and there now exist methods by which contract performance may be excused without payment of damages, provided neither party is truly at fault. Under limited circumstances, a contract also might be rendered void or voidable under various similar theories, including impossibility, frustration of purpose, and impracticability.[13] These concepts originated in English law.[14] Although they have some commonalities with the civil law concepts of force majeure or hardship, the civil law concepts are "far narrower"[15] in the sense that they are unavailable if technical performance is possible. On the other hand, civil law doctrines may be more generous in some circumstances.[16] The U.S. doctrines are defined carefully in both

---

11. FORCE MAJEURE AND FRUSTRATION OF CONTRACT 8 (E. McKendrick, ed. 1991).

12. "When a party by his own contract creates a duty or charge upon himself, he is bound to make it good, if he may, notwithstanding any accident by inevitable necessity, because he might have provided against it by his contract." Paradyne v. Jane, (1647) Aleyn 26.

13. *See generally* FORCE MAJEURE AND FRUSTRATION OF CONTRACT (E. McKendrick ed. 1991); 2 CHITTY ON CONTRACTS §§ 1521–1570 (26th ed. 1989); FARNSWORTH ON CONTRACTS §§ 9.5–9.9 (1990).

14. Anson, ANSON'S LAW OF CONTRACT, 506–507 (1979). For U.S. law, *see* Becker, *Force Majeure and State Intervention in U.S. Law*, 1985 INT'L Bus. Law. 283 (1985); Nicolas, *Force Majeure and Frustration*, 1927 AM. J. COMP. L. 231 (1979).

15. B. Nicholas, FRENCH LAW OF CONTRACT 196 (1982).

16. FORCE MAJEURE AND FRUSTRATION OF CONTRACT 7 (E. McKendrick, ed. 1991).

the U.S. *Restatement (Second) of Contracts*[17] and the Uniform Commercial Code.[18]

The doctrine of impossibility was introduced in the 1863 English case of *Taylor v. Caldwell*.[19] Taylor had rented a music hall from Caldwell, which burned down prior to the scheduled concert. The court held that in contracts where performance depends on the continued existence of a given person or thing, "a condition is implied that the impossibility of performance arising from the perishing of the person or thing shall excuse the performance."[20] Both parties were excused from their obligations.

When, subsequent to contract formation, an unforeseen event renders performance impossible, common law courts often hold that the promisor is excused from performing. This is an exception to the general rule that the promisor must perform or pay damages for the failure to perform.[21] A prerequisite for application of this theory, however, is that the risk had not been allocated within the contract itself or in trade usage or custom related to the transaction.[22]

Two related concepts appear in the *Restatement (Second)*, Section 261 entitled "Discharge by Supervening Impracticability." Its contents are self-explanatory:

---

17. RESTATEMENT (SECOND) OF CONTRACTS (1979).

18. U.C.C. (1979). A review of the authorities reveals that the English doctrine of frustration, which contains what in the United States might be called "impossibility," "impracticability," or "frustration of purpose," is rather narrower than the U.S. doctrines, although modern English have and continue to widen it. *See generally* FORCE MAJEURE AND FRUSTRATION OF CONTRACT (E. McKendrick, ed. 1991); Battersby, *Frustration — A Limited Future*, 134 SOLIC. L. J. 354 (March 1990).

19. 122 ENG. REP. 309 (K.B. 1863). *See also* FARNSWORTH ON CONTRACTS § 9.5 (1990); J. Calamari & J. Perillo, CONTRACTS 2D. 479 (West Hornbook series, 1982).

20. *See* J. Calamari & J. Perillo, CONTRACTS 2D. 479 (West Hornbook series, 1981) (Statement of Justice Blackburn).

21. *Id.* at 477.

22. *Id.* at 470.

Where, after a contract is made, a party's performance is made impracticable *without his fault* by the occurrence of an event, the non-occurrence of which was a basic assumption in which the contract was made, his duty to render that performance is discharged, unless the language or the circumstances indicate the contrary.

The Uniform Commercial Code, in Section 2-615, entitled "Excuse by Failure of Presupposed Conditions," also employs the term "impracticable" as encompassing "impossible." Although in both the *Restatement* and the U.C.C. the concept is termed "impracticable," courts have been reluctant to accept anything short of impossibility as an excuse for performance.[23]

Frustration of purpose likewise was detailed in early English case law. In *Krell v. Henry*,[24] an apartment was rented for two days because it afforded a good view of King Edward VII's coronation procession. When the coronation was canceled due to the king's illness, the landlord sued for the rent. The defendant was excused from his payment, despite the fact that the plaintiff made no promise that the coronation would proceed.[25]

The current U.S. statement of the principle derived from *Krell v. Henry* and other cases is found in Section 265 of the *Restatement (Second) of Contracts*:

Where, after a contract is made, a party's principal purpose is substantially frustrated without his fault by the occurrence of an event, the

---

23. *Id.* at 491.

24. 2 K.B. 740 (1903).

25. A definition of the English doctrine of frustration was given by Lord Radcliffe. "Frustration occurs whenever the law recognizes that without default of either party a contractual obligation has become incapable of being performed because the circumstances in which performance is called for would render it a thing radically different from that which was undertaken by the contract." Davis Contractors Ltd. v. Fareham Urban District Council, (A.C., 1956, at 696 and 729). In the various Suez Canal cases, however, the closure of the Suez Canal was not considered by the English courts as a sufficient cause for excusing non-performance of the contract obligations affected. More recently, and along the same lines, *see* The Chrysalis (1983), 1 W. L. R. 1469; The Evia (1983), A. C. 736; The Wenjiang (1983), 1 LLOYD'S REP. 400.

non-occurrence of which was a basic assumption on which the contract was made, his remaining duties to render performance are discharged, unless the language or the circumstances indicate the contrary.

As with impracticability, courts will not apply the doctrine of frustration unless the frustration is "total or nearly total."[26] Under Section 272 of the *Restatement*, restitution, meaning placing the parties in their pre-contractual positions, may be awarded. Awards also may be made to reliance interest as justice requires.[27]

In the socialist countries, the concept of force majeure has some peculiar connotations, due to the fact that one of the contracting parties is often the state itself.[28] As extensive comparative analyses on the subject of force majeure already are available,[29] the treatment here

---

26. *See* J. Calamari & J. Perillo, CONTRACTS 2D. 479 (West Hornbook series, 1982), at 495, quoting Lloyd v. Murphy, 153 P.2d 47 (1944).

27. RESTATEMENT (SECOND) OF CONTRACTS § 272 (1979), entitled "Relief Including Restitution."

28. Rajski, *Basic Principles of International Trade Law in Certain European Socialist States and of East-West Trade Relations*, 1978 DROIT ET PRATIQUE DU COMMERCE INTERNATIONAL 9 (1978); Sokolow, *La Force Majeure dans les contrats entre sociétés occidentals et centrales commerciales soviétiques*, 1978 DROIT ET PRATIQUE DU COMMERCE INTERNATIONAL 323 (1978); Strohbach, *Force Majeure and Hardship Clauses in International Commercial Contracts and Arbitration*, 1984 J. INT'L ARB. 39 (1984).

29. Among the most important comparative surveys are FORCE MAJEURE AND FRUSTRATION OF CONTRACT (E. McKendrick, ed. 1991); 2 K. Zweigert & H. Kötz, AN INTRODUCTION TO COMPARATIVE LAW 159 (2d ed. 1987); Goff, *Force Majeure and Frustration*, LA VENDITA INTERNAZIONALE, QUADERNI DI GIURISPRUDENZA COMMERCIALE n. 39, 301 (1981); Lesguillons, *Frustration, Force Majeure, Imprévision, Wegfall der Geschäftsgrundlage, Unmöglichkeit, Changed Circumstances*, 1986 J. INT'L ARB. 29 (1986); Brabant, LE CONTRAT INTERNATIONAL DE CONSTRUCTION 292 (1981); Green, *Force Majeure in International Construction Contracts*, 13 INT'L BUS. LAW. 505 (1985); Schmitthoff, *Frustration of International Contracts of Sale in English and Comparative Law*, in PROBLEMES DE L'INEXECUTION ET DE LA FORCE MAJEURE DANS LES CONTRATS DE VENTE INTERNATIONALE 127–158 (Assoc. Int. Sc. Jur., Helsinki, 1961).

is brief. It is, however, important to emphasize that the various national concepts of force majeure, although theoretically quite different, have some commonalities.[30] First of all, the event constituting a force majeure situation must not only always be outside the control of the obligee, but also *unforeseeable* and *irresistible*. It must be such as to make the discharge of an obligation objectively impossible. It is insufficient that the performance of an obligation becomes simply particularly difficult, or, in any case, more difficult than was originally contemplated at the time of the contract's execution. Second, the consequence of force majeure, in all municipal laws where it is present, is the extinction of the obligation, not the suspension of its performance for a given period of time.[31]

The practice of international business contracts, on the other hand, overcomes the restricted boundaries within which national laws confine the effects of force majeure, so that the concept has acquired a new dimension in international trade usage.[32] To describe that dimension we will analyse: (1) the practice of the international business contracts; (2) the efforts of codification of such practice through con-

---

30. "[A]ttentive readers will repeatedly have noticed that the practical results . . . are much more often in agreement than one would expect in view of their theoretical starting points." 2 K. ZWEIGERT & H. KÖTZ, AN INTRODUCTION TO COMPARATIVE LAW 200 (2d ed. 1987). "The respective provisions of civil and common law of impossibility seem irreconcilable at first glance. This impression is misleading." Marcatonio, *Unifying the Law of Impossibility*, 8 HAST. INT'L & COMP. L. REV. 41 (1984).

31. An exception to this rule is Art. 1256, para. 2, of the Italian Civil Code, which allows a suspension of performance.

32. The existence of an international or transnational notion of force majeure is widely recognized. *See*, inter alia, Delaume, *Excuse for Non-Performance and Force Majeure in Economic Development Agreements*, 10 COLUM. J. TRANSNAT'L. 242 (1971); Delaume, *Change of Circumstances and Force Majeure Clauses in Transnational Loans*, 1981 DROIT ET PRATIQUE DU COMMERCE INTERNATIONAL 333 (1981); Bruner, *Allocation of Risks in International Construction: Revisiting the Murphy's Law, the FIDIC Conditions and the Doctrine of Force Majeure*, 1986 INT'L CONSTR. L. REV. 259 (1986); Myers, *Government Influence on International Construction Contracts*, 13 INT'L BUS. LAW. 105 (1985).

tract models and forms prepared by international organizations, industry associations, or individual companies, including the model force
majeure clause prepared by the International Chamber of Commerce;
(3) the concept of force majeure as contained in the Vienna Convention; and (4) International Chamber of Commerce (ICC) arbitration
practice.

A. *The Practice of International Business Contracts Concerning Force Majeure*

Several analytical surveys of the use of force majeure clauses in
international business contracts have been published in Europe.[33] It
is clear that a force majeure clause, often very detailed, is almost
invariably included in an international business contract, irrespective
of its proper or selected governing law. Even when the proper or
selected governing law is, for example, that of England, clauses that
refer to the French term force majeure are common.[34] The expression
"force majeure" is always written in French, even if the contract is
written in a different language. This is due to the fact that in this area
the international trade usages found their inspiration in the French
legal tradition.[35]

---

33. We refer specifically to the surveys of Kahn, *Force majeure et contrats
    internationaux de longue durée*, 1975 Clunet 474–485 (1975) and of
    Fontaine, Droit des Contrats Internationaux 211–268 (1989). *See also*
    Draetta, *La prassi dei contratti internazionali in tema di clausole penali
    e di clausole limitative della responsabilità*, 2 Diritto del Commercio
    Internazionale 527 (1987). Examples of force majeure clauses in in-
    ternational trade practice also are reported by Frignani, Il Diritto del
    Commercio Internazionale 345 (1986) and by Brabant, Le Contrat
    International de Construction 405 (1981).

34. "I regret the introduction of foreign words into English statutes and
    orders without any definition of them being given." Sankey, J.,
    Hackney Borough Council v. Dore, [1922] 1 K.B. 431, A similar dis-
    approval can be found in Matsoukis v. Priestmen, [1915] 1 K. B. 681,
    685.

35. The French term appears in English and U.S. cases and even statutes,
    sometimes with reference to its meaning in French law. *See id.*

Force majeure clauses generally are drafted in such a way as to offer first a definition of the concept, followed by a non-exhaustive, "including but not limited to" list of the events that the parties agree to constitute force majeure. After the list, these clauses usually describe the behavior expected from the party affected by a force majeure event. Typically, there is a specific obligation to take all possible measures to remove the force majeure condition, or to minimize its impact on the performance of the contract.

Force majeure clauses generally contemplate either the suspension of the duty to discharge an obligation or the extension of the time of performance. Such an extension normally is for a period corresponding to the duration of the force majeure condition. Sometimes, force majeure clauses specify that if, after the expiration of a given period, a force majeure condition still exists, one or both parties may terminate the contract. More often, however, the parties agree to a renegotiation of the contract to adapt it to the new circumstances. As an alternative to a renegotiation, or in case of its failure, force majeure clauses occasionally contemplate recourse to arbitration or some other kind of alternative dispute resolution, such as a mini-trial or a technical expertise procedure. Sometimes, the party affected by the force majeure condition may recover from the other party extra costs incurred as a consequence (e.g., cost of idle equipment, additional rental costs, etc.), thus allocating to the other party the risk of the occurrence of the force majeure event. It is evident that broad force majeure clauses of the type described above overlap with hardship clauses, in that their effect is to adapt a contract to changed circumstances.[36]

By agreeing to such broad force majeure clauses, parties to international contracts appear to be willing to adopt a "de-nationalized" or transnational notion of force majeure in lieu of the generally narrower corresponding concepts contained in the proper or selected law of the contract. This intent is particularly apparent in the frequently encountered force majeure clauses that refer to what is *internationally regarded as force majeure,*[37] or *generally recognized as force majeure,*[38]

---

36. § 6.5 *infra.*

37. *See* Kahn, *Force majeure et contrats internationaux de longue durée,* 1975 CLUNET 474 (1975).

38. *See* Fontaine, DROIT DES CONTRATS INTERNATIONAUX 215 (1989).

or to those force majeure causes *recognized as such by the ICC arbitration practice.* Parties to international contracts thus appear to be aware of the existence in international trade usages of a concept of force majeure that is independent of any specific national law, and they increasingly are willing to adopt that concept.

The first characteristic of force majeure clauses in international contracts is that they generally are very detailed and more articulated than their domestic counterparts. Analyzing their content more closely, other recurring features can be observed. First, the requisites for a given event to constitute force majeure are less restrictive in international trade practice than in municipal laws. For example, the requirements of municipal systems that an event of force majeure not be attributable to the obligee and must be irresistible often are replaced by the reference to events that are *beyond the control of the parties*, or even only *beyond the reasonable control of the parties.* In this way, the requirements of party innocence and irresistibility are not evaluated in the abstract, that is, objectively, but with respect to the specific subjective position of a given party and its particular professional background.[39]

In other cases, events of force majeure are defined as events that do not necessarily render contract performance impossible, but that hamper the *normal* discharge of the contract obligation, or make it

---

39. In commenting on the expression "beyond the reasonable control of the parties," Kahn, *Force majeure et contrats internationaux de longue durée*, 1975 CLUNET 474, 476–477 (1975), very appropriately states that almost all the obstacles can in theory be overcome, applying the necessary resources. However, "*une communauté d'entrepreneurs n'est pas une communauté d'héros*" (a community of businessmen is not a community of heroes), hence formulae of this kind imply that in the economic context in which businesspeople operate it is not possible to apply any resource irrespective of cost. As Kahn observes, this acknowledgment of the relevance of economic and social factors is alien to the traditional concept of force majeure as an act of God that made the performance of the contract absolutely impossible. In their more modern formulations, force majeure clauses basically achieve the result of providing a conventional risk allocation between the parties, which is ultimately a function of their respective bargaining positions.

exorbitant from an industrial or commercial stand-point.[40] The over-lap with hardship changes is clear here as well.[41] Even the require-ment of the unforeseeability of the event, always present in municipal law, sometimes is attenuated in international trade practice and, in certain cases, omitted entirely.[42]

The list of specific force majeure events included in international contracts has evolved in such a way as to include, in addition to the classical events of natural calamities and wars, impediments to the ability of the parties to fulfil their obligations due to (1) the increas-ing participation of states or their entities in business activities (au-thorizations, approvals, concessions, and regulations) or (2) turmoil of a social nature (strikes, lock-outs). In this way, a force majeure event becomes any event that prevents a party from performing at the due date, and is beyond its control, thus including, in the most extreme cases, difficulties in the sourcing of raw materials or in their transpor-tation or accidental damage to production equipment or processes.[43]

Another important feature of force majeure clauses in the practice of the international business contracts is a formal obligation of the party affected to provide notice of a force majeure event. Failure to provide such notice often results in the drastic consequence of the inability to rely on the force majeure clause to excuse non-performance. However, such a drastic consequence does not appear automatically to result from a failure to provide timely notice; there usually must be an express provision in the contract.[44]

---

40. *See* Fontaine, *Les clauses de force majeure dans les contrats inter-nationaux*, 1979 Droit et Pratique du Commerce International 475 (1979).

41. § 6.6 *infra*.

42. *See* Fontaine, Droit des Contrats Internationaux 215 (1989).

43. Interpetrol Bermuda Ltd. v. Kaiser Aluminum International, Inc., 719 F.2d 992 (9th Cir. 1983) (deals with "economic force majeure").

44. This is basically the opinion expressed by Kahn, *Force majeure et contrats internationaux de longue durée*, 1975 Clunet 474, 477–478 (1975), and Fontaine, Droit des Contrats Internationaux 225 (1989). It is interesting to observe, in this connection, that Art. 79, paragraph 4, of the Vienna Convention provides that the party breaching a notice

As to the consequences of the force majeure event, the general rule is that it implies first of all a disclaimer of liability for the effects of such event, i.e., normally for the delay in performance, or — with respect to certain types of obligation — for the failure to perform. This exclusion of responsibility implies that the obligee is not liable for damages, as it would be under the general doctrine of breach of contract. The ultimate consequence is that the risk connected with the occurrence of the force majeure event is shifted from the obligee to the other party of the contract.

The burden of proving the existence of a force majeure event almost invariably is placed on the party relying on it. If an obligee produces satisfactory evidence in this respect, the result is that the party is not liable for breach of contract. With respect to *obligations de résultat*, of course, this is the only way an obligee could be excused. In *obligations de moyens*, the other party still must attempt to prove the fault of the obligee.[45]

Contrary to most municipal laws that adopt a notion of force majeure, in international trade practice, force majeure does not necessarily result in the termination of a contract. More often, performance is merely suspended for the duration of the force majeure condition. Normally, upon the cessation of a force majeure condition, the contract revives without consequence. If a force majeure event is or becomes permanent, then termination of a contract is sometimes provided for, but more often the parties provide for renegotiation or recourse to arbitration to adapt the contract to the changed circumstances. In conclusion, unlike the approach of municipal systems, in which force majeure traditionally has the effect of terminating the contract, international trade practice evolved in the direction of preserving the agreement to the extent possible.

---

obligation must simply reimburse the other party's damages caused by such a breach. The right to be excused from performance, however, remains.

45. Lesguillons, *Frustration, Force Majeure, Imprévision, Wegfall der Geschäftsgrundlage, Unmöglichkeit, Changed Circumstances*, 1986 J. Int'l Arb. 520 (1986).

B. *International Contract Models and Forms*

International trade usages of force majeure are contained in, and at the same time influenced by, models and forms of international contracts. This is the case, indirectly, of the FIDIC contract forms for civil works and for electrical and mechanical works. In their latest version, the forms contain an express reference to force majeure. In addition, force majeure issues are dealt with in detail by the clauses concerning *excepted risks* and *special risks*.[46] In other words, the FIDIC forms emphasize a particular risk allocation, in the sense that for certain events the risk is shifted from the obligee to the other party of the contract, normally the owner.[47]

Force majeure situations are more specifically addressed in the contract model issued by the International Law Association for foreign investments in developing countries. This contract model contains a force majeure clause that provides for different consequences of a force majeure event depending on whether it affects a private party or a state.[48]

Other force majeure clauses, drafted along the lines of international practice as described above, are contained in the contract model prepared by the Economic Commission for Europe of the United Nations

---

46. FARNSWORTH ON CONTRACTS § 9.9a (1990) recommends to U.S. draftspersons that they eschew the term "force majeure" in favor of less legally connotative terms like "exemptions" or "changed circumstances."

47. As to the FIDIC Contract Model For Civil Works (4th ed. 1987), *see* Clause 65 (Special Risks). As to the FIDIC Contract Model For Electrical And Mechanical Works (3d ed. 1987), *see* Clause 44. A comment to such clauses, although in their earlier version, is included in Wallace, THE INTERNATIONAL CIVIL ENGINEERING CONTRACT, 44–46, 53–55, 162–168 (1974).

48. *See* Art. 17 of the contract model adopted by the International Law Association on the occasion of its 56th Conference held in New Delhi from December 28th, 1974 to January 4th, 1975.

(E.C.E.),[49] some industry associations,[50] governmental agencies in charge of foreign trade,[51] and private companies.[52]

Document No. 421 of the International Chamber of Commerce, which contains a rather elaborate model force majeure clause for international contracts, warrants special attention.[53] This clause, to which contract parties may expressly refer, is largely inspired by the de-

---

49. Art. 13 of the General Conditions for the Export and Import of Solid Fuels of August 1958; Art. 20 of the General Conditions for the Erection of Plant and Machinery Abroad, No. 5740 of August 1963.

50. *See* Arts. 23 and 24 of the Contract for Canadian and United States of America Grain in Bulk, No. 30, prepared by the Grain and Feed Trade Association; Art. 19 of the International Contract for Skins, No. 5, prepared by the Hide and Skins Sellers' Association; Art. 7 of the Conditions of Sale, C.I.F., prepared by United States Steel International, in A. Lowenfeld, INTERNATIONAL PRIVATE TRADE, 153, 165, 171 (1975); Clause 17 of the Refined Sugar Association Contract, in FORCE MAJEURE AND FRUSTRATION OF CONTRACT 9 (E. McKendrick, ed. 1991).

51. *See* Art. 9 of the USSR Standard Sales Contract Form; Art. 12 of the USSR Standard Purchase Contract Form; Art. 9 of the general terms and conditions adopted by the Algerian government agency Sonatrach, as applied to the contract of October 9th, 1969 between Sonatrach and El Paso, reprinted in LES HYDROCARBURES GASEUX ET LE DEVELOPEMENT DES PAYS PRODUCTEURS 393 (1974); Art. 24 of the Association Contract of 1980 between Tunisian Enterprise for Petroleum Activities (ETAP) and Occidental of Tunisia, Inc., reprinted in PETROLEUM LEGISLATION, NORTH AFRICA Suppl. 56 at 13; Arts. 2.7 and 3 of the 1979 Model Production Contract between Pertamina and Private Companies, reprinted in PETROLEUM LEGISLATION, ASIA AND AUSTRALASIA Suppl. 72.

52. Art. IV of the General Conditions of Sale of Westinghouse Electric Corporation, published in A. Lowenfeld, INTERNATIONAL PRIVATE TRADE 179 (1975); Art. 23 of the Joint Operating Agreement of December 20th, 1977 between the British National Oil Corporation (BNOC), Texas North Sea U.K. Ltd., and Texaco North Sea U.K. Co., reprinted in PETROLEUM LEGISLATION, EUROPE, Suppl. 54.

53. This document, published in 1985, originates from the study of force majeure clauses by Van Ommeslaghe, *Les clauses de force majeure et d'imprévision (hardship) dans les contrats internationaux,* 1980 REVUE DE DROIT INTERNATIONAL ET DE DROIT COMPARÉ 15 (1980). It is appended to this chapter as Appendix 3.

finition of force majeure contained in the Vienna Convention. To that definition, however, it adds a non-exhaustive list of force majeure events. In the ICC clause, the consequences of force majeure are the exclusion of liability for non-performance, a reasonable extension period in which performance must occur, and the right of either party to terminate the contract in case the force majeure condition continues beyond that period.

These contract models constitute an impressive testimony of how deeply a transnational concept of force majeure is consolidated and accepted in international trade practice.

C. Article 79 of the Vienna Convention on the International Sale of Goods

The Vienna Convention, although it applies solely to sales contracts, reflects the existence of international trade usage in the area of force majeure. Article 79 appears to mark an evolution with respect to the corresponding Article 74 of the previous 1964 Uniform Law on the International Sale of Goods (ULIS). While the latter was inspired by the traditional concept of force majeure, the Vienna Convention adopts some of the more recent developments, at least when it defines force majeure as an "impediment beyond [the] control" of a party, in connection with which such party "could not reasonably be expected to have taken the impediment into account at the time of the conclusion of the contract or to have avoided or overcome it or its consequences."

When a party can prove that failure to perform an obligation is due to an "impediment beyond its control," it is no longer liable for non-performance. The term "impediment" has been interpreted to include not only cases of absolute impossibility of performance, but also those where performance is so onerous that it cannot be reasonably expected from an obligee.[54] Furthermore, the formula adopted by Article 79 of the Vienna Convention tends to reconcile the civil law and common law notions of breach of contract.[55] Its reference to "impediments,"

---

54. J. Honnold, Uniform Law for International Sales under the 1980 United Nations Convention 443 (1982).

55. Marcatonio, *Unifying the Law of Impossibility*, 8 Hastings Int'l & Comp. L. Rev. 41 (1984).

rather than to the more generic term "circumstances" used by the prior 1964 ULIS Convention, generally is interpreted in the sense that the seller cannot be excused for non-performance on the basis of its ignorance of any defects in the goods being sold.[56]

D. *International Chamber of Commerce Arbitration Practice with Respect to Force Majeure*

ICC arbitration practice has played a very important role in the development of international trade usages with respect to force majeure. Many ICC arbitral awards appear to adopt the classic notion of force majeure as an event that is outside the control of the obligee and is at the same time unforeseeable and irresistible. For example, a 1974 ICC arbitral award recognized that the repeal of an export authorization issued by a government agency constituted a force majeure event on the basis of the "general principles of law."[57] A change in the applicable exchange control laws has been denied the benefit of force majeure event, because, according to the ICC Arbitral Tribunal, such a change was not unforeseeable in that specific case,[58] since the obligee was an agency of the same government that issued the new exchange control regulations. The arbitrators argued not only that the event was foreseeable but that it was also within and not beyond the control of the obligee. In other words, they considered that the autonomous legal personality of the government agency was not sufficient to insulate its liability from that of the government issuing the

---

56. *See* J. Honnold, Uniform Law for International Sales under the 1980 United Nations Convention 430 (1982). Some doubts are expressed, though, by Nicholas, *Force Majeure and Frustration*, 27 Am. J. Comp. L. 249 (1979), who believes that under some circumstances, a seller that is only an intermediary can be excused for defects in the goods it ignored. Bianca-Bonell, Commentary on the International Sales Law — The 1980 Vienna Sales Convention, 572–595 (1987), provides an exhaustive commentary to Art. 79 of the Vienna Convention.

57. ICC Award No. 2478 of 1974, 1975 Clunet 925 (1975).

58. ICC Award No. 3093/3100 of 1979, 1980 Clunet 951 (1980). This award is particularly interesting in that it offers a systematic reconstruction of the notion of force majeure in international trade law.

exchange control regulations. This arbitral award does not appear to be in line with the predominant tendency of arbitral tribunals, which is not to pierce the "corporate veils" of public agencies with respect to the government of which they are a part.[59]

In another ICC case, national exchange control regulations, coupled with the decrease in the market price of the oil an obligee had agreed to purchase, were deemed to be neither unforeseeable nor irresistible events, and were thus inadequate to excuse performance.[60]

The regulations of some Arab countries that imposed a boycott on Israeli goods[61] did not constitute, according to another ICC arbitral award,[62] a force majeure event that would excuse the obligee from its maintenance obligations with respect to products it exported to an Arab country. The obligee had argued that the Jewish religion of the maintenance engineer prevented him from working in the countries where the products had to be maintained. The arbitrators easily found that the boycott provisions of the Arab country in question were not irresistible, and perhaps not even unforeseeable.

Finally, the threat of a third party to seize oil that an obligee had agreed to purchase under an invalidation of title suit was not sufficient to excuse performance, according to another ICC arbitral decision.[63] The obligee claimed that he had received such a threat from

---

59. An award dated July 3, 1958 by the Arbitral Tribunal for USSR Foreign Trade considered that a foreign trade government agency was not responsible for a decision of the USSR central bank in the area of exchange control. In this respect, *see* Fouchard, L'ARBITRAGE COMMERCIAL INTERNATIONAL 200 (1965); Domke, *The Israeli-Soviet Oil Arbitration*, 1959 AM. J. INT'L L. 787 (1959). The House of Lords in England took a similar position when it considered that a Polish sugar exporter was not liable for breach of contract when the Polish government cancelled the export licenses already granted: Czarnikow Ltd. vs. Centrala Handru Zalgranicznego "Rolimpex," [1978] 2 ALL E. R. 1043.

60. ICC Award No. 2216 of 1974, 1975 CLUNET 917 (1975).

61. These regulations are published in PALESTINE YEARBOOK OF INTERNATIONAL LAW Vols. 3, 4 (1986 and 1987).

62. ICC Award No. 1782 of 1973, 1975 CLUNET 923 (1973).

63. ICC Award Nos. 2142 of 1974, 1974 CLUNET 982 (1974); No. 2139 of 1974, 1975 CLUNET 929 (1975).

a third party entitled to exploit the oil field prior to subsequent na-
tionalization measures.

As to the consequences of force majeure, ICC arbitrators generally
are inclined to recognize the suspension of a duty to perform, but
only for the duration of a force majeure condition. In one specific
case, such a condition consisted of a war.[64] In another case, the tribunal stated that the lack of timely notice, as contractually agreed,
determined the forfeiture of the right to claim force majeure.[65]

The EEC Court of Justice also has developed a concept of force
majeure, with specific reference to EEC agricultural law.[66]

This survey suggests that while the contractual practice seems
to be oriented toward a substantial broadening of the force majeure
notion, ICC arbitral practice is still reluctant to acknowledge the
existence of a general principle of law in this respect, which could be
applicable even in the absence of an express contractual provision.
Most ICC arbitrators still insist that a force majeure condition be
unforeseeable, irresistible, and beyond the control of the obligee, as
the classical French doctrine requires. It therefore can be concluded
that events that do not determine the absolute impossibility of performing the obligation can be qualified as force majeure in international
contracts only when expressly provided for by the parties. A number
of typical force majeure clauses are appended to this chapter.

---

64. ICC Award No. 1703 of 1971, 1974 CLUNET 894 (1974).

65. ICC Award No. 2478 of 1974, 1975 CLUNET 925 (1975). For a more
complete survey of the ICC arbitration practice with respect to force
majeure, *see* Melis, *Force Majeure and Hardship Clauses in International Commercial Contracts in View of the Practice of the ICC Court
of Arbitration*, 1984 J. INT'L ARB. 214 (1984). With specific respect to
ICC arbitral decisions concerning force majeure in international sales
contracts, *see* Derains, *La jurisprudence arbitrale de la CCI en matière
de vente internationale: expérience et perspectives*, in LA VENDITA
INTERNAZIONALE, QUADERNI DI GIURISPRUDENZA COMMERCIALE, No. 39, 343,
352–355 (1981).

66. *See* FORCE MAJEURE AND FRUSTRATION OF CONTRACT 213–229 (E.
McKendrick, ed. 1991). Off. J. Eur. Comm. No. C 259/10 of October
6, 1988.

4.3 Other Limitations of Liability Based on the Degree of Fault

Force majeure constitutes a cause of exclusion of the liability for breach of international contracts, affecting the entitlement to damages itself. The negotiators of international contracts have broadened the concept by defining as force majeure a number of events that are not necessarily unforeseeable, irresistible, and beyond the control of an affected party. In this manner, the practice has created the practical result of shifting the risk of the occurrence of such events from the party suffering them to the other party. Economically, this reflects the framework of the overall risk allocation agreed upon by the parties to international business contracts.

Other than force majeure, cases of total disclaimers of liability for breach of contract are only very infrequently contained in international business contracts. This reflects the general disfavor in which municipal laws hold broad disclaimers of liability. Municipal systems generally adopt as a general principle that contractual obligations must be undertaken with a certain degree of seriousness, to which broad exclusions of liability are antithetical.[67]

Total disclaimers of liability discussed here must be kept distinct from contractual provisions that define the scope of an obligation. Such provisions eliminate any obligation at all beyond the agreed scope. Redefinitions of the scope of an obligation and limitations remedies are not infrequent in practice. Limitations of warranty and maintenance obligations are common, as are clauses stating that delivery terms are indicative only, thus negating possible penalties or other forms of compensation for late delivery. It would be clearly erroneous to characterize such provisions as exclusions of liability for late delivery. Instead, it is the delivery obligation itself that does not contemplate a firm delivery term. Obviously, courts applying the law of a contract would fix the term in the event of dispute.

---

67. *See* Bernardini, *La patologia dei contratti internazionali*, 1984 GIURIS-PRUDENZA PIEMONTESE 799 (1984), offering a comparative analysis of the various practical solutions to the problem of reconciling the freedom of the parties to determine the content of their contractual relationships with the need to avoid abuse.

Although total disclaimers of liability, other than for force majeure, are rare in international contract practice, similar results are more frequently obtained through limitations of damages for breach.[68] There are, however, contractual provisions frequently contained in international contracts by which liability for breach is limited or avoided in specific circumstances. Clauses that exclude liability depending on the degree of diligence applied by a party are common. Classic examples are clauses providing that a party is liable only for "gross negligence" or "wilful misconduct." In civil law systems, such clauses sometimes are void or unenforceable as being against public order or other statutory provisions. In some civil law countries, such as Italy and France, liability cannot be excluded when fraud, willful misconduct, or gross negligence is present. Other countries, such as Belgium, Japan, and Mexico, prohibit only exclusions of liability for fraud or willful misconduct.[69] The common law countries regulate such clauses by statute and by common law doctrines.[70]

All these provisions are evidence of the general antipathy shown by national legal systems toward exclusions and limitations of lia-

---

68. § 4.4 *infra.*

69. Interesting comparative surveys of the municipal laws in this respect are published in 1985 INT'L TRADE L. REV. 479 (1985). *See also* Fontaine, DROIT DES CONTRATS INTERNATIONAUX 171–210 (1983); Eörsi, *The Validity of the Clauses Excluding or Limiting Liability*, 23 AM. J. COMP. L. 215 (1975); Von Hippel, *The Control of Exemption Clauses. A Comparative Study*, 15 INT'L & COMP. L. Q. 591 (1967).

70. In England, the doctrine of the breach of a fundamental term, in the presence of which an exclusion of liability is presumed to be invalid, has now been largely replaced by the Unfair Contract Terms Act. The presumption is now rebuttable. "There is a strong, though rebuttable, presumption that in inserting a clause of exclusion or limitation in their contract the parties are not contemplating breaches of fundamental terms and such clauses do not apply to relieve a party from the consequences of such a breach." Suisse Atlantique Société d'Armement Maritime S.A. v. N.V. Rotterdamsche Kolen Centrale, [1967] 1 A.C. 427. The doctrine is now primarily a rule of construction. Photo Production Ltd. v. Securicor Transport Ltd., [1980] A.C. 827. In the United States, the doctrine of unconscionability, introduced by the U.C.C., has played a significant role.

bility. This antipathy is at the source of a number of other municipal law provisions that, although not prohibiting exclusions or limitations of liability, establish mechanisms aimed at protecting the weaker party that accepts them. Examples of such measures are the formal requirements to which certain "adhesion" or "leonine" clauses (including clauses limiting liability) must be submitted.[71] In most countries, exclusion clauses of this kind are interpreted against their drafter, i.e., according to their narrower meaning (interpretatio contra proferentem),[72] or their effect is mitigated by the recourse to the principle of good faith and its negative counterpart, "unconscionability."[73]

Limitations of liability that depend on various degrees of negligence by the obligee can be conceived only with respect to the *obligations de moyens*, because only for the latter are the notions of fault or negligence relevant. It would be impossible to conceive any such limitation of liability with respect to the *obligations de résultat*, be-

---

71. In Italy, for example, Art. 1341 of the Civil Code requires that such leonine clauses (*clausule leonine*) be specifically and separately approved by the other party when they are included in contracts. The U.C.C. requires that contractual provisions that disclaim the warranties implied by the U.C.C. be "conspicuous." U.C.C. § 2-316(2). Some provisions in contracts governed by the U.C.C. must be separately signed. U.C.C. § 2-205.

72. For example, the principle of interpretatio contra proferentem is codified by Art. 1370 of the Italian Civil Code. Article 5 of the German Law on the Regulation of Standardized Contracts (*Gesetz zur Regelung der Allgemeinen Geschäftsbedingungen ABGB*) contains the contra Proferentem rule. *See generally* Holmes and Thürman, A *New and Old Theory for Analyzing Standardized Contracts*, 17 GA. J. INT'L & COMP. L. 323 (1987). The principle is a rule of construction in the common law countries, particularly where a clause is a part of a standard contract or a result of unequal bargaining positions. For English law, *see* Houghton v. Trafalgar Ins., [1954] 1 Q. B. 247; Hollier v. Rambler Motors (A.M.C.) Ltd., [1972] 2 Q.B. 71. For U.S. law, *see* RESTATEMENT (SECOND) OF CONTRACTS § 206 (1979).

73. J. O'Connor, GOOD FAITH IN ENGLISH LAW 20–23 (1990); FARNSWORTH ON CONTRACTS § 4.28; U.C.C. § 2-302. Slawson, *Unconscionable Coercion: The German Version*, 89 HARV. L. REV. 1041 (1976).

cause these are not affected by any consideration as to the faulty or negligent behavior of an obligee.

Municipal laws often define liability as "objective" (in civil law countries), or "strict" or "absolute" (in common law countries). Such definitions are often "jus imperii," i.e., they are contained in "public order" statutory provisions that may not be varied by private agreement.[74]

They thus may render void contract provisions that exclude liability when a contract breach is attributable to simple negligence. The applicable law in such cases would prevent inquiry as to the degree of fault by a party in breach of contract, and would impose strict or absolute liability. Also, uniform laws codified by international treaties may contain provisions aimed at prohibiting certain exclusions or limitations of liability.[75]

4.4 Clauses Limiting Damages Amounts

Many limitations of liability do not affect the entitlement to damages, but only their quantification. Such clauses, as opposed to those

---

74. Civil law systems contain many "imperative norms", i.e., rules that may not be varied by private agreement. These norms may be found in statutes, code provisions, and code general clauses. Whether a norm is jus imperii sometimes is revealed in its source, but the question is often one of judicial interpretation. Article 6 of the French Civil Code provides that "[o]ne cannot by agreements between individuals derogate from *lois* which involve *ordre public* or *bonnes moeurs*." Article 1133 of the French Civil Code, Art. 1343 of the Italian Civil Code, Art. 138 (1) render void contracts contrary to public order and good morals. The common law countries accomplish the same ends by statute and judicial doctrine. We use the term "public order" to include all invalidating municipal public norms.

75. *See, e.g.,* Art. 23, para. 1, of the Warsaw Convention (Convention for the Unification of Certain Rules Relating to International Carriage by Air, signed in Warsaw on October 12th, 1929, as amended at The Hague on September 28th, 1955); Arts. 29 and 41, para. 1, of the CMR Convention concerning carriage by road; Art. 31 of the Bruxelles Convention of April 23, 1970 on the transport contract; Art. 10 of the EEC directive on the product liability.

that limit liability, as discussed above, assume that a breach exists, with the consequent entitlement to damages by the other party. Their effect is thus solely to affect the quantification of damages.

Normally, such clauses do not totally exclude damages reimbursement. Such an exclusion would have practically the same effect as an exoneration from liability itself, and as such, probably would be void or unenforceable under the law applicable to a contract. The same conclusion can be drawn when damages are reduced to a nominal amount,[76] or when a limitation clause is drafted in excessively vague terms.[77] In all these cases, the enforceability of a liability limitation clause must be scrutinized carefully in the light of the public order or other overriding provisions of the applicable law.

In the practice of international contracts, the obligation to reimburse damages frequently is limited by less extreme means. Although limitations assume a number of forms depending on the transaction, some particular types of performances have become common practice. For example, the liability of the engineer in an international construction contract customarily is limited to the amount of the compensation due to the engineer.[78] Liability for defective design often consists only in the obligation to re-do incorrect drawings.[79]

---

76. In addition to the general hostility of municipal laws to limitation of liability clauses, U.C.C. § 2-316 and § 3 of the British Unfair Contract Terms Act require that disclaimer clauses be "reasonable." As to U.S. law, *see generally* Phillips, *Unconscionability and Article 2 Implied Warranty Disclaimers*, 62 CHI.-KENT L. REV. 199 (1985); *Article Two Warranties in Commercial Transactions*, 64 CORNELL L. REV. 30, 170 (1978).

77. For example, in England the courts have held that a clause excluding liability for any damage that could be covered by insurance was too vague and ambiguous, and thus unable to exonerate an obligee from liability in case of his negligence. Price v. Union Lighterage Company Ltd., [1904] 1 KB 412.

78. For an example, *see* M. Fontaine, DROIT DES CONTRATS INTERNATIONAUX 180–181 (1989).

79. A major international engineering company has the following clause in its standard terms and conditions for professional engineering services: "In the performances of services hereunder, the Engineer shall exercise that degree of skill and care as required by customarily accepted pro-

In some other cases, a maximum amount of reimbursable damages is agreed by the parties. Often, such a ceiling is set as a percentage of the total contract value, up to the entire contract value, or coincides

---

fessional engineering practices and procedures. Should the Engineer breach said obligation, the Client's sole and exclusive remedy is to have the Engineer correct any of the Engineer's defective engineering and design work without charge to the Client. The Engineer shall not be liable for incidental or consequential damages. The Engineer's liability for breach of its obligations shall be limited to the breaches reported to the Engineer within four years after the substantial completion of the Engineer's services, provided the Engineer shall have received written notice of such breach within thirty days after its discovery by the Client or after the Client should have discovered the breach using due diligence. The Client and the Engineer agree that the risk of the Project is to be borne by the Client and therefore the Client agrees that in addition to the limits set forth above, the Client shall limit the Engineer's liability to anyone other than the Client. Therefore, the Client shall pay on behalf of the Engineer all sums of money which the Engineer shall become legally obligated to pay as damages for all claims from any and all third parties, if such arise out of the Engineer's performance of this Agreement, plus expenses related thereto. The Client shall have the right and duty to defend any such claim, suit or arbitration request brought against the Engineer by a third party and to designate an attorney to handle such proceedings. Any liability, claim or expenses which is covered by the Engineer's General Public Liability, Workmen's Compensation, or automobile Liability Insurance are excluded from the above, and the Engineer shall indemnify and hold harmless the Client to such extent."

This clause is particularly interesting in that it contains many of the elements discussed above. For example: (1) the reference to a degree of diligence that must be in conformity with the generally accepted professional standards, which has the practical effect of limiting the cases where a liability for breach of contract can arise; (2) the limitation of the amount of reimbursable damages to the payment of the costs of re-doing the defective drawings; (3) the exclusion of indirect and consequential damages; (4) the time limits within which a claim for damages can be brought; and (5) the clear risk allocation in favor of the engineer even for tort liability, with a wide formulation that may end up conflicting with some public order provision of the applicable law.

with the value of the products or services affected by a contract breach.[80]

However, there is also the possibility that the ceiling be established by reference only, as in the case of the supplier, who, in the case of a breach due to the fault of its sub-suppliers, limits its liability for damages to the amount recovered from such sub-suppliers. Contractual ceilings that confine damages to those not "indirect" or "consequential" frequently are contained in international contracts.[81]

Finally, it should be mentioned that some clauses limit the time within which a claim for reimbursement of damages can be asserted. The rationale for such provisions is related to the need for certainty in international business relationships, which requires that the risk of disputes not be protracted too long.[82]

From the summary above, it is clear that a major task of the lawyer who negotiates and drafts international contracts is to ensure the consistency of limitation of liability contractual provisions with the public order provisions of the applicable law, particularly as they relate to the good-faith principles that generally permeate civil law and, to a lesser extent, common law systems. It can be concluded that some general principles appear to be widely acknowledged in the trans-

---

80. Article 62.2 of the FIDIC conditions for electrical and mechanical work (3d ed. 1987) limits, for example, the amount of the reimbursable damages to the entire contract value. A clause included in the standard terms and conditions for sale of locomotives of a large multinational company, instead, relates the amount of reimbursable damages to the products affected by the breach: "The total liability of the Seller (including its subcontractors) on any claim, whether in contact, tort (including negligence) or otherwise, arising out of, connected with or resulting from the manufacture, sale, delivery, resale, repair, replacement or use of any equipment or the furnishing of any services shall not exceed the price allocable to the equipment or services or part thereof which gives rise to the claim." *See also* the examples cited by M. Fontaine, Droit des Contrats Internationaux 187 (1989).

81. § 3.4 *supra*.

82. An example is reported in note 79 *supra*. Additionally, it is common practice in international merger and acquisition contracts for claims of a purchaser of unrecorded or contingent liabilities of an acquired company to expire after a given period of time from the closing date.

national practice of international contracts. The most important of these is that the validity of clauses limiting liability is affected by concepts related to morality, bona fides, good faith, and the civil law concept of abuse of right (in French: *abus de droit*) of the limitation.[83] There is an abuse, and consequent difficulties of enforcement, when a party's interest in diligent good-faith performance of a contract is hindered by attempts of the other party to unfairly limit or exclude liability for breach.

4.5 Liquidated Damages and Penalty Clauses

A. The Concept of Liquidated Damages

Liquidated damages clauses deserve special consideration.[84] By means of such clauses, damages for breach are contractually pre-

---

83. While the common law does not recognize a separate doctrine of abuse of right, it is subsumed in the more general concept of good faith, and finds its conceptual equivalent in torts containing the word "malice" or "malicious." J. O'Connor, GOOD FAITH IN ENGLISH LAW 68, 81–84 (1990).

84. The term "liquidated damages" is unique to common law systems. Some confusion may arise because the French words *clause pénale* and the English words "penalty clause" sound similar, but they have totally different meanings. The correct English translation of *clause pénale* is "liquidated damages clause" and not "penalty clause." For example, ICC Award No. 3267 of 1979, 1980 CLUNET 980 (1988), mentions the word *pénalité* meaning in reality "penalty." For some comparative analyses, *see* G. Treitel, REMEDIES FOR BREACH OF CONTRACT: A COMPARATIVE ACCOUNT 208–244 (1988); Thilmany, *La clause pénale en droit belge: droit matériel et droit international privé*, 1982 DROIT ET PRATIQUE DU COMMERCE INTERNATIONAL 447 (1982); Ellington, *Penalty Clause: England, id.* at 507; Hanotian, *La clause pénale en droit américain, id.* at 515; Benjamin, *Penalties, Liquidated Damages and Penal Clauses in Commercial Contracts: A Comparative Study of English and Continental Law*, 1960 Int'l & COMP. L. Q. 600 (1960). The common law distinction between liquidated damages and penalties has created great problems of interpretation. De Galard, *Les pénaltés de retard dans les contrats internationaux de construction*, 1986 INT'L TRADE L. REV. 136 (1986) outlines that many late delivery penalties have in practice a punitive function, to the extent they are not the re-

determined so that a damaged party need not prove its loss in the event of a breach, and will receive the agreed upon amount irrespective of the amount of actual damages. These clauses have the desirable qualities of predetermining damages, of limiting liability for default to a predictable level, and of pressuring a debtor to perform.[85] Unless the parties agree otherwise, liquidated damages are paid even if no actual damages are suffered as a consequence of the breach. Strictly speaking, liquidated damages clauses do not constitute limitations of liability. They merely establish a level of damages that is simultaneously a maximum and a minimum. Liquidated damages clauses, however, do constitute an important form of contractual regulation of liability for damages.

B. Liquidated Damages Clauses in Municipal Law

Municipal legal systems are not generally as averse to liquidated damages clauses as toward other limitation of liability contractual provisions. However, basic differences in their treatment exist from country to country. Many municipal systems disapprove of liquidated damages clauses if their function is not to ensure the prompt determination and payment of damages resulting from a contract breach, but to deter breach in the first place. Conceptually, the rationale for disapproval of such clauses is that they constitute the exercise of a punitive function by a private party, result in the undue enrichment of the party not in breach, and contain the potential for possible abuses by a stronger party. Legal systems that draw such a distinction usually do so in cases where the agreed compensation is disproportionate to the amount of actual damages likely to be suffered as a consequence of breach. In all systems, the choice is between "certainty and justice."[86]

---

sult of an estimation of the potential damage deriving from the delay in delivery. The recognition that liquidated damages clauses are in fact penalties (in the English legal sense) is more apparent in German law than in other civil law systems. § 340 (2) BGB.

85. G. Treitel, REMEDIES FOR BREACH OF CONTRACT: A COMPARATIVE ACCOUNT 212–213 (1988).

86. Id.

The common law countries generally provide for the literal enforcement of liquidated damages clauses. They achieve the balance between certainty and justice by refusing to enforce undesirable clauses altogether, by means of the distinction between "liquidated damages," which are strictly enforced, and "penalties," which are unenforceable.[87] A stipulated sum is a penalty "where it is in the nature of a threat fixed *in terrorem* of the other party."[88] In both English and U.S. law, two general concepts help draw the very fine line between liquidated damages and penalties. First, stated simply, penalties are "too high" and liquidated damages are not.[89] Second, liquidated damages are forecast in situations where actual damages would be difficult to prove and uncertain in amount.[90] Numerous economic analyses of contract law have argued the economic inefficiency of the common law rules.[91] Legal analysts have commented on the relative inflexibility of the common law approach as compared with that of the civil law.[92] En-

---

87. In the United States, U.C.C. § 2-718 (1) provides that "a term fixing unreasonably large liquidated damages is void as a penalty."

88. McGregor on Damages § 443 (15th ed. 1988); Dunlop Pneumatic Tyre Co. v. New Garage and Motor Co., [1915] A.C. 79.

89. A stipulated sum is a penalty if it is "extravagant and unconscionable in amount in comparison with the greatest loss that could conceivably be proved to have followed from the breach." Dunlop Pneumatic Tyre Co. v. New Garage and Motor Co., [1915] A.C. 79, 87. United States courts focus on the "reasonability of the stipulated sum." Farnsworth on Contracts § 12.18 (1990); Restatement (Second) of Contracts § 356 (1979).

90. McGregor on Damages § 252 (15th ed. 1988); Farnsworth on Contracts § 12.18 (1990); Restatement (Second) of Contracts § 356 (1979).

91. *See generally* Schwarz, *The Myth that Promisees Prefer Supracompensatory Remedies: An Analysis of Contracting for Damage Measures*, 100 Yale L. J. 369 (1990); Goetz & Scott, *Liquidated Damages, Penalties and the Just Compensation Principle*, 77 Colum L. Rev. 554 (1977).

92. "The common law rules for distinguishing between penalties and liquidated damages manage to get the worst of both worlds. They achieve neither the certainty of the principle of literal enforcement, since there is always some doubt as to the category into which the clause will fall,

forcement of liquidated damages clauses seems to be the modern trend.[93]

The common law systems either enforce liquidated damages clauses or disregard them altogether.[94] In many civil law municipal systems, however, courts may reduce the agreed amount of damages if they find them to be clearly excessive, or even increase them, when they appear to be merely nominal.[95] For example, French (since 1975), Austrian, Italian, Portuguese, Soviet, Swiss, and German (only with respect to relationships between merchants) laws provide for the possibility of judicial reduction of liquidated damages. French law also provides for their increase.[96]

National laws also vary as to the extent that liquidated damages are payable in addition to other remedies available to the damaged party, as opposed to being its exclusive remedy.[97] In this respect, legal systems generally disapprove of the payment of the liquidated damages as an alternative to performance. Thus, while under some municipal

---

nor the flexibility of the principle of enforcement subject to reduction, since there is no judicial power of reduction." G. Treitel, REMEDIES FOR BREACH OF CONTRACT: A COMPARATIVE ACCOUNT 223 (1988).

93. FARNSWORTH ON CONTRACTS §12.18 (1990).

94. If a stipulated sum is found to be a penalty, an aggrieved party may recover whatever damages the party can prove, irrespective of a penalty clause. MCGREGOR ON DAMAGES § 448 (1988); FARNSWORTH ON CONTRACTS § 12.18 (1990). It has been held in Canada, however, that no more than the invalid stipulated sum may be recovered. Elsley v. J.G. Collins Insurance Agencies, Ltd., (1978) 83 D. L. R. (3d) 1.

95. Professor Treitel describes this approach to be the majority view, and finds the common law countries and Belgium (C.C. 1134; C.C. 1152) to be in the minority. G. Treitel, REMEDIES FOR BREACH OF CONTRACT: A COMPARATIVE ACCOUNT 224 (1988).

96. Code Civil 1152 (2) grants courts the right to reduce liquidated damages that are "manifestly excessive" and to increase those that are "manifestly derisory." "Considerable difficulty has arisen in controlling the power to reduce excessive penalties." G. Treitel, REMEDIES FOR BREACH OF CONTRACT: A COMPARATIVE ACCOUNT 226 (1988).

97. A survey of different laws in the area of liquidated damages is included in 1982 DROIT ET PRATIQUE DU COMMERCE INTERNATIONAL 443 (1982).

laws, a damaged party may claim either specific performance or liquidated damages, in some others, both remedies may be claimed.[98]

C. Liquidated Damages Clauses in International Trade Practice

Possibly as a reaction to the differing attitudes of municipal laws toward liquidated damages clauses, negotiators and drafters of international contracts have developed their own, more uniform approach. Those following this approach, of course, must always be mindful of the public order provisions of municipal laws on the matter, including those aimed at protecting the weaker party to a contract against so called "vexatory" or "leonine" clauses.[99]

It is not always clear whether a provision of local law regarding liquidated damages has the nature of a public order provision, thus prevailing over private agreements. Scholars and courts have expressed conflicting opinions and decisions on the subject, so that the issue is far from settled.[100]

---

98. Civil codes generally define situations where amounts greater than liquidated damages may be claimed. G. Treitel, REMEDIES FOR BREACH OF CONTRACT: A COMPARATIVE ACCOUNT 215–218 (1988). In common law systems, the drafting of liquidated damages clauses is very important in this respect.

99. *See, e.g.*, the aforementioned Arts. 1341 and 1342 of the Italian Civil Code, which require specific and separate approval of "vexatory" clauses when included in standard printed contract forms, U.C.C. § 2-302, which introduces the notion of unconscionability, as well as similar provisions included in the British Unfair Contract Term Act of 1977, in the German AGBG on the general conditions of contract, in the Spanish law of July 23rd, 1908 on loans with excessively high interest rates, and in the French law of January 10th, 1978 (together with the decree of March 24th, 1978 containing implementing regulations thereof).

100. As to French law *see* Mercadal, *L'article 1152 al.2 du Code Civil est-il d'ordre public international francais?* 1979 DROIT ET PRATIQUE DU COMMERCE INTERNATIONAL 285 [1979], where it is argued that the statutory provision granting the court the right to reduce a stipulated sum when found excessive is a French public order provision. Francon, *La clause pénale en droit francais*, 1982 DROIT ET PRATIQUE DU COM-

In any case, the practice of international contracts is very well developed.[101] Liquidated damages clauses have been studied by UNCITRAL[102] with the aim of developing a uniform law on the matter. The Council of Europe has issued a resolution on the subject,[103] and an as yet unratified Benelux Convention has the objective of achieving a uniform treatment of liquidated damages in the three Benelux countries by the introduction of common national laws.[104]

These efforts by international organizations specifically concern liquidated damages clauses. Other contract forms prepared at the international level include model clauses within a broader context. This is the case of the Guidelines for Industrial Projects in Developing

---

MERCE INTERNATIONAL 481 (1982), where it is argued that a less rigorous approach is justified, particularly when a liquidated damage clause is included in an international contract. According to an English court decision, Godard v. Gray, L. R. 6 Q. B. 139, English law provisions on liquidated damages are of a public order nature, while two rather old court decisions, one in Germany and another in Switzerland, have concluded differently with respect to the similar provisions in those countries (OLG Hamburg, December 23rd, 1902, STEUFFERT ARCHIV 63 [1902]; Tribunal Fédéral, February 25th, 1915, RECUEIL OFFICIAL, Vol. 41, II, 138).

101. The most important comparative surveys include Fontaine, DROIT DES CONTRATS INTERNATIONAUX 127–170 (1989). *See also* De Galard, *Les pénalités de retard dans les contrats internationaux de construction* 1986 INT'L TRADE L. REV. 131 (1986).

102. *See* the two Reports of the Secretary General of UNCITRAL, entitled "Liquidated Damages and Penalty Clauses," dated respectively, April 25th, 1979 (Doc. A/CN 9/161) and February 12th, 1981 (Doc. A/CN 9/ WG 2WP 33). The full text of the draft UNCITRAL convention and model law on liquidated damages is published in 1982 DROIT ET PRATIQUE DU COMMERCE INTERNATIONAL 542 (1982).

103. Council of Europe, Clauses pénales en droit civil, 1972 (three volumes of 91, 15, and 14 pages respectively). The text of the resolution of the Council of Europe is published in 1982 DROIT ET PRATIQUE DU COMMERCE INTERNATIONAL 541 (1982).

104. The text of the Benelux Convention is published in 1982 DROIT ET PRATIQUE DU COMMERCE INTERNATIONAL 540 (1982).

Countries prepared by UNIDO,[105] the contract models issued by the United Nations Economic Commission for Europe,[106] as well as the FIDIC standard forms for civil works and for electromechanical works.[107]

It is possible to identify some recurring features of the liquidated damages clauses in international contracts. As evidenced by the above-mentioned UNCITRAL study,[108] such clauses are more frequently used when: (1) proving the breach of contract is relatively easy, e.g., delays in delivery; (2) a logical base exists on which the estimated damage can be calculated, e.g., a percentage of the contract price for each week of delay; (3) it is difficult or costly to quantify the actual damage deriving from the breach; and (4) a breach is not so serious as to justify termination. Liquidated damages clauses normally are used for *obligations de résultat*, and not for *obligations de moyens*, because their automatic application would appear inconsistent with the

---

105. Publication UNIDO 10/149, at 22, where the practice of international construction contracts in the area of late delivery penalties is reported (i.e., from .0001 to .001 percent of the contract price per day of delay in delivery, up to a maximum ranging from 5 to 10 percent of such price).

106. *See, e.g.*, Art. 7.3 of the ECE Standard Contract No. 188, as well as the ECE contract models for the Supply of Plant and Machinery for Export, and for the Supply and Erection of Plant and Machinery.

107. Article 47.1 of the FIDIC form for civil works (4th ed. 1987) provides for the payments of certain amounts "as liquidated damages . . . and not as penalty" for the case of late delivery, while Art. 31.1 of the FIDIC form for electromechanical works refers to a "reduction" of the contract price as opposed to liquidated damages. For a comment on such FIDIC clauses, *see* D. Wallace, THE INTERNATIONAL CIVIL ENGINEERING CONTRACT 87 (1974). Other standard forms prevailing in the international trade practice, which contain references to liquidated damages, are those concerning the trade of commodities issued by the trade associations respectively concerned, such as the British Wool Confederation, the Cocoa Association of London, the Grain and Feed Trade Association, the Federation of Oil, Seed and Fats Associations, the London Metal Exchange, the Refined Sugar Association, and the Timber Federation of the U.K.

108. UNCITRAL Report of February 12th, 1981, mentioned above, at 24–25.

need to determine whether or not the breach is attributable to the fault of an obligee, as is typical of *obligations de moyens*.[109]

Another conclusion that can be derived from the practice, as analyzed by the UNCITRAL survey, is that liquidated damages clauses tend to be used when performance is delayed, or when the performance does not reach certain technical parameters (performance penalties), rather than when there is no performance at all. Finally, liquidated damages clauses often are used in countertrade agreements (to sanction, for example, the obligation to buy goods for a value corresponding to that of the goods sold) or in long-term supply contracts (to sanction the obligation to buy or sell a given amount of goods or services periodically at the due dates).

Generally, liquidated damages clauses contemplate the payment of an agreed amount of money. Some liquidated damages provisions, however, provide for payments that are less definite, e.g., set-off of other amounts due and/or payments in kind.[110]

Aside from these very general features of liquidated damages clauses in international trade practice, specific clauses present some unusual aspects. For example, some clauses provide that: (1) a damaged party still must prove that it has suffered actual damages in order to collect liquidated damages; (2) a damaged party is entitled to the payment of actual damages if they are greater than the liquidated damages provided in the contract; (3) liquidated damages are in addition to other remedies, such as the termination; and (4) in certain cases, the payment of liquidated damages can be demanded as an alternative to specific performance.[111] It is clear that clauses drafted as above can-

---

109. *See* M. Fontaine, DROIT DES CONTRATS INTERNATIONAUX 155 (1989).

110. *See* the examples quoted by M. Fontaine, DROIT DES CONTRATS INTERNATIONAUX 150 (1989). Fontaine, however, queries whether in these cases the clause has still the nature of a liquidated damages clause. One of his examples deals with the case of a patent licensee that, by virtue of the clause, is authorized to suspend the payment of the royalties when third parties infringe the licensed patents without any reaction from the licensor.

111. *See* the examples quoted by M. Fontaine, DROIT DES CONTRATS INTERNATIONAUX 146 (1989). When the obligee can avoid the consequences of the breach by paying a certain amount of money (in French: *indemnité de dédit*), the clause has the same effect as a liquidated damages clause,

not be properly considered liquidated damages clauses, but, as is often the case, the pragmatism of the drafters of international contracts appears to prevail over concerns of a conceptual nature.

Some lessons for the negotiator and drafter of international contracts can be drawn from the examples discussed above. First, any reference to the necessity of proving actual damages should be eschewed in order not to dilute the intended effect of a liquidated damages clause. On the contrary, an express statement that liquidated damages are due irrespective of the existence of actual damages is advisable. Second, it always should be made clear that the payment of the liquidated damages is the sole remedy for the breach they are intended to compensate. Other remedies, such as actual damages and termination, should be disclaimed (assuming, of course, that a liquidated damages clause in its proper sense is what the parties want). Finally, the means of payment should be described specifically particularly as to whether only cash payments are to be made or whether set-offs are permitted under a different portion of the contract or on draw-down of a bank guarantee. On the last point, it is not infrequent for the party entitled to the payment of liquidated damages to insist on a bank guarantee or bond. An interesting ICC arbitral award demonstrates that it is possible for parties to agree on a guarantee, and that the adequacy of its amount cannot be challenged by arbitrators.[112]

It can be concluded that liquidated damages clauses are a common feature of international contracts. They ensure the prompt payment of a given amount of money and avoid lengthy and costly investigations of the amount of damages actually incurred. Their use, in fact, is so conspicuous that in one ICC arbitration the determination of actual damages was made with reference to the normal practice with respect to liquidated damages clauses, establishing the actual damages as if there were a liquidated damages clause in the contract.[113]

The drafters and negotiators of international contracts appear to be attempting to reach a uniform customary treatment of liquidated

---

though being conceptually different, to the extent there is in fact a readjustment of the price and not a breach of contract in its proper sense.

112. ICC Award No. 3267 of 1979, 1980 CLUNET 962 (1980).
113. ICC Award No. 2139 of 1974, 1975 CLUNET 930 (1975). *See also* commentary by Derains, 1975 CLUNET 933 (1975).

damages clauses in international trade, and to avoid the differences in municipal law. The efforts by international organizations such as UNCITRAL and the Council of Europe, discussed above, have the same aim.

D. Late Delivery Penalties

Because there is rarely a doubt as to whether there is a delay in delivery, late delivery penalties are the most frequent type of liquidated damages provisions in international contracts. The only dispute in the case of late delivery is whether a delay can be excused or whether an extension of time should be granted. Late delivery penalties may apply to the delivery of goods or services in sales and construction contracts, or to the payment of money, such as installments under a loan agreement. In this last case, the penalties are called "penalty interest" clauses and consist of the payment of a higher interest rate on the amounts overdue than the interest rate agreed upon for the loan. Some late delivery penalties are combined with bonuses to provide an incentive for earlier delivery. Such provisions frequently are contained in international construction contracts. It has been observed that these schemes pertain rather to the mechanism of determination of the price than to the area of liquidated damages.[114]

It can be said that late delivery penalties are almost the rule in international contracts, especially construction contracts. Forms of penalty include payment of: (1) a lump sum; (2) a constant or progressive percentage of the contract price; or (3) a percentage of the price of the delayed goods or service. Penalties are imposed for each temporary unit of delay (day, week, or month) in delivering the goods or services contemplated by the contract. Sometimes, a grace period is provided for, during which no delay penalties are applicable. Sometimes, delay penalties are established with respect to intermediate delivery or completion milestones, in addition to sanctioning the delay at the time of final delivery or completion. In such cases, an obligee should be able to recover intermediate penalties paid if the final ob-

---

114. M. Fontaine, Droit des Contrats Internationaux 167 (1989). De Galard, *Les Pénalités de retard dans les contrats internationaux de construction*, 1986 Int'l Trade L. Rev. 134 (1986), suggests that a bonus for early delivery should always be provided for when there is a late delivery clause.

119

ligation is performed in a timely manner. Otherwise, such intermediate penalties should be deducted from final penalties. A contract clause that provides for payment of both intermediate and final penalties probably will be considered abusive or be otherwise void or unenforceable under the law applicable to a contract.[115]

E. Ceilings for Late Delivery Penalties

Late delivery penalty clauses often contain ceilings. These normally are defined as maximum percentages (generally from 5 to 10 percent) of the contract value. Penalties for late delivery cannot be assessed beyond such ceilings, irrespective of the actual delay in delivery.

Ceilings pose several problems of interpretation and application. There is a widely held view among practitioners and, more often, clients, that the effect of a ceiling is to automatically cap liability for breach of a delivery obligation. According to this view, an obligee would not be liable to pay amounts higher than a ceiling even if delay exceeds a reasonable time or even if delivery never occurs. When interpreted in such a way, a penalty ceiling would have the same function as a limitation of liability clause. We do not share this view because it does not distinguish between the functions of late delivery penalty clauses and those that limit liability.

The most probable function and purpose of ceilings in late delivery penalty clauses is to entitle a creditor to receive *only* the agreed amount in the event of delay. A creditor, unless otherwise agreed, *cannot* claim damages above the agreed penalty (even if the actual damages were higher). Other remedies that otherwise would be available under the applicable law, such as termination, interruption of payments — the basis of the exceptio inadimpleti contractus (no performance in favor of a party which in turn does not perform), or the drawing down of performance bonds and other forms of guarantee, also are foreclosed.

When a late delivery penalty clause has no ceiling, evidently the intention of the parties is to prevent the foreclosing of such alternative remedies *for the entire duration of the delay*, the only limits being

---

115. De Galard, *Les Pénalités de retard dans les contrats internationaux de construction*, 1986 INT'L TRADE L. REV. 131, 134 (1986), states that intermediate penalty clauses are based neither on any general principle of law nor on any logic, but are only a product of a superior bargaining situation and an abuse of dominant position.

those dictated by good faith, reasonableness, and equity. It is obvious in connection with this last point that under any legal system there always will be a time beyond which a creditor can claim to no longer have an economic interest in receiving the delivery of the goods or services contemplated by the contract.

On the other hand, ceilings in late delivery penalty clauses normally are established as a percentage of the contract value. Late delivery penalties in international construction contracts, for example, typically accrue for a duration of approximately two months before the ceiling is reached.

What happens if the delay exceeds the two months, or whatever duration corresponds to the ceiling? Some international contracts include express provisions in this respect. For example, there may be a *cap to total liabilities* in the contract, in which case, obviously, the function of the ceiling is precisely that of limiting liability, thus generating the kinds of problems discussed above.

Other contracts contemplate that a ceiling only operates as a cap to liability for late delivery (or to the combination of the liability for late delivery and the liability for not meeting certain technical specifications). The parties to such contracts clearly intend to cap only late delivery penalties (and/or performance penalties). In such contracts, it is understood that all other remedies (termination, draw-down of guarantees, etc.) would be available to the damaged party in the event of a total failure of performance (or of such delayed performance that would be the equivalent). Finally, some contracts expressly provide that if a delay is of a duration so that penalties exceed a ceiling, the other party may terminate the contract or take other measures described in the contract.

In all the above cases, the answer to the question of delays that result in penalties exceeding a ceiling is given by the parties themselves. More often, however, contracts are silent in this respect, and the interpreter is left with a problem with no easy solution. We believe, however, that the solution cannot be that the ceiling is the maximum amount of penalties due by the obligee irrespective of the duration of the delay in delivery, or even if there is no delivery at all.

Such a conclusion would be irrational because once a ceiling had been exceeded, an obligee would have no interest in accelerating delivery. A delay of three months (assuming the ceiling is reached after two months) or three years would imply the same financial consequences. A creditor then would be deprived of any guarantee that an obligee should do the obligee's best to deliver the delayed goods or services as promptly as possible. Consequently, the meaning and purpose of ceilings, in the absence of express provisions of the parties, should be found elsewhere.

The solution most consistent with the requirements of international trade is found in the function of ceilings. In reality, ceilings are established in the interest of creditors, not obligees. In other words, the purpose is to identify the maximum time within which a creditor is prepared to tolerate delay and to be compensated only with the agreed late delivery penalty. If a ceiling, for example, is two months, it means that even when faced with a delay of up to two months, a creditor still is interested in receiving the delivery of the contractually contemplated goods or services, and accepts that the damages be calculated as liquidated damages through the formula specified in the late delivery penalty clause. At the same time, during the two-month period, the creditor accepts that remedies otherwise available for breach of contract are foreclosed.

One could object that this construction is inconsistent with the stated purpose of late delivery penalty clauses, which is to predetermine damages for late delivery. It could be argued that if the parties established a ceiling for the late delivery penalties, they do not want an obligee to incur other liability. This argument, however, would be incorrect. Late delivery is a contract breach of a continuous nature. Furthermore, it becomes more serious with the passage of time. A delay of one week constitutes a less serious breach than a delay of two weeks, up to the point when the breach is so serious as to justify termination.

A late delivery penalty is not a remedy for the breach constituted by late delivery in general because there is no single breach. The remedy is intended only for that specific delay corresponding to the temporary unit taken into consideration by the late delivery penalty clause. If a penalty consists of a given amount of money for each week of delay, a creditor can receive only that amount even if there is a delay of a week, or two or three weeks. Within these limits, a creditor implicitly agrees not to consider a delay so serious a breach as to warrant termination or other remedies for breach. This waiver, however, only operates within the limits of the ceiling. For example, if the ceiling is hit after eight weeks of delay, this means that for the specific breach constituted by a delay of eight weeks the delay penalty fully operates as a liquidated damages clause. If a delay in delivery is longer, for example, ten weeks, then a creditor is confronted with a different and more serious breach than an eight-week delay. For such a breach, the parties did not provide a liquidated damages clause because by definition the late delivery penalty clause contemplated a ceiling corresponding to eight weeks of delay.

When faced with this different and more serious contract breach, the late delivery penalty clause provided for in the contract, according to the example we have chosen, ceases to perform its function of providing the parties with a predetermination of the damages in case of late delivery. The damaged party reacquires its right to all the remedies generally available to it. This argument can be carried a step further to the point of interpreting the establishment of a ceiling as an expression of the intention of the parties not to consider a delay kept within the limits of a ceiling as one of those "serious" or "material" breaches that, according to many municipal laws, are a prerequisite for a termination of a contract. Conversely, once a ceiling is exceeded, any further delay would justify termination of the contract, with all related consequences in terms of damages and otherwise. It is probably clear at this point that it would be imprudent to assume that payment of the penalty corresponding to the ceiling is the maximum risk for the obligee, irrespective of the duration of the delay in delivery.

A final remark concerning a development in the practice of the application (rather misapplication) of late delivery penalties needs to be made. There are those situations where creditors entitled to receiving delivery of goods or services purposely delay taking steps that would allow timely delivery (such as acceptance and testing) in order to apply the late delivery penalties, as if they were a kind of discount on the price due in any case. This type of behavior, which is unfortunately not infrequent, even when it does not constitute, in and of itself, a breach of the duties of cooperation by the creditor, constitutes an abuse that places itself beyond any rule of law.[116]

---

116. De Galard, *Les Pénalités de retard dans les contrats internationaux de construction*, 1986 INT'L TRADE L. REV. 131, 136 (1986), strongly criticizes these abuses, which are, in practice, more frequent than one would wish. Indeed, international contractors are aware of buyers (frequently, they are agencies of third-world governments) who engage in these practices, and have learned to adjust their prices accordingly.

Appendix 1. Force Majeure Clause Contained in an Economic Development Contract (A)

"Article 24. *Force Majeure.*

24.1 Neither of the Parties, shall be held responsible for losses or damages resulting from an act or event beyond its control such as a case of force majeure, including but not limited to, strikes, rebellions, civil insurrection, war, blockade, floods, earthquakes and/or all other circumstances of a similar kind, as well as measures imposed by public authorities.

24.2 In the case of force majeure, the obligations of the defaulting Party are suspended, to the extent such force majeure affects the obligations, until such time as the effects cease, subject to the following conditions:

(a) The defaulting Party must notify the other Party within a short time of the presence of Force Majeure. The Party must use its best efforts to overcome the effects.

(b) In the case where the effects of a case of force majeure — by their nature or their duration — have a material effect on the present Contract, the Parties will consult each other to follow-up the situation in what appears to them to be the best way.

24.3 In case of Force Majeure, the obligations affected by Force Majeure shall be automatically extended for a period equal to the delay occasioned by Force Majeure.

If, due to a case of Force Majeure, either Party could not perform its obligations as provided hereunder for a period of six (6) months, the Parties shall meet as soon as possible to examine the contractual impact and the continuance of the respective obligations.

In case the Parties cannot reach agreement, the consequences relating to said Force Majeure shall be submitted to arbitration as provided in Article 27.

24.4 In no case will inability to make payments be considered as a case of Force Majeure."

Appendix 2. Force Majeure Clause Contained in an Economic Development Contract (B)

"Article 9. *Force Majeure.*

Any obligation of one of the parties and the corresponding obligation of the other party shall be temporarily suspended for the period during which one of the parties shall be unable to perform the said obligation:

— in the event of a case of Force Majeure or an act of God such as, in particular:

— fire, flood, atmospheric disturbances, storms, tornado, earthquake, soil erosion, landslide, lightning, epidemic, etc.

— war, riot, civil war, insurrection, acts of a public enemy, an act of government, administrative decision, etc.

— strike, lock out, etc.

provided that the party asserting a case of Force Majeure must prove that the circumstances constitute a case of Force Majeure;

— and in the following circumstances that the parties hereby agree to assimilate, for purposes of this Agreement, to cases of Force Majeure:

— serious accidental damage to operations or equipment affecting, in Algeria, the natural gas production facilities in the field, transportation by the principal pipeline system, treatment, liquefaction, storage and loading operations; transportation by LNG tankers; and in the United States of America, unloading, storage, regasification, transportation in the principal pipeline or pipelines leading from regasification facilities and in the principal pipeline systems transporting the gas intended for the Purchaser's Principal Customers, of such a nature that the consequences of said damage cannot be overcome by the use of reasonable means at a reasonable cost. The term 'Principal Customer' shall mean any customer whose annual purchases of the gas which is the subject of this Agreement shall equal at least ten (10) percent of the annual contractual quantity set forth in paragraph 1) of Article 6. The Purchaser agrees to consult and collaborate with the Seller during the negotiation and the drafting of the Force Majeure clauses which are to be included in the agreements between the Purchaser and its Principal Customers.

— an act of a third party affecting the facilities and operations enumerated above, such that said act or its consequences cannot be overcome by the use of reasonable means at a reasonable cost.

The party affected shall as soon as possible following the occurrence of one of the events enumerated above, give notification to the other party by letter, or by telephone or telex confirmed by letter in both cases.

It is agreed that no event shall release the Seller or the Purchaser from its obligations existing on the date of notification, including, in particular, the obligation of the Purchaser to pay the amounts due at that time as payment for the quantities of LNG theretofore delivered.

In any case, the parties shall take all useful measures to ensure resumption of the normal performance of this Agreement within the shortest possible time.

Prior to restoration of the normal situation, the undertakings of the parties shall continue to exist to the extent that their performance is physically possible.

As soon as any cause of Force Majeure or event assimilated thereto shall cease to exist, each of the parties may request that the quantities of LNG not delivered by reason of one of the above-mentioned events, be sold or purchased, as applicable, as make-up quantities within the shortest possible time and to the extent permitted by the capacity of the respective facilities of the parties and the possibilities of marketing such quantities of LNG. The said quantities will be paid for by the Purchaser at the contractual sales price provided in Article 7, which price shall be deemed to be FOB loading port."

Appendix 3. ICC Document No. 421

FORCE MAJEURE (EXEMPTION) CLAUSE

Grounds of relief from liability.

1. A party is not liable for a failure to perform any of his obligations in so far as he proves:

— that the failure was due to an impediment beyond his control; and

— that he could not reasonably be expected to have taken the impediment and its effects upon his ability to perform into account at the time of the conclusion of the contract;
and

— that he could not reasonably have avoided or overcome it or at least its effects.

2. An impediment within paragraph (1) above, may result from events such as the following, this enumeration not being exhaustive:

(a) war, whether declared or not, civil war, riots and revolutions, acts of piracy, acts of sabotage;

(b) natural disasters such as violent storms, cyclones, earthquakes, tidal waves, floods, destruction by lightning;

(c) explosions, fires, destruction of machines, of factories, and of any kind of installations;

(d) boycotts, strikes and lock-outs of all kinds, go-slows, occupation of factories and premises, and work stoppages which occur in the enterprise of the party seeking relief;

(e) acts of authority, whether lawful or unlawful, apart from acts for which the party seeking relief has assumed the risk by virtue of other provisions of the contract; and apart from the matters mentioned in paragraph 3, below.

3. For the purposes of paragraph (1) above, and unless otherwise provided in the contract, impediment does not include lack of authorisations, of licences, of entry or residence permits, or of approvals necessary for the performance of the contract and to be issued by a public authority of any kind whatsoever in the country of the party seeking relief.

Duty to notify.

4. A party seeking relief shall as soon as practicable after the impediment and its effects upon his ability to perform became known

to him give notice to the other party of such impediment and its effects on his ability to perform. Notice shall also be given when the ground of relief ceases.

5. The ground of relief takes effect from the time of the impediment or, if notice is not timely given, from the time of notice. Failure to give notice makes the failing party liable in damages for loss which otherwise could have been avoided.

Effects of grounds of relief.

6. A ground of relief under this clause relieves the failing party from damages, penalties and other contractual sanctions, except from duty to pay interest on money owing as long as and to the extent that the ground subsists.

7. Further it postpones the time for performance, for such period as may be reasonable, thereby excluding the other party's right, if any, to terminate or rescind the contract. In determining what is a reasonable period, regard shall be had to the failing party's ability to resume performance, and the other party's interest in receiving performance despite the delay. Pending resumption of performance by the failing party the other party may suspend his own performance.

8. If the grounds of relief subsist for more than such period as the parties provide [the applicable period to be specified here by the parties], or in the absence of such provision for longer than a reasonable period, either party shall be entitled to terminate the contract with notice.

9. Each party may retain what he has received from the performance of the contract carried out prior to the termination. Each party must account to the other for any unjust enrichment resulting from such performance. The payment of the final balance shall be made without delay.

Force Majeure clause — model reference clause.

Parties who wish to incorporate this clause by reference to their contracts are recommended to use the following wording:

"The Force Majeure (Exemption) clause of the International Chamber of Commerce (I.C.C. Publication n. 421) is hereby incorporated in this contract."

Appendix 4. Limitation of Liability Clause Contained in an International Contract for the Supply of a Nuclear Power Plant

Article 9. *General limitations of liability.*

9.1 Contractor's total liability to . . . for all claims of any kind, whether alleged or based upon contract, tort (including negligence), strict liability or otherwise, for any loss or damage arising out of, connected with, or resulting from this Contract or from the performance or breach thereof, or from the design, manufacture, sale, delivery, resale, installation, Construction Management Service, repair or use of the Plant or component thereof or related services covered by or furnished under this Contract shall in no case exceed fifty million dollars. In applying this limitation, any damages paid or payable to . . . by Contractor, as well as any cost incurred, under Article 8 (Warranties, Warranty Periods, Remedies) and Article 15 (Patents) and any refund of the Contract Price required by law shall be credited against Contractor's total liability to . . . .

9.2 In no event, whether as a result of breach of contract, tort liability (including negligence), strict liability or otherwise, and whether arising before or after commercial operation of the Plant, shall Contractor be liable for damages caused by reason of unavailability of the Plant. Plant shutdowns or service interruptions (including loss of anticipated profits, loss of use of revenue, inventory or use charges, cost of purchased or replacement power, cost of capital, or claims of customers), or other special, incidental, or consequential damages of any nature. Further, . . . shall indemnify Contractor and its Suppliers against any third party claims of the type identified in the preceding sentence.

9.3 . . .'s exclusive remedies and Contractor's sole obligations with respect to the Plant, or nonconformities in or damage to or resulting from the Plant, whether . . .'s claim is alleged or based on contract obligation, tort (including negligence), strict liability or otherwise, shall be those specifically provided in Article 8 (Warranties, Warranty Periods, Remedies) and Article 15 (Patents) and Contractor shall have no further or other obligations arising out of the Plant.

9.4 The provisions of this Article 9, Article 13 (Protection Against Nuclear Liability) and of other Articles of this Contract providing for limitation of or protection against liability of Contractor shall also protect Contractor's Suppliers, and shall apply to the full extent permitted by law and regardless of fault and shall survive either termination or cancellation, as well as completion of the work hereunder.

9.5 The above provisions of this Article shall apply, notwithstanding any other provisions of this Contract or of any other agreement.

Appendix 5. Limitation of Liability Clause Contained in an International Contract for the Supply of a Diesel Locomotive

A. The total liability of Seller (including its subcontractors) on any claim, whether in contract, tort (including negligence) or otherwise, arising out of, connected with or resulting from the manufacture, sale, delivery, resale, repair, replacement or use of any equipment or the furnishing of any service shall not exceed the price allocable to the equipment or service or part thereof which gives rise to the claim.

B. In no event shall Seller (including its subcontractors) be liable for any indirect or consequential damages, including, but not limited to, damages for loss of revenue, cost of capital, claims of customers for service interruptions or failure of supply, and costs and expenses incurred in connection with labor overhead, transportation or substitute facilities or supply sources.

Appendix 6. Limitation of Liability Clause Contained in an International Contract for the Supply of a Gas Power Plant

(1) Except as provided in Paragraph (3) and (4) below, the total liability of the Seller (including its suppliers and subcontractors) on all claims of any kind whether in contract, warranty, tort (including negligence), strict liability or otherwise arising out of, connected with or resulting from the manufacture, sale, delivery, repair, replacement or use of any equipment or the furnishing of any service shall in no event (except for costs incurred under Article 9, "Warranties"; and Article 11, "Patents") exceed the price allocable to the equipment or service which gives rise to the claim and shall terminate upon the expiration of the warranty of the equipment or service giving rise to the claim.

(2) In no event shall the Seller (including its suppliers and sub-contractors) be liable for any special or consequential damages including, but not limited to, damages for loss of anticipated profits or revenue, loss of goods, cost of capital, claims of Purchaser's customers for service interruptions or plant shutdown or failure of supply, cost incurred in connection with obtaining replacement power, costs and expenses incurred in connection with labor, overhead, general administration, transportation, substitute facilities, supply sources or other similar damages.

(3) With regard to conceptual design services to be furnished pursuant to Article 2 (2) a., Seller's total liability on all claims of any kind, whether in contract, tort (including negligence), strict liability or otherwise for any loss or damage arising out of, connected with or resulting from the conceptual design services or from the performance or breach thereof, is limited exclusively to correction of Seller's drawings or engineering calculations where errors are shown to exist. It shall, in no case, exceed the portion of the Contract price allocable to the specific conceptual design services which give rise to the claim and shall terminate upon completion of the period for which the conceptual design services are to be utilized.

(4) With regard to advisory services for education and training services, the Seller's liability on any claim of any kind, including negligence, for any loss or damage arising out of, connected with, or

resulting from this Contract, shall in no case, exceed that which is provided under the warranty, Article 9(6).

(5) The provisions of this Contract providing for limitation of or protection against liability shall apply to the full extent permitted by law and regardless of fault or negligence.

Appendix 7. Limitation of Liability Clause Contained in an International Contract for the Supply of Maintenance Services

Limitation on contractor's liability.

Notwithstanding any other provision of this Contract (including indemnity)

(i) The Contractor shall not be liable to the Company for:

(*a*) Indirect damages caused to the Company such as loss of production, loss of profit, loss of orders, claims of customers of the Company, down-time costs, cost of replacement power or consequential damages of any nature.

(*b*) Any and all losses and damage occasioned by Special Risks.

(ii) Except as provided in sub-paragraph (iii) of this Article regarding Operation and Maintenance Services. Contractor's total liability on all claims of any kind shall in no case exceed the price of the works or portion of the works that give rise to claim and shall terminate upon the expiration of the Warranty Period of the works or portion of the works giving rise to the claim; and

(iii) The liability of the Contractor, its Agents, Employees, Sub-Contractors and Suppliers with respect to any and all claims arising out of the performance or non-performance of obligations in connection with Operation and Maintenance Services furnished hereunder shall not exceed the price specified in the Contract to be paid for such Operation and Maintenance Services and shall in no event include incidental or consequential damages of any nature.

Appendix 8. Limitation of Liability Clause Contained in an Offer Responding to an International Tender

Governing conditions.

We have reviewed the terms and conditions of sale set forth in the Tender Document namely 'Instructions for Tendering' and the General Conditions of Contract for Purchase of Goods (1972) and find them generally acceptable. However, we respectfully submit that the General Conditions of Contract for Purchase of Goods (1972) included in the Tender Documents are not readily applicable in total to the supply of locomotives proposed here in. Application of these terms and conditions without modification or additions would necessitate strained interpretations resulting in possible misunderstanding and would be, in some respects, at variance with the usual terms under which the . . . Company have undertaken projects of this nature in the past per attached Standard Conditions of Sale.

For instance, we might point out that the *terms do not* cover title passage of the equipment which we propose to be F.O.B. factory nor *provide any reasonable limitations of liability.* While we note the rate of liquidated damages for delay, they are much higher then usual and normally would not apply until after the first 30 days of any delay."

Chapter 5. Contractual Self-Protections Against Breach

5.1 General

One of the most significant developments in the practice of international business contract law is the adoption of a broad range of mechanisms by which parties may protect themselves against breach without the involvement of municipal legal systems. There are almost no long-term relational international contracts that do not provide for the more common of these self-protection mechanisms. Certainly the most common device, the performance bond, is virtually always included. Although extra-judicial guarantees are contained in many purely domestic contracts, their use, application, and enforcement are used more extensively and with greater particularity internationally.

Before discussing the forms of these self-protective devices, some general considerations are appropriate. The international business community does not have structures and institutions of its own to ensure adequate enforcement of contractual rights. Such structures are presently the monopoly of national legal systems.

Consequently, although parties try to "de-localize" international contracts as much as possible in order to overcome the inadequacies and differences in domestic laws at the level of the substantive regulation of their relationships, they necessarily must rely on the substantive regulations of national jurisdictions. This is true even when "de-localized" international commercial arbitration is selected for the settlement of disputes: ultimately a domestic court must execute the arbitral award if a losing party does not comply;[1] and only national courts can grant interim relief measures during arbitration proceedings.[2]

---

1. *See generally* Sandrock, *Prejudgment Attachments: Securing International Loans or Other Claims of Money*, 21 INT'L LAW. 1 (1987).

2. *See generally, id.*; Shenton, Buhart, Kuehn, Ughi, Freimuller, *Attachments and Other Court Remedies in Support of Arbitration*, 1984 INT'L BUS. LAW. 101, 111, 115, 119 (1984) (with respect to British, French, German, Italian, and Swiss Law). As to U.S. law, *see* Von Mehren, *The Enforcement of Arbitral Awards Under Conventions and United States Law*, 1983 YALE J. WORLD PUB. ORDER 343, 362 (1983). "The general

We have seen that international contracts generally are more complex and of longer duration than domestic contracts. Also, they are apt to have larger underlying economic interests. This results in very high levels of risk when such contracts go awry. It is therefore essential for parties to international contracts to have at their disposal quick and effective mechanisms to protect themselves against breach. Although municipal systems ultimately provide the only available enforcement procedures, in most cases these systems are an unsatisfactory choice. If the parties are of different nationalities, one of them is always at a disadvantage before a foreign national court. The proceedings and languages are unfamiliar, which may result in perceptions of discrimination; judges in national courts often are perceived by foreign parties as being partial. In addition to being unfamiliar and potentially unfriendly, some national legal systems are very rudimentary. This is the case in many countries where courts are not independent. This circumstance is even more troublesome when the state itself (or one of its agencies) is a party to an international contract with a foreign private party. Finally, domestic enforcement procedures, being either excessively cumbersome or costly, are not always in tune with the requirements of parties to international contracts.

This state of affairs has created the growth of self-protection, which has become customary in international trade practice. It is an inevitable result of an absence of truly transnational mechanisms for the judicial enforcement of contractual rights and the widely perceived need for quick and effective ways to deal with non-performance or defective performance.

This situation is not unique to the legal regime of international business contracts. It characterizes all legal systems governing nonstructured communities. The relationship of public international law and the international community of states, where few effective enforcement agencies exist, is perhaps the most obvious example. It is thus no surprise that self-protection devices are conspicuous in inter-

---

rule is that interim awards are not enforceable." Brody, *An Argument for Pre-Award Attachment in International Arbitration Under the New York Convention*, 1985 CORNELL INT'L L. J., 99 (1985). Certain internal regulations of arbitral institutions do refer to interim relief measures, *e.g.*, Art. 8.5 of ICC arbitral regulation and Art. 26 of UNCITRAL arbitral regulations.

national relations. An important example is the right of individual or collective self-defense contained in Article 51 of the United Nations Charter as an "inherent" right (in the French text: *droit actuel*), i.e., as a right under customary international law that exists independent of the Charter itself.[3] A few recent examples are the 1981 Israeli attack on Iraqi nuclear reactors,[4] the 1985 Israeli raid on Tunisia,[5] and the 1986 U.S. raid on Libya.[6]

Structured legal systems, such as those of nation states, have effective judicial and enforcement institutions, so that self-help or self-protective devices have only a residual role.

5.2 Bank Guarantees and Guarantee Bonds

Important and typical forms of self-protection found in international contracts are bank guarantees or guarantee bonds, identified as "on demand," "on first call," or "unconditional." They will be referred to as "bonds" or "guarantee bonds."[7] Bonds are issued by an institutional guarantor to a beneficiary on the instruction of a party to the contract. They are invariably a part of international construction

---

3. *See* Alibert, DU DROIT DE SE FAIRE JUSTICE DANS LA SOCIÉTÉ INTERNATIONALE DEPUIS 1945 (1983). *See also* the decision of the International Court of Justice in Nicaragua v. United States, where the court said: "It will therefore be clear that customary international law continues to exist and to apply, separately from international treaty law, even where the two categories have an identical content." [1986] I.C.J. 14, 96, reprinted in 25 I.L.M. 1023, 1064 (1986).

4. *See* 18 UN CHRONICLE No. 8, at 5 (1981).

5. *See* 22 UN CHRONICLE Nos. 10/11, at 3 (1985).

6. *See* 23 UN CHRONICLE No. 4, at 46 (1986).

7. The term "bank guarantee," though widely used in international trade practice, is not entirely accurate because such guarantees are given not only by banks but also by insurance companies, mainly in the United States. *See generally* Dohm, LES GARANTIES BANCAIRES DANS LE COMMERCE INTERNATIONAL (1986); Kozolchyk, *Bank Guarantees and Letters of Credit: Time for a Return to the Fold*, 11 U. PA. J. INT'L BUS. L. 1 (1989); Stoufflet, *La garantie bancaire à première demande*, 1987 CLUNET 265 (1987). Rubino Sammartano, *Performance Bonds: Primary or Secondary Obligations?*, 1982 INT'L BUS. LAW. 125 (1985); R. Sammartano, *Perfor-*

contracts, but also frequently are contained in contracts for the international sale of goods and contracts for the supply and installation of infrastructure facilities, such as communications and electrical generating stations. The beneficiary and the obligee are parties to the underlying international contract, in which the obligee normally undertakes the obligation to deliver goods or services to the beneficiary for monetary compensation. The obligee instructs the guarantor to issue the bond in compliance with a specific obligation in the underlying international contract. The contract generally includes the express wording of the bond. Since the language of the bond determines both the conditions under which it may be drawn down and its cost, negotiators of international contracts take great care that bonds are clear and accurate.

This triangular relationship (obligee/guarantor/beneficiary) frequently becomes quadrangular in situations where a beneficiary wants a bank of its own country to issue a bond. In these situations, a counter-guarantee from a bank of the obligee's country normally is obtained. In the United States, because of restrictions on the ability of banks to issue guarantees, guarantee bonds normally assume the form of "stand-by" letters of credit. Their function and effect is largely the same as guarantee bonds issued by banks in other countries.

Guarantee bonds serve a number of purposes. The most common types of guarantee bonds are bid, performance, advance payment, and maintenance bonds. Bid bonds are issued at the time a tender offer for bid to provide the international supply of goods or services is submitted. They are designed to give the entity soliciting them some security that an offer will not be withdrawn before its stated date of expiration and that a contract will be negotiated and executed by a successful bidder. The amount of a bid bond normally does not exceed 5 percent of the price stated in the bid.

Problems connected with bid bonds are related to the fact that bids in connection with public tenders are required to be stated as offers.

---

mance Bonds and Injunctions, THE LAW SOCIETY GAZETTE, February 4th, 1981; Jordan, *Guarantee Bonds: Their Use in International Contracts*, 1982 INT'L CONTRACTS 172 (1982); Niggeman, *How to Stop Fraudulent Payment Demands out of First Demand Bank Guarantees — a Comparative Study*, 1981 INT'L CONTRACTS 558 (1981).

All municipal legal systems contain the "mirror image rule" for the formation of contracts — offers without qualification form contracts upon acceptance without variation. Bidders virtually always are required to bid against a set of general terms and conditions that are attached to tender documents. Should a bidder find some of those terms and conditions unacceptable, it can neither negotiate them after acceptance, nor refuse to sign a contract, since this would create exposure to a draw-down of the bid bond.

The only way an offeror can avoid such risks and still protect its interest to be bound only by terms and conditions it considers commercially acceptable is to insert appropriate qualifications into its offer. This solution is not without risks either, since many international tenders provide for the automatic rejection of bids qualified in any way. This creates a dilemma for offerors who are not prepared to accept, in their entirety, the often "leonine" or "adhesive" general terms and conditions included in tender documents.[8] Which is the lesser evil between not qualifying an offer, thus risking draw-down of a bid bond if attempts to eliminate unacceptable terms and conditions after acceptance are unsuccessful, or qualifying the offer and thus risking automatic rejection of the bid?

Of course, a bidder may always "bid against the documents," setting the price of its offer to reflect the general terms and conditions. In addition to the possible unlawfulness of compliance, there are several practical problems with such an approach. First, it is very difficult to put a cost on the sometimes ludicrous terms and conditions that find their way into international tender documents.[9] Second, any reasonable cost allocation may make a bid uncompetitive against less cautious bidders. The more pragmatic solution to the dilemma often consists of formulating comments and observations to the tender documents as "requests for clarifications." This permits more flexibility during the negotiation phase, where the offeror who has been awarded

---

8. Acceptance of general terms and conditions sometimes is unlawful in the country of a bidder. United States bidders for contracts in some Arab countries, for example, often are confronted with terms the acceptance of which would violate the U.S. anti-boycott laws.

9. Bidders sometimes are asked to surrender rights to basic technology, to agree to heavy delay penalties with no excuse by reason of force majeure, and to waive all limitations of liability.

the contract undoubtedly enjoys a position of greater relative strength. If such requests are properly drafted, an offeror may be able to maintain that the offer was predicated on a favorable interpretation of the disputed clauses included in the general terms and conditions, and thus avert draw-down of a bid bond.

The duration of a bid bond cannot exceed that of an offer. In principle, a bid bond should expire when the offer itself expires prior to acceptance. Some customers, in order to force offerors to extend the duration of offers, threaten to draw-down bid bonds unless offers are extended. This is simply an abusive practice that has been consistently criticized by the business community and by commentators.[10] On the other hand, if an offer is accepted, the duration of a bid bond normally is considered to be extended until the other bonds contemplated by the contract (usually a performance bond) are issued.

Performance bonds are issued to guarantee proper performance of a contract by the obligee. These bonds are issued by a guarantor on behalf the obligee to a beneficiary. The amount of a performance bond is approximately 10 percent of the contract value. In the United States, however, performance bonds frequently are issued in much higher amounts (often as much as 100 percent of the contract value). Such amounts would be highly exceptional in international practice.

Advance payment bonds are intended to guarantee that performance of a contract by an obligee matches the advance payments made by the beneficiary to the obligee. Advance payment bonds thus generally are reduced proportionally to the percentage of actual work performed compared with the total work to be performed.

Finally, maintenance or warranty bonds are intended to guarantee performance of post-installation obligations. Generally, such bonds guarantee contracts to provide maintenance, overhaul, and repair services with respect to work performed.

Typically, each of these bonds (performance bonds, advance payment bonds, and maintenance bonds) has the same duration as the obligations contemplated in an underlying contract. Consequently, it would be improper for a beneficiary to condition the release and ter-

---

10. Dubisson, *Le droit de saisir les cautions de soumission et les garanties de bonne exécution*, 1977 Droit et Pratique du Commerce International 433 (1977).

mination of bonds on the physical return of the documents incorporating them.[11]

The conditions under which guarantee bonds can be drawn-down or "called" are of particular significance for the parties to international contracts. Although the principles that follow apply generally to all types of bonds, they refer specifically to performance bonds. This is because performance bonds have created the most problems in practice.

From the point of view of their draw-down, bonds belong to two categories. The first category comprises bonds defined as "conditional" or "on default." In this case, draw-down is conditional upon (1) production by a beneficiary of sufficient evidence of a contract breach by an obligee and upon (2) the judicial determination of breach. These conditional bonds are traditional guarantee obligations. They perform the function of a collateral security aimed at guaranteeing the beneficiary that a sufficient amount of money will be made available to the beneficiary in case the contract is breached. It is a matter of negotia-

---

11. *Id.* at 442. *See also* Art. 4 (b) of the Uniform Rules for Contractual Guarantees, issued by the International Chamber of Commerce in 1978 (ICC Publication No. 325), as well as the commentary to the various models of bank guarantees elaborated by the ICC in 1982 and published in a so-called *Brochure explicative*, which can be found in 1982 Droit et Pratique du Commerce International 713 (1982). Article 4 (b) prescribes that unless an expiration term is expressly provided for, the bond remains in force until the end of the sixth month following the completion date originally contemplated by the underlying contract. This provision, clearly unacceptable for the beneficiary of the bond, has been a contributor to the above Uniform Rules' difficulties in the international trade practice. Actually, they are very seldom adopted by parties to international contracts. It must be pointed out that great difficulties may arise for foreign parties from some local laws with respect to the duration of the bond. For example, the regulations of Syria and Turkey oblige local banks, when acting as guarantors, to consider bonds as having an unlimited duration (*see* the March 21, 1973 decision of the Board of Directors of the Commercial Bank of Syria), or as expiring after ten years (*see* the circular dated November 1976 issued by the Turkish Central Bank, which is being systematically enforced by the Turkish Court of Cassation, Turkey's highest court), irrespective of the actual duration agreed upon by the parties.

tion whether a party may prove greater damages in addition to the draw-down of a bond or whether the amount of a bond constitutes liquidated damages.

A second category of bonds is called "unconditional," "on demand," or "on first call."[12] They can be drawn-down by a beneficiary at any time during their duration, upon simple request (i.e., without the necessity of alleging, proving, or even mentioning a contract breach).[13] The guarantor under an unconditional bond is obligated to pay in accordance with the terms of the bond as soon as the beneficiary so requests.

The unconditional guarantee bond is a relatively new form of guarantee. It has been widely adopted in the international trade practice in recent years, however, and has become virtually standard in some areas such as Africa and the Middle East. There it has completely replaced the conditional bonds previously used. This is particularly the case with respect to contracts in which a government is the purchaser of goods or services. In spite of the fact that unconditional bonds clearly place one party at a disadvantage, they have become accepted in the highly competitive environment of international construction and infrastructure contracting. In these fields, many companies from recently industrialized countries (especially Asia) adopt very aggressive commercial postures.

The right to draw-down an unconditional bond protects a beneficiary against less scrupulous contractors. This is an important consideration for purchasers in less developed countries who perceive themselves as having been victimized by sharp contractors. On the other hand, it places obligees at the mercy of less scrupulous purchasers and owners. Typical in this respect is the "pay or extend" practice, which consists of a threat by the beneficiary to draw-down a bond unless a guarantor extends it beyond its original expiration. This blackmailing practice is regrettably not uncommon, and results in many guarantee bonds assuming a quality of immortality.

---

12. These terms (in German: *auf erstes Anfordern*; in French: *première demande*; in Italian: *a prima domanda*) are used in literal translation in the languages in which most international contracts are written.

13. For this reason, unconditional guarantee bonds, colorfully and by no means inaccurately, sometimes are called "suicide bonds."

The only remedy available to an obligee in the face of an abusive draw-down is recourse to local courts. An obligee may seek an injunction preventing a guarantor from paying. If an injunction is not requested or is denied, a guarantor will pay the amount of the bond upon a beneficiary's demand. The primary obligee then must resort to litigation to determine whether a breach of contract occurred and a bond was wrongfully drawn-down. Litigation is always lengthy and expensive. The benefit to the obligee is unpredictable, particularly when the dispute is submitted to a court in the country of the beneficiary. Moreover, since the texts of guarantee bonds seldom specify the applicable law, the issue always arises of whether such law should be the same as that applicable to the contract or the law of the forum.

It is understandable, therefore, that parties whose obligations are protected by guarantee bonds typically attempt to introduce some kind of procedure into a contract that establishes — even in a very simplified way — the existence of a breach as a condition to a draw-down of the bond.[14] These attempts, which are aimed at making the bonds less unconditional and less subject to arbitrary decisions of the beneficiary, are only seldom successful. Thus, it can be said that the practice of unconditional bonds is well established in international trade.

5.3 Guarantee Bonds in Municipal Law

Since unconditional bonds are a creation of the international trade practice, domestic laws have not dealt with them in a comprehensive

---

14. Many scholars propose the introduction of a quick and simple referee procedure, aimed at determining when a bond is being unduly drawn-down. *See, e.g.,* Ruccellai, *Arbitration as an Instrument of Guarantee in International Undertaking Contracts for the Performance of Construction Contracts,* in ICCA — NEW TRENDS IN THE DEVELOPMENT OF INTERNATIONAL COMMERCIAL ARBITRATION AND THE ROLE OF ARBITRAL AND OTHER INSTITUTIONS 259 (P. Sanders, ed. 1983); Dubisson, *Le droit de saisir les cautions de soumission et les garanties de bonne exécution,* 1977 DROIT ET PRATIQUE DU COMMERCE INTERNATIONAL 433 (1977). The latter, however, is in favor of a solution of the problem, which should be offered by the international banking system through some kind of self-restraint. *Id.* at 449. At the present stage, any likelihood of a solution appears to be very remote.

way. There are almost no specific statutory provisions regarding unconditional bonds,[15] and the attitudes of courts vary from country to country. These different attitudes tend to surface when an obligee, to avoid the risk of an improper draw-down of a bond, seeks an injunction from a local court to prevent payment by a guarantor, or less frequently, to prevent a beneficiary's requesting the draw-down.

Litigation of this sort has created a conspicuous body of case law in a number of countries, all of which centers around limitations imposed by local public policy considerations on the enforceability of unconditional bonds and the existence of protection available against fraudulent draw-downs. Several excellent comparative studies of this case law are available.[16] A survey of them suggests that:

1. Many municipal legal systems find it difficult to enforce guarantees payable on simple demand.

2. Even less restrictive systems have introduced measures to protect against fraudulent draw-down.

3. Litigation deals with the evidence to be provided by an obligee requesting interim relief measures.

The enforceability of unconditional guarantees was recognized earlier in Germany than in other countries. However, German courts are willing to enjoin payment in cases of "manifest abuse" (*rechtsmissbräuchlichen*) in the presence of "liquid" evidence, i.e., conclusive evidence of the fraudulent behavior of a beneficiary.[17] The ability to

---

15. Exceptional are the Czechoslovakian law of December 4th, 1963 (Arts. 665–675), the 1978 Yugoslav law on bank guarantees (Arts. 1083–1087), and the former East German law on the economic international contracts of February 10th, 1976 (252–255), which all deal specifically with guarantee bonds.

16. *See* the works cited in note 4 *supra*, as well as G. Von Westphalen, Die Bankgarantie im Internationalen Handelsverkehr (1982); Bonelli, *Le garanzie bancarie nel commercio internazionale*, 1 Diritto del Commercio Internazionale 127 (1987); Poullet, *La jurisprudence récente en matière de garantie bancaire dans les contrats internationaux*, 1982 Banca Borsa Titoli di Credito 397 (1982).

17. *See* Blau & Jedzig, *Bank Guarantees to Pay upon First Written Demand in German Courts*, 23 Int'l Law. 725 (1989); Mülbert, *Neueste Ent-*

enjoin guaranteeing banks has been limited by a 1987 decision of the Frankfurt Appellate Court holding that an injunction cannot be granted based merely on an obligee's right to demand a refusal of payment.[18]

French courts have been more reluctant to admit that the payment of a bond can be totally divorced from the determination of breach of the underlaying contract. The result is that the French case law is far from being settled.[19]

In Italy, although scholars generally have viewed the enforcement of unconditional bonds with favor, the courts have shown some uncertainty, granting injunctions only in the presence of clear bad faith by a beneficiary. Italian court decisions range from cases of a very liberal approach in granting interim relief measures to cases of their emphatic denial.[20]

Consistent with the more formal approach of common law systems, courts in England and the United States show no hesitation in admit-

---

wicklungen des materiellen Rechts der Garantie auf erstes Anfordern, ZEITSCHRIFT FÜR WIRTSCHAFTSRECHT UND INSOLVENZPRAXIS 1101 (1985); Mülbert, MISSBRAUCH VON BANKGARANTIEN UND EINTSWEILGER RECHTSCHUTZ (1985); Käser, *Garantieversprechen als Sicherheit im Handelsverkehr*, in GARANTIEVERTRÄGE IM HANDELSVERKEHR 25 (1972).

18. Judgment of April 22, 1987, OLG (discussed in Blau & Jedzig, *id.*, at 730.)

19. *See* Bouloy, *Note sous l'arrêt de la Cour d'Appel de Paris du 27 octobre 1981*, 1981 JURIS-CLASSEUR PERIODIQUE 19702, II (1981); Gavalda-Stoufflet, *Note sous l'arret du Tribunal de Grande Instance de Paris du 13 mai 1980*, 1980 RECUEIL DALLOZ SIREY 488 (1980); Vasseur, *Garantie indépendente*, REPERTOIRE DALLOZ-DROIT COMMERCIALE (1984); Contamine-Raynaud, *Les rapports entre la garantie à première demande et le contrat de base en droit français*, ETUDES DEDIEES A RENEE ROBLOT 413 (1984).

20. *See* Portaled, *Fidejussione e garantie-vertrag nella prassi bancaria*, LE OPERAZIONI BANCARIE 1043 (G. Portale, ed. (1978); Portale, *Nuovi sviluppi del contratto autonomo di garanzia*, 1985 BANCA BORSA TITOLI DI CREDITO 169, I (1985); Benatti, *Il contratto autonomo di garanzia, id.*, at 171, I (1982); Grippo, *La garanzia automatica in bilico tra "tecnica" e "politica"; tendenze della giurisprudenza, id.*, at 83, II (1985); Sesta, *Pagamento a prima richiesta*, 1985 CONTRATTO E IMPRESA 939 (1985); Maccarone, *Contratto autonomo di garanzia*, DIZIONARIO DI DIRITTO PRIVATO, III, DIRITTO COMMERCIALE E INDUSTRIALE 379 (1981).

ting and enforcing unconditional guarantees. The English courts in particular seem more reluctant than their European counterparts to grant injunctions against guarantors.[21] In the United States, a slightly increased flexibility in granting interim relief measures is a result of the United States-Iranian disputes.[22] Some less developed countries also have been developing their case law on the matter.[23]

---

21. RD Harbottle (Mercantile) Ltd. v. Nat'l Westminster Bank Ltd., [1977] 2 All E.R. 862; Howe Richardson Scale Ltd. v. Polimex-Cekop and National Westminster Bank Ltd., [1978] 1 LLOYD'S REP. 161; Edward Owen Engineering Ltd. v. Barclays Bank International, [1978] 1 All E.R. 976. These three leading English cases have been called the "hard as granite trio." Kozolchyk, *Bank Guarantees and Letters of Credit: Time for a Return to the Fold*, 11 U. PA. J. INT'L BUS. L. 1. 51 (1989). *See also* Elland & Goldsmith, *Performance Bonds in the English Courts*, 1978 DROIT ET PRATIQUE DU COMMERCE INTERNATIONAL, 151 (1978); Putnam, SURETYSHIP GUARANTEES INDEMNITIES AND PERFORMANCE BONDS (1981); Williams, *On Demand and Conditional Performance Bonds*, 1981 J. BUS. L. 8 (1981); Trimble, *The Law Merchant and the Letter of Credit*, 1981 HARV. L. REV. 1007 (1981); Penn, *Performance Bonds: Are Bankers Free from the Underlying Contract?*, 1985 LLOYD'S MAR. & COMM. L. REV. 132 (1985).

22. "Recent decisions concerning Iranian credits establish that a demonstrably fraudulent demand for payment is essential for an injunction against payment. In the absence of an actual demand, payment injunctions were universally denied as premature, though many courts required banks to furnish their customers notice before honoring Iranian demands." Kimball & Sanders, *Preventing Wrongful Payment of Guarantee Letters of Credit — Lessons from Iran*, 39 BUS. LAW. 417 (1984). *See generally id.*, which contains much useful drafting advice; Note, *The Role of Stand-by Letters of Credit in International Commerce: Reflections After Iran*, 20 VA. J. INT'L L. 459 (1980); Note, *Enjoining the International Stand-by Letter of Credit: The Iranian Letter of Credit Cases*, 1980 HARV. INT'L L. J. 189 (1980); Weisz & Blackman, *Stand-by Letter of Credit After Iran: Remedies on the Account Party*, 1982 U. ILL. L. REV. 355 (1982).

23. El-Hakim, *Les pays du Proche-Orient*, LES GARANTIES BANCAIRES DANS LES CONTRATS INTERNATIONAUX 398 (Feduci, ed. 1981); Kronfol, *Legal Theory and Practice of Guarantee Bonds in the Arabian Gulf*, 1984 INT'L CONSTRUC. L. REV. 218 (1984).

5.4 The Proper Law of Guarantee Bonds

Because of the differing approaches of municipal laws to guarantee bonds, the determination of the applicable law is critical. Both the enforceability and the availability of interim relief measures are questions of the proper law of a bond.[24] The identification of the proper law of the bonds must be made in accordance with local conflict of law provisions. In contracts to which members of the European Community are parties, the applicable law is determined by the 1980 Convention on the Law Applicable to Contractual Obligation.[25] Article 3 of the Contractual Obligations Convention emphasizes the parties' freedom to submit an international contract to the law of their choice, while Article 4 (1) provides that the law of contracts in which there is no choice-of-law clause is the law of the country with which the contract is "most closely connected."[26] Article 4(2), however, provides for a presumption that the country most closely connected is the country of habitual residence of the party that is to effect "the performance which is characteristic of the contract." The concept of "characteristic performance" is not defined, but it is a Swiss legal concept that basically deems as "characteristic" the performance of the party that does not pay money.[27] Many scholars, however, are of the opinion that it is not easy to clearly identify the "characteristic performance" with respect to guarantee bonds, and prefer to search for the most closely connected law, taking into regard the overall circumstances. This latter approach is that contained in Article 4 (5) of the Contractual

---

24. Some commentators have recommended that choice of law clauses be negotiated in guarantee bonds and stand-by letters of credit. Kimball & Sanders, *Preventing Wrongful Payment of Guarantee Letters of Credit — Lessons from Iran*, 39 INT'L LAW. 417, 439 (1984).

25. "Convention on the Law Applicable to Contract Obligations," 23 O. J. Eur. Comm. (No. L266) 1 (1980) [hereinafter Contractual Obligations Convention].

26. Contractual Obligations Convention, Arts. 3 and 4 (1).

27. T. Hartley, CIVIL JURISDICTION AND JUDGEMENTS 45 (1984); Gabor, *Emerging Unification of Conflict of Laws & Rules Applicable to International Sale of Goods: UNCITRAL and the New Hague Convention on Private International Law*, 7 Nw. J. INT'L L. & BUS. 696, 703 (1986).

Obligations Convention. The end result is that in the majority of European cases, the law governing the underlying contract between the obligee and the beneficiary is identified as the proper law of the bond as well.[28]

Apart from domestic conflict of law provisions, international arbitration institutions tend to determine the proper law of contractual obligations themselves, applying criteria that appear to them most appropriate under the specific circumstances. For example, an ICC arbitral tribunal has ruled that the law applicable to guarantee bonds in the absence of an express choice of law provision is the law of the guarantor. The arbitration panel considered that the selection of such law was more in line with both international usage and Article 10 of the Uniform Rules for Contractual Guarantees issued by the ICC in 1978.[29]

5.5 Emerging Principles Governing Guarantee Bonds in International Trade Practice

In contrast with the scarce and contradictory provisions of municipal laws, international trade practice concerning guarantee bonds has developed a substantial body of general principles. These principles can be derived primarily from international arbitrations, attempts by international institutions to codify the rules governing guarantee bonds, and descriptions of uniform usages. The discussion that follows identifies the most important of these principles. First, it is clear that when

---

28. *See* Bonelli, *La Convenzione di Roma del 19 giugno 1980 e la legge applicabile alle operazioni bancarie*, Verso una Disciplina Comunitaria Della Legge Applicabile ai Contratti 96 (T. Treves, ed. 1983). In many international contracts, the selected applicable law is that of the purchaser under a contract of sale or the owner under a construction contract. The submission of a bond to that law does not provide sufficient protection to the obligee against abuses by the beneficiary. Hence the efforts of developing some lex mercatoria concepts.

29. ICC Publication No. 325 (Art. 10: "if the bond does not specify the applicable law, such law is the law of the place of establishment of the guarantor"). ICC Case No. 3316, 1980 Clunet 971, 1980.

international arbitrators have had to decide issues related to unconditional guarantee bonds, they have shown no hesitation in enforcing their unconditional nature. If unconditionality is thought to have been agreed, international arbitrators have ruled consistently that guarantors must pay upon demand, without investigating the legal basis of the demand for payment.[30]

It therefore can be stated that unconditional guarantee bonds, although sometimes questioned in municipal courts, have acquired full citizenship in the lex mercatoria. It should be stressed, however, that international arbitration courts take special care to keep the relationship between guarantor and beneficiary distinct from that of obligee and beneficiary. The unconditional nature of guarantee bonds generally is deemed to affect only the relationship between guarantor and

---

30. In ICC Arbitration Case No. 3316, 1980 CLUNET 970 (1980), with a commentary by Derains, the arbitrators concluded that unconditional bonds create obligations that are sui generis because guarantors must pay in any case once a bond is drawn-down. In this case, the bank (guarantor) had raised five objections to avoid payment on demand, namely that (1) the term "unconditional" did not mean "on call" but "irrevocable," (2) the text of the bond included a reference to the underlying contract, thus the bank could not be free on such contract, (3) unconditional guarantee for indefinite amounts do not conform to international trade usages, (4) in case of doubt, the scope of an obligation must be construed in favor of an obligee, and (5) only in exceptional cases can a guarantee be unconditional. With respect to this last objection, the arbitral tribunal stated that unconditional bonds now universally are accepted and should be enforced as such. The same conclusions were reached, although indirectly, in ICC Arbitration Case No. 3896, 1983 CLUNET 914 (1983). Finally, in ICC Arbitration Case No. 4555, 1985 CLUNET 964 (1985), the arbitrators clarified what is meant by "unconditional" bond, stating that even the so-called "operative clauses" (conditioning the entry into force of the bond upon the issuance of a letter of credit by the beneficiary with respect to the payment owed to the obligee under the underlying contract) contravene the unconditional nature of a bond. In this case, the arbitrators considered that the obligee acted wrongly in refusing to issue a bond based on the failure by the obligee to issue the letter of credit. *See also* ICC Arbitration Case No. 5721, 1990 CLUNET 1020, 1026 (1990).

beneficiary. However, international arbitrators have consistently stated that an unconditional bond does not give to a beneficiary "an abstract right to cash an amount of money"[31] with respect to an obligee. In other words, a draw-down must always be justified by a legitimate reason, normally a breach of contract by an obligee.

In effect, therefore, an unconditional bond is a "pay now — litigate later" device. It authorizes its beneficiary to obtain an amount of money from a guarantor "on a provisional basis," without having to produce evidence of entitlement on the basis of the underlying contract.[32] In this respect, guarantee bonds constitute a form of self-protection typical of the international trade practice. They entitle the beneficiary to an interim relief measure for which the beneficiary is the sole judge. As with all interim relief measures, two requisites of legitimacy must concur:

1. A valid claim against the obligee, normally derived from a breach of contract, must exist; and

2. There must be a degree of urgency, i.e., there must be a danger that by not drawing-down a bond, a beneficiary's claims may be in jeopardy.

---

31. ICC Arbitration Case No. 3896, 1983 CLUNET 915 (1983), quoting a commentary from Stoufflet to the decisions of the Paris Tribunal of November 24, 1981 and March 25, 1981 (1982 JURIS CLASSEUR PERIODIQUE 19876, II, (1982)).

32. ICC Arbitration Case No. 3316, 1980 CLUNET 974 (1982), expressly refers to the possibility for the obligee to sue the beneficiary who illegally drew-down the bond and obtain the reimbursement of its amount. *See also* Derains, 1980 CLUNET 976 (1980). Substantially along the same lines is ICC Arbitration Case No. 3896, 1983 CLUNET 915 (1983), where the risks for the beneficiary, deriving from an illegal draw-down, are duly underlined. ICC Arbitration Case No. 3267, 1980 CLUNET 962 (1980), is an example of how an arbitration court would evaluate whether or not a draw-down is justified (the court decided the question affirmatively). Another interesting ICC case, ICC Arbitration Case No. 3055, 1981 CLUNET 957 (1981), reminds us that a beneficiary can enforce claims against an obligee irrespective of the existence or validity of a bond. In this case, the bond had expired, and the beneficiary's claim for late delivery penalty was nevertheless enforced.

The lex mercatoria principles, however, clearly include liability of a beneficiary in the absence of the requisites above and in the event of fraud.[33]

In sum, guarantee bonds constitute a form of self-protection for one party to an international contract, enabling it to obtain an agreed sum upon a breach or alleged breach. Contractors have only a limited recourse to national courts to obtain interim relief. It is no surprise, therefore, that ICC arbitral tribunals are slow to deny this party autonomy, and do not consider the unconditional nature of "on demand" bonds and the limited availability of injunctive relief as incompatible.[34]

---

33. As to the requisite of urgency, for example, the arbitrators in the ICC Arbitration Case No. 3896, 1983 CLUNET 917 (1983), found the absence of the requisite urgency when a beneficiary drew-down a bond only as a reaction to the commencement of an arbitration proceeding against it by an obligee. On the other hand, the existence of urgency has been recognized in the presence of attempts by the obligee to obtain a court injunction to block the payment of a bond, ICC Arbitration Case No. 4126, 1984 CLUNET 934 (1984), with a commentary by Jarvin, 1984 CLUNET 937 (1986).

34. The arbitrators in ICC Arbitration Case No. 3896, 1983 CLUNET 914 (1983), emphasized that an obligee, by agreeing to an unconditional bond, did not waive its right to oppose a fraudulent draw-down. In ICC Arbitration Case No. 4126, 1984 CLUNET 936 (1984), the arbitrators stated that if a local court denied the requested injunction, the matter could not be raised again in the arbitration proceeding, according to the *ne bis in idem* principle. In this connection, the arbitrators made reference to Art. 8 (5) of the ICC Rules of Arbitration, which provides that "before the file is transmitted to the arbitrator, and in exceptional circumstances even thereafter, the parties shall be at liberty to apply to any competent judicial authority for interim or conservative measures, and they shall not by so doing be held to infringe the agreement to arbitrate or to affect the relevant powers reserved to the arbitrators." In contrast, Art. 26 of the UNCITRAL Arbitration Rules entitles the arbitral tribunal to take "any interim measures it deems necessary in respect of the subject matter of the dispute." On this point, *see* Goldman, *The Complementary Role of Judges and Arbitrators in Ensuring that International Commercial Arbitration is Effective*, TRAVAUX DU COLLOQUE POUR LE 60EME ANNIVERSAIRE DE LA COUR D'ARBITRAGE CCI 40 (1983).

Between beneficiary and obligee, only a breach of contract entitles a beneficiary to draw-down a bond, even if it is unconditional. The practical effect of the bond is to give a beneficiary the possibility of self-protection while still allowing the intervention of a local court to prevent abuse. In both cases, the jurisdiction to which the contract is submitted must evaluate the presence of liability. If a bond has been drawn-down and subsequent litigation does not establish liability, a beneficiary must return the amount of the bond improperly drawn-down and will be liable for further damages incurred by an obligee as a consequence.[35] Conversely, if an obligee obtains an injunction preventing payment of a guarantee bond, and subsequently a court establishes a breach of contract, the beneficiary is entitled to damages for both the breach and those resulting from its inability to obtain the amount of the guarantee bond.

Since many international contracts select arbitration for the settlement of disputes, international arbitral tribunals often make the types of decisions described above. In this connection, some interesting principles have evolved, specifically as to the relationship between interim relief proceedings and subsequent breach litigation. Also, arbitral tribunals have developed principles regarding the relationship between the amount of a bond and actual damages. The first issue to be addressed by international arbitrators was whether draw-down of a bond in the course of litigation regarding a substantive breach of a contract constituted an unjustifiable widening of the dispute under prevailing international arbitration usages. In one case, ICC arbitrators considered such a draw-down impermissible in the absence of any danger to a beneficiary's claim.[36] In yet another case, ICC arbitrators supported a draw-down in circumstances where there was a legitimate risk that an obligee might be successful in obtaining interim conserva-

---

35. *See* Derains on ICC Arbitration Case No. 3316 of 1979, as well as the unpublished 1979 arbitral award discussed in 1980 CLUNET 977 (1980).

36. The arbitrators, ICC Arbitration Case No. 3896, 1983 CLUNET 917, 918 (1983), expressed the opinion that the existence of bonds and their availability for draw-down in case of need is their required function. A draw-down by the beneficiary in a situation where the beneficiary's legitimate interests are not in danger would only have the effect of widening the pending dispute and complicating the task of the arbitral tribunal. With respect to such award, *see also* Jarvin, 1983 CLUNET 918 (1983).

tive measures blocking the bond.[37] Consequently, it can be said that international arbitration practice supports the proposition that a draw-down of a bond is impermissible when a beneficiary is not in a particular situation of urgency. Without urgency, draw-downs of bonds have the effect of unduly widening a dispute.

As to the relationship between the amount of a bond and damages, arbitral tribunals have distinguished between cases where a bond is intended by the parties to serve as liquidated damages, and those where a bond serves only to induce proper performance *ad terrorem*. In the first situation, arbitrators have stated that in the presence of a contract breach, beneficiaries may draw-down bonds without having to produce evidence as to the amount of damages actually incurred. In the second situation, the amount of a bond is determined by a court in relation to damages actually incurred by a beneficiary.[38]

Finally, the fact that the amount of a bond and the amount of damages actually incurred by a beneficiary need not necessarily be related has been indirectly affirmed by some arbitral tribunals in awards determining that the expiration of a bond does not cause the expiration of an obligee's liability for damages for breach of the contract underlying the bond.[39]

---

37. ICC Arbitration Case No. 4126, 1984 CLUNET 934, 937 (1984), with an interesting commentary by Jarvin, 1986 CLUNET 937 (1984).

38. In ICC Arbitration Case No. 3267, 1980 CLUNET 961 (1980), arbitrators had to decide whether the amount of the bond drawn-down could be entirely retained by a beneficiary as liquidated damages without having to prove the amount of the damages actually incurred, or whether it constituted a penalty, the amount of which could be revised by the arbitrators in relation to damages finally determined. The arbitrators, based on the language of the contract and the bond, concluded that the bond amount was intended as liquidated damages, but stated that should it not have been the case they would have felt free to revise the amount of the bond upwards or downwards. *See also* the interesting commentary by Derains, 1980 CLUNET 969 (1980).

39. In ICC Arbitration Case No. 3055, 1981 CLUNET 938 (1981), the arbitrators stated that guarantee bonds are not intended to benefit obligees. They only benefit the other party, and the contractual rights enjoyed by such party are not affected by the existence of guarantee bonds. *See also* Derains, 1981 CLUNET 938, 939 (1981), quoting unpublished ICC

5.6 Attempts to Codify the Transnational Rules Governing Guarantee Bonds

There have been several attempts to codify a set of rules to govern guarantee bonds. They have not been particularly successful, and are worth mentioning more for their failure than their achievement.

We already have mentioned the Uniform Rules for Contractual Guarantees issued by the International Chamber of Commerce on June 20th, 1978 (ICC Publication No. 325). These rules were followed in 1982 by model forms for the various types of bonds, together with extensive commentary.[40] This "moribund"[41] codification effort is of very limited utility because it only covers conditional bonds. This is consistent with the generally negative attitude of the ICC toward unconditional bonds, an attitude expressly stated in the Introduction to the Uniform Rules.[42] Even if some of the Uniform Rules are likely to be applicable to unconditional bonds in practice, there is no question that they are not "drafted to apply thereto."[43] This is expressly recognized

---

Arbitration Case No. 3515 of 1980, where it is stated that a bond is not capable of being drawn-down after a beneficiary is compensated by breach of contract damages. Conversely, if a party draws-down a bond, it cannot request damages again (presumably, if the amount of the bond was to be intended as liquidated damages). The beneficiary cannot be compensated twice.

40. *Model Forms for Issuing Contract Guarantees Under the ICC Uniform Rules for Contract Guarantees*, ICC Publication No. 406 (1982); a French text was published at 1982 Droit et Pratique du Commerce International 713 (1982).

41. Byrne, *Fundamental Issues in the Unification and Harmonization of Letter of Credit Law*, 37 Loy. L. Rev. 1, 3 (1991).

42. The Introduction to the ICC Uniform Rules specifies that they were drafted based on "the need to justify a claim under guarantee, to invest guarantee practice with a moral content." The drafters of the Introduction then clarify that "it has not been found advisable to make provisions for so-called simple or first demand guarantees, under which claims are payable without independent evidence of their validity."

43. Article 9 of the ICC Uniform Rules, for example, lists documents that a beneficiary should be required to produce in support of a request for draw-down. It is clear, therefore, that the Rules are not intended to be

in their text; hence the limited success of the Uniform Rules in international trade law. Additionly, certain aspects of the regulations regarding conditional bonds favor obligees so openly that the possibility of them becoming the basis of a widely accepted set of rules for international bonds is diminished.[44] Another deficiency of the ICC Uniform Rules is that they do not address the crucial issue of whether a bond is tied to its underlying contract or is totally independent.

The performance bond model adopted in connection with the UNIDO contract forms and prepared in 1979 by the UNIDO Secretariat is worthy of mention.[45] This model submits to the attention of a group of experts two types of performance bonds to be used in connection with the UNIDO contract forms — those on demand and those on default. The choice appears to be left to a beneficiary. The UNIDO model only indicates that, should the beneficiary opt for an unconditional bond (termed as "simple and unambiguous as regards when and how it can be called"), the amount of such bond should constitute liquidated damages. The UNIDO model for unconditional bonds provides that they can be drawn-down "without any objections and enquiry whatsoever regarding the grounds for the non-fulfillment of obligations and without asking for any reason as to whether the amount is lawfully asked for by the Purchaser or not." The unconditional nature of such bonds could not be better stressed.

---

applicable to unconditional guarantees. In perspective, it would perhaps have been preferable for the ICC to address the practice of unconditional bonds, rather than pretend that such practice is minimal. While specifying that "the Rules do not encourage the use of such [unconditional] guarantees," the drafter added, with an optimism hardly justifiable in light of the practice, that "there is evidence of a decline in their use in certain areas as their economic disadvantages are more fully understood." The reality is that the sellers and contractors are acutely aware of the economic disadvantages of the unconditional bonds, but they often lack the bargaining power to oppose the routine requests for such bonds by buyers or owners.

44. *See* note 7 *supra* with respect to the duration of the bond.
45. "Type of Performance Bond That Might be Included in the UNIDO Model Forms of Contract." Note, UNIDO Secretariat, doc. 1D/WG. 306/3 of November 23rd, 1979, submitted to the group of experts in charge of the drafting of the UNIDO contract forms for plants for the production of fertilizers.

As noted before, codification efforts to date are still unsatisfactory. More work to formulate the texts of bonds that will be widely accepted by the international business community needs to be undertaken. Such a codification is in progress, and it is hoped that the international organizations and other institutions, such as international trade associations, presently at work will be able to perform this task. An effort to draft a uniform law or convention on bank guarantees and stand-by letters of credit currently is being undertaken by UNCITRAL and the ICC in conjunction.[46] The objective of these efforts should be to limit the still extant plague of international business life — abusive or fraudulent draw-down of bonds — while preserving the risk transferring aspects of guarantee bonds that parties may choose to negotiate.[47]

5.7 Other Types of Self-Protection Remedies Against Contract Breach

A. *Exceptio Inadimpleti Contractus*

Contractual guarantees are not the only forms of self-protection included in international business contracts. Some doctrines of municipal contract law also are seen as forms of permissible self-protection, and are encountered more frequently in an international context than in a purely domestic one.

Perhaps the most notable of these is the civil law doctrine known as the "exceptio inadimpleti contractus" ("exceptio") and its rough common law counterparts.[48] According to the civil law principle, which

---

46. *Stand-By Letters of Credit and Guarantees: Report to the Secretary-General,* 21 UNCITRAL at 9, U.N. Doc. A/CN.9/301 (1988). *See generally* Byrne, *Fundamental Issues in the Unification and Harmonization of Letter of Credit Law,* 37 Loy. L. Rev. 1, 3 (1991).

47. "To restore the balance of fairness, the bank guarantee must return to its documentary origins and rely on the guarantor's verification of documentary compliance as a prerequisite of payment to the beneficiary." Kozolchyk, *Bank Guarantees and Letters of Credit: Time for a Return to the Fold,* 11 U. Pa. J. Int'l Bus. L. 1 (1989).

48. The principle is called *Einrede des nicht erfüllten Vertrags* in German and *eccezione di inadempimento* in Italian. The French term *exception*

was contained in Roman law, a party may refuse to perform contractual obligations to the extent the other party does not fulfil its own obligation. This principle is expressly contained in the German[49] and Italian[50] civil codes. Although there is no specific French statutory provision, the courts consider the exceptio to be a well-established principle of law.[51]

The effect of the exceptio is to paralyze an action for breach of contract. It does not terminate or cancel a contract, but is "temporary and provisional non-performance."[52] The remedy is wholly private; action by a judicial authority is not required for a party to invoke it.[53] The importance of the exceptio's autonomous nature is greater in the civil law than in the common law. In the latter, we have seen that the very concept of contract is tied to remedies and breach. Common law parties "declare" a contract terminated upon the serious failure of performance by the other party. In civil law countries, termination is an extreme sanction tied inextricably to the court system.[54]

---

d'inexécution is preferred by the French Ministry of Justice to the Latin, but in all three countries the Latin phrase is commonly in use.

49. § 320 BGB.

50. Cod. Civ. Arts. 1460 and 1461.

51. *See generally* the cases reported in 1984 CLUNET 429 (1984); B. Nicholas, FRENCH LAW OF CONTRACT 207–210 (1982). The exceptio is truly an exception (in the English sense) in that it is an exception to the general distaste for self-help remedies that characterizes the French legal system.

52. B. Nicholas, FRENCH LAW OF CONTRACT 208 (1982). It is a "dilatory plea" that produces a "waiting position." G. Treitel, REMEDIES FOR BREACH OF CONTRACT: A COMPARATIVE ACCOUNT 310 (1988), citing respectively L. Enneccerus & H. Lehmann, RECHT DER SCHULDVERHÄLTNISSE (15th ed. 1958) and 2 H., L., and J. Mazeaud, LEÇONS DE DROIT CIVIL 1, No. 1132 (5th ed. 1980).

53. B. Nicholas, FRENCH LAW OF CONTRACT 207 (1982). In this respect, the Latin word *exceptio* and the French word *exception* are misleading, both implying a defense.

54. In the absence of express agreement, termination in French and Belgian law requires a judgment. C. C. Art. 1184 (France) and C. C. 1184 (Belgium).

The exceptio deals with problems related to the order of performance as well. It is obviously inapplicable as a practical matter to *obligations de moyens*. The only general limitation to the exercise of the exceptio is the good-faith principle. This requires that a refusal to perform in reliance on the exceptio is commensurate, as to its practical effects, with the extent of the contract breach of the other party.

Normally, the exceptio is invoked in contractual situations where the respective obligations of the two parties are performed concurrently. When performance is to occur at different times, suspension of performance is considered, rather than the exceptio, as a self-protection remedy.

There are no obvious conceptual counterparts to the exceptio in common law systems. In these systems, no sharp distinctions are drawn between remedies for refusal to perform and those for termination.[55] In this respect, as in many areas of contract law, U.S. law is somewhat closer to the civil law than is English law. In both systems, a party may terminate a contract in the event of a "serious," "substantial," or "material" breach by the other party.[56] In both systems, however, a party in breach may "cure" its breach. The right of a party to cure in U.S. law is more extensive than in English law.[57]

The exceptio is a part of public international law as well, where it has been codified by Article 60 of the Vienna Convention on the Law of Treaties.[58]

---

55. *See generally* G. Treitel, Remedies for Breach of Contract: A Comparative Account 245–317 (1988), where the conceptual difficulties with comparative analysis in this area are discussed in detail. For the common law principles applied with specific reference to construction contracts, *see* De Belder, *Repudiating a Construction Contract for Late Payment*, 1987 Int'l Construc. L. Rev. 27 (1987).

56. Farnsworth on Contracts §§ 8.15–8.17 (1990); Chitty on Contracts §1616 (1990).

57. G. Treitel, Remedies for Breach of Contract: A Comparative Account 370–375 (1988); Restatement (Second) of Contracts § 237 (1979); U.C.C. § 508.

58. Article 60 of the Vienna Convention on the Law of Treaties (*see* U.N. Doc A/CONF. 39 (27, at 289) (1969)), provides that a material breach of

The simplicity and autonomous nature of this self-protection has made it particularly suitable for situations involving international business contracts. In international trade law, the exceptio applies both to relational contracts that contemplate performance of a continuous and prolonged nature, such as technical assistance agreements, and to contracts contemplating instantaneous performance, such as sales contracts. In this respect, the 1980 Vienna Convention on the International Sale of Goods contains a number of provisions regarding what in the common law would be called "anticipatory breaches." Since these provisions permit suspension prior to a failure of performance by a party, they are much wider than the civil law exceptio principle.[59]

Article 71 of the U.N. Convention on Contracts for the Sale of Goods (the Vienna Convention)[60] provides that either party may suspend the performance of its obligations if it becomes evident that the other party will not perform a substantial part of its own obligations.

---

a bilateral treaty by one of its parties entitles the other party to terminate the treaty or to partially or totally suspend its application. This article applies also to multilateral treaties. However, a distinction is drawn between measures that can be collectively adopted by all the other parties and measures that can be adopted only by the individual party damaged by the breach. The third paragraph of the above-mentioned Article 60 defines "material breach" as a repudiation of the treaty or the violation of a provision that is essential for the attainment of the object or purpose of the treaty. The International Court of Justice has pronounced that Article 60 of the Vienna Convention must be considered as a codification of existing international law (*see* advisory opinion of June 21, 1971 rendered on the legal consequences for the states of the continued presence of South Africa in Namibia, notwithstanding Resolution 276 of 1970 by the Security Council, [1971] I.C.J. 16), thus confirming that the exceptio has always constituted a general rule of public international law.

59. It is interesting to note that the previous convention for international sales of goods, the 1964 Uniform Law for the International Sale of Goods (U.L.I.S.) did not include a form of the exceptio. It is evident that the 1980 Vienna Convention represents an increased awareness of the issue on the part of the international business community.

60. *See generally* J. Honnold, UNIFORM LAW FOR INTERNATIONAL SALES UNDER THE 1980 UNITED NATIONS CONVENTION (1982).

This remedy may be invoked if there is a "serious deficiency" in the other party's "ability to perform," "credit worthiness," or "conduct in preparing to perform or in performing" the contract. This language is very broad, and goes far beyond the statutory civil provisions that expressly contemplate the exceptio.[61] Under the 1980 Vienna Convention, a party may invoke the exceptio even on the basis of the delayed passing of procurement orders to the suppliers by the other party, or delayed sourcing of raw materials or manpower, because this activity would fall within the notion of "conduct in preparing to perform the contract."

Article 72 of the Vienna Convention provides that either party may terminate a sales contract when it is clear that the other party "will commit a fundamental breach of contract."[62] If time allows, a terminating party must give "reasonable notice" to the other party to allow the latter to provide adequate assurance of performance. No notice is required, however, if the other party has expressly stated its unwillingness to perform. Here, too, the Vienna Convention seems to go further than most civil laws that expressly contemplate the exceptio. Civil law systems normally require that a party can terminate the sales contract only after the term for performance by the other party has expired, and notice has been duly given.[63]

Article 73 of the Vienna Convention deals with contracts for delivery of goods by installments. If a breach concerns only one installment, the party not in breach has the option to terminate the contract (1) with respect only to that installment, and on "good grounds," (2) with respect to all future installments, and even (3) with respect to all contract obligations, including those already performed.

---

61. *See, e.g.*, Art. 1461 of the Italian Civil Code.

62. The "fundamental" breach requirement is borrowed from U.S. law, where a breach must be of a serious nature to warrant the application of the doctrine of anticipatory breach. RESTATEMENT (SECOND) OF CONTRACTS §§ 253, 250 (1979); U.C.C. § 2-610. The requirement is less clear in English law. G. Treitel, THE LAW OF CONTRACT 655 (7th ed. 1987).

63. *See, e.g.*, Art. 1517 of the Italian Civil Code. The Vienna Convention approach is similar to the approach of German law, where the notice requirements of § 326 BGB prior to a termination are inapplicable when a party states an intention not to perform.

This possibility of retroactive termination, again, goes further than the majority of civil municipal law provisions.[64]

With respect to contracts for sale, the Vienna Convention, as we have seen, has codified principles similar to the civil law exceptio principle and the common law doctrine of anticipatory breach. It is thus clear that the right of a party not to perform in the face of non-performance by the other party to an international contract is a part of the lex mercatoria. With respect to construction, distribution, or technical assistance contracts, there are presently no international uniform laws. Yet, there is a little doubt about the adoption of the exceptio by the international trade practice with respect to such contracts.[65]

In 1976,[66] an ICC Arbitral Tribunal stated that a contractor who abandons a jobsite as a consequence of one or more material breaches by an employer would be acting in accordance with the "well established usages regarding construction contracts." Another ICC Arbitral Tribunal decided in 1980 that the exceptio must be considered as an integral part of the general principles of law constituting the lex mercatoria.[67]

The decision of the International Centre for the Settlement of Investment Disputes (ICSID) Arbitral Tribunal, dated October 21, 1983,

---

64. For a detailed and accurate commentary of Arts. 71–73 of the Vienna Convention, *see* Bianca-Bonell, COMMENTARY ON THE INTERNATIONAL SALES LAW — THE 1980 VIENNA SALES CONVENTION 513–537 (1987).

65. With respect to international construction contracts, many scholars maintain that the contractor is entitled to abandon the jobsite in the presence of an unjustified interruption of the progress payments by the employer. *See* Brabant, LE CONTRAT INTERNATIONAL DE CONSTRUCTION 252, 253 (1981); Rubino-Sammartano, *International Construction Agreements — Employer's Breach and Consequent Right of the Contractor to Withhold Delivery of the Site*, 1983 INT'L BUS. LAW. 143 (1983); De Belder, *Repudiating a Construction Contract for Late Payment*, 1987 INT'L CONSTRUC. L. REV. 27 (1987).

66. ICC Arbitration Case No. 2583, 1977 CLUNET 951 (1977). In the specific case, however, the arbitrators stated that the delay by the employer in opening a letter of credit in favor of the contractor did not constitute a material breach likely to justify recourse to the exceptio. Along the same lines, *see* ICC Arbitration Case No. 1675, 1974 CLUNET 895 (1974).

67. ICC Arbitration Case No. 3540, 1981 CLUNET 920 (1981).

in *Klöckner v. République Unie du Cameroun et SOCAME* is worthy of mention. In that case, the arbitrators stated that the exceptio had found its route into the general principles of international trade law. Article 42(1) of the Washington Convention, which established the ICSID, makes reference to the principle. As a consequence, arbitrators held that the exceptio may be invoked by either party, at any moment, during the life of the contract or even during the arbitration or judicial proceeding, without the need for previous notice to the opposing party.[68]

The exceptio is understood by, and is an integral part of, the work of negotiators and drafters of international contracts. Article 69 of the FIDIC conditions for civil works, for example, entitles a contractor to "terminate his employment under the Contract" if material breaches of contract are committed by an employer. In general, however, express exceptio clauses in international contracts are infrequent. The exceptio normally is considered as derived from general principles of law and does not need to be expressly elaborated. Furthermore, in an international contract, the exceptio normally protects the party that delivers goods or performs services and does not pay money — the "characteristic" performer in the sense of the EC Contractual Obligations Convention. The party that pays money generally is protected by bank guarantees. Given the fact that such other party is often the stronger of the two, it is understandable that there are not many express exceptio provisions in international contracts.

The stronger position of the creditor of the non-monetary obligation is at times reflected in clauses *preventing* the other party from invoking the exceptio. These "required to work" clauses provide that a contractor must continue to perform diligently even while the contractor has claims pending towards the employers. As has been correctly pointed out, "these *requirement to work*" clauses should not automatically be considered to mean that the owner has the right to do whatever the owner wants, including breaching the contract by such acts as delaying or failing to pay the contractor, while requiring the

---

68. This ICSID arbitration decision is published in 1984 CLUNET 428 (1984). In his comment on this decision, Galliard states that the *exceptio* is a principle of law inherent in any contractual relationship contemplating reciprocal obligations 1984 CLUNET 142 [1984].

contractor to continue performance. There is a major difference between an owner requiring a contractor to continue performance during a dispute and the requirement that a contractor continue performance where the owner has clearly breached the contract. The owner's obvious breach automatically gives the contractor the right to terminate the contract."[69] The distinction between the two cases, though, may not be easy to draw in specific instances.

B. Documentary Credit and Vesting of Plant and Contractor's Equipment

There are other forms of self-protection in the international trade law that are not necessarily always considered in the context of protective devices.

Letters of credit, while primarily conceived as a mechanism to effect payments, also serve the purpose of guaranteeing a buyer's or employer's payment obligations. A letter of credit is merely the commitment of a bank to pay an agreed sum on behalf of a contractual debtor, as soon as a creditor (the seller or the contractor) presents to the bank certain documents, such as shipping documents and test certificates. Letters of credit are issued on the instruction and at the cost of a party paying money. Letters of credit can be "confirmed" by a second bank, selected by the seller or contractor. Confirmed letters of credit obviously offer a stronger protection to the creditor of a payment obligation. A confirming bank normally is located in the country of the party receiving funds. Its use, therefore, effects both the second financial guarantee and ease of enforcement.

International practice in the area of documentary credit is sizeable and has been memorialized by the International Chamber of Commerce in a 1984 publication entitled "Rules and Uniform Practices Concerning Documentary Credits."[70] Many interesting legal issues could be discussed in connection with letters of credit, such as the kind of liability to the bank, the assignability of the credit, etc. A

---

69. R. Sammartano-Grey, *Constructor's Duty When Owner is in Breach*, 1987 INT'L BUS. LAW. 117 (1987).

70. *See also* Brabant, LE CONTRAT INTERNATIONAL DE CONSTRUCTION 256 (1981); Kurkela, LETTERS OF CREDIT UNDER INTERNATIONAL TRADE LAW (1985).

discussion of these issues can be found in the specialized treatises on the subject.

Another form of self-protection typical of international construction agreements is the right of an employer to have the works completed by a third party, at the contractor's expense, where the contractor fails to perform. The frequent inclusion of such clauses in international contracts appears to be justified by the interest of the employer to have the works promptly completed prior to lengthy and costly litigation proceedings. The FIDIC conditions for civil works expressly provide for such a right of the employer.[71]

Finally, a last form of self-protection available to the employer in an international construction contract is offered by the "vesting of plant and contractor's equipment" clause. Such clauses, in effect, grant private pre-judgment attachment rights to one party. By means of these frequently encountered clauses, employers acquire the right to "attach" a contractor's goods at a job site in the event of breach by the contractor. The employer then may sell the goods so taken and apply them against the damages it ultimately may be awarded.

The description of the more common forms of self-protection in international business contracts contained in this chapter is by no means intended to be exhaustive. Its purpose is rather to stress the relative importance that self-protection has assumed in the lex mercatoria as compared to municipal law, the more structured framework of which leaves less room and less necessity for the principles of self-protection. This is undoubtedly one of the more interesting aspects of the development of the lex mercatoria, and it probably deserves more attention than that received so far.

---

71. FIDIC § 63.

III. THE ADAPTATION OF INTERNATIONAL BUSINESS CONTRACTS

Chapter 6. Changed Circumstances and Contract Adaptation

6.1 General

In Part I, the most common "pathological" aspects of international contracts — breach, non-performance, and defective performance — were discussed. In Part II, we will examine contract adaptation, the change or adaptation of contractual provisions during the course of performance. Contract adaptation can occur in two ways: the terms of a contract may change because circumstances change, or because one of the parties makes a unilateral decision to change them. The former possibility is the subject of Chapter 6; the latter of Chapter 7.

Contract adaptation is the legal avatar of the ubiquitous economic concept of equilibrium. It is a process that returns the relationship of parties to a contract to an agreed original position when changed circumstances after the execution of an agreement have created an imbalance or disequilibrium in their relative economic positions. It normally is applicable to long-term, "relational" contracts.

Contract adaptation normally occurs, as we shall see, because parties to a contract choose for it to occur by specifically providing for changed circumstances in an agreement. It also can occur, however, by the operation of law. The attitudes of national legal systems vary widely with respect to the latter possibility. The concept of contract adaptation by operation of law as treated here is distinct from that involving an imbalance of the relative positions of parties to a contract that exists at the time of execution.[1]

---

1. A strong distaste for this second situation is found in most civil law systems, although it is present in many specific areas. It was known in Roman Law as *laesio* (in French: *lésion*). The concept was developed under Thomistic influence in the Middle Ages, and is present in one form or another in many civil law systems. 2 K. Zweigert & H. Kötz, AN INTRODUCTION TO COMPARATIVE LAW 68–70 (2d ed. 1987). It gives a remedy to a disadvantaged party in situations where the rights and obligations of the parties are grossly disproportionate; for example, in the case of the laesio ultra dimidii, when the value of one party's performance is less than one half of what the other party originally believed it to be at the time a contract was executed. The French doctrine

6.2 Adaptation Clauses in International Business Contracts

Several noteworthy surveys of the law surrounding adaptation clauses, particularly with respect to hardship clauses, have shown that their use is more frequent in international contracts than in purely national contracts.[2] This is due to the fact that international contracts are more likely to be of a long-term, relational nature, usually including obligations that are continuing, periodic, and differentiated.[3] Moreover, international contracts are performed in an uncertain political

---

of *lésion* is applicable only to sales of land and a decedent's estate, but it is spiritually present in many other areas by statute. B. Nicholas, FRENCH LAW OF CONTRACT 131–137 (1982). The German equivalent, BGB § 138, para. 2, is more generally applicable, and the Austrian version, 934 AGBG, is applicable to *all* contracts. There is no real common law counterpart, although one might argue that roughly the same function is accomplished by the judicial inclusion of implied terms, by statutes applicable to certain types of transactions (primarily consumer transactions), and by the criminal law. Certainly, a more disproportionate relationship increases the application of the U.S. concept of unconscionability, embodied in U.C.C. § 2-302.

2. CONTRACT LAW TODAY: ANGLO-FRENCH COMPARISONS 195–241 (D. Harris & D. Tallon, eds. 1989); Horn, ADAPTATION AND RENEGOTIATION OF CONTRACTS IN INTERNATIONAL TRADE AND FINANCE — STUDIES IN TRANSNATIONAL ECONOMIC LAW No. 3 (1985), with particular reference to the contribution from Böckstiegel, *Hardship, Force Majeure and Special Risks in International Contracts, id.* at 159; Oppetit, *L'adaptation des contrats internationaux aux changement des circonstances: la clause de hardship,* 1974 CLUNET 794 (1974); Fontaine, DROIT DES CONTRATS INTERNATIONAUX — AYALYSE ET REDACTION DE CLAUSES, 211, 249 (1989); Silard, *Clause de maintien de la valeur dans les transactions internationales,* 1972 CLUNET 214 (1972); Schmitthoff, *Hardship and Intervener Clauses,* 1980 J. BUS. L. 82 (1980).

3. Examples of long-term international contracts include construction agreements, turnkey agreements, international output or requirements contracts, agreements for the sale of infrastructure equipment, such as telecommunications facilities, concession and work contracts for the development of primary products, agency and distribution agreements, franchise agreements, management agreements, technical consulting

and economic environment that changes more rapidly and frequently than the context in which internal contracts operate.

The relational nature and long duration of international contracts create an aversion to the risks associated with the passage of time always being borne by the party negatively affected. French scholars and courts have long made a distinction between contracts such as sales contracts that must be performed immediately, or within a very short time, and where a party intends to bear the risk of unforeseen events (aleatory contract, in French: *contrats aléatoires*), and long-term contracts, which the parties do not want to be *aléatoires*.[4] One of the characteristics of these long-term contracts is that the parties generally intend that unforeseen events be handled through contract adaptation, which re-establishes the balance between the parties, rather than through termination or the impossible task of considering all contingencies in the future.[5]

---

agreements, finance agreements, countertrade agreements and joint venture agreements.

4. As to the concept of aleatory contracts in French law, *see* B. Nicholas, FRENCH LAW OF CONTRACT 44 (1982).

5. French scholars were the first to make the distinction. *See, e.g.*, Fouchard, L'ARBITRAGE COMMERCIAL INTERNATIONAL 437 (1965), where it is maintained that international arbitrators generally assume that international contracts are not of an aleatory nature, and thus find that it is fair and equitable that they contain an implied clause protecting the parties against currency devaluation. Professor Kahn distinguishes between "exchange contracts," where the parties immediately discharge their reciprocal obligations, and "production or supply contracts," which are essentially more long-term, relational contracts. With respect to these latter contracts, Kahn identifies an emerging principle of law in international practice aimed at offsetting, through the process of contract adaptation, the imbalances created by changed circumstances. Kahn, *Lex Mercatoria et pratique des contrats internationaux*, LE CONTRAT ECONOMIC INTERNATIONAL, TRAVAUX DES VII JOURNÉES D'ÉTUDES JURIDIQUES JEAN DABIN 180 (1977); Kahn, *Force Majeure et contrats internationaux de longue durée*, 1975 CLUNET 467–468 (1975). Along the same lines, *see* Goldman, *La lex mercatoria dans les contrats et l'arbitrage internationaux: réalité et perspectives*, 1979 CLUNET 494 (1979) and Loquin, L'AMIABLE COMPOSITION EN DROIT COMPARE ET INTERNATIONAL

It is not surprising, therefore, that commercial entities frequently negotiate provisions in international contracts clauses that are designed to preserve their relationship as circumstances change during the course of performance which may alter the balance of rights and obligations originally existing. Such provisions may be described in two classifications: those aimed at maintaining the original economic value of each party's obligations and those aimed more generally at adapting a contract to unforeseen changes of circumstance.

A. *Clauses Aimed at Maintaining the Original Economic Value of the Parties' Obligations Unchanged*

Provisions of the first type consist generally of price revision clauses based on extraordinary cost increases, and exchange variation clauses by which a contract price can change depending on the variation of the exchange rate of the currency in which the price is denominated. Both of these clauses are intended to equitably allocate risks of a monetary nature, such as those connected with inflation or currency devaluation.

With respect to price variations based on cost increases, several standard clauses have been developed. They generally provide for an automatic price revision depending on the variation of certain parameters or indices agreed on by the parties. Some contractual provisions of this kind are highly complex, referring to a variety of indices and

---

284 (1980). In the United States, much of the discussion of long-term contracts has centered around economic analysis. "Relational" contracts frequently are analyzed in terms of transaction costs, and are defined as those contracts in which the costs of writing or enforcement make it impossible to consider all contingencies that may arise. *See, e.g.,* Goetz & Scott, *Principles of Relational Contracts,* 67 VA. L. REV. 1089 (1981); Macneill, *Contracts: Adjustment of Long-Term Economic Relations Under Classical, Neoclassical, and Relational Contract Law,* 72 NW. U. L. REV. 854 (1978); Posner & Rosenfield, *Impossibility and Related Doctrines in Contract Law*: An Economic Analysis, 6 J. LEG. STUD. 83 (1977). Many European commentators believe that a purely economic analysis is insufficient. CONTRACT LAW TODAY: ANGLO-FRENCH COMPARISONS 220 (D. Harris & D. Tallon, eds. 1989).

assigning different weight to them.[6] Of course, price revision clauses are incompatible with fixed price contracts. In fixed price contracts, parties damaged by cost inflation only may avail themselves of exchange variation clauses. On the other hand, the existence of a price revision clause can be interpreted as negating the parties' intention that a contract should be adapted due to unforeseen changed circumstances in the absence of a specific hardship clause.[7] Municipal systems place restrictions on the use of price revision clauses, but they are usually of a limited nature.[8]

Exchange variation clauses provide protection against currency fluctuations, i.e., against the risk of an unfavorable alteration of the exchange rate of the currency in which a contract price is denominated with respect to another currency of reference, a basket of different currencies, or gold. Exchange variation clauses are not always enforceable under national or international legislation.[9]

---

6. On price revision clauses, *see*, among others, Fresle, Variation and Escalation Clauses, in ADAPTATION AND RENEGOTIATION OF CONTRACTS IN INTERNATIONAL TRADE AND FINANCE 149 (N. Horn, ed. 1985).

7. Generally, ICC arbitral tribunals have found that when no express price revision clause is included in a contract, the parties wanted a fixed price contract. Worthy of mention is ICC Arbitration Case No. 3267, 1980 CLUNET 962 (1980), in which a clause providing for a possible price increase depending on the rise in certain indexes was not interpreted to permit a price reduction faced when the same indexes fell.

8. In French law, price revision clauses must be precise, independent, and have a direct relationship with the objective of the clause. The Cour de Cassation has disapproved of clauses that adjust prices to be similar to those of competitors, of those that depended on the "will" of a party. French legislation has seriously limited the choice of indexes that may be used in price revision clauses governed by French law. CONTRACT LAW TODAY: ANGLO-FRENCH COMPARISONS 223 (D. Harris & D. Tallon, eds. 1989). English courts are generally more permissive in this respect, and have limited price revision indexes only if they are so irrelevant to the contract as to constitute a wager. Brogden v. Marriott, (1836) 5 L. J. C. P. 302.

9. An example of an international agreement limiting the enforceability of exchange variation clauses is Article VIII, § 2 (b) of the International Monetary Fund Agreement. *See generally* Schwab, *The Unenforceability*

ICC arbitrators consistently have enforced clauses that protect against the currency devaluation, and "gold clauses" in particular.[10] At the same time, however, they have denied adjustment of the contract price in the absence of an express contract provision dealing with the matter.[11] Currency devaluations occurring after the due date of a particular payment, however, can be recognized as a source of compensation to a creditor in addition to interest payment. In other words, international arbitrators appear to consider that when a contract is denominated in a particular currency, the parties must bear the risk of that currency's fluctuation unless they have provided otherwise. If, however, a payment in a given currency is overdue, the late debtor should compensate the creditor through interest and also be responsible for losses due to exchange fluctuations. The applicable base currency in such situations is normally that of the country of the creditor. For example, in a recent ICC partial award,[12] the arbitrators had to

---

of International Contracts Violating Foreign Exchange Regulations: Article VIII, Section 2(b) of the International Monetary Fund Agreement, 71 Va. J. Int'l L. 967 (1985). On the limitations to which exchange variation clauses are submitted in many municipal laws, *see* Malaurie, *Les clauses monétaires stipulées dans un contrat international*, 1966 Clunet 571 (1966); Leboulanger, *Remarques sur la règle dite order public appliquée aux stipulations de garantie monétaire dans les contrats internationaux*, 1963 Clunet 68 (1963); Ugeux, *Extranéité, risques de change et euro-dévises*, 1976 Droit et Pratique du Commerce International 265 (1976). Many models of international contracts expressly exclude price variation depending on variation of the exchange rate of the currency in which the price is denominated. *See, e.g.*, Art. 72 of the FIDIC model contract for civil works.

10. ICC Arbitration Case No. 2142, 1974 Clunet 892 (1974); No. 1704, 1978 Clunet 979 (1978).

11. ICC Arbitration Case No. 1990, 1974 Clunet 901–902 (1974); No. 2520, 1976 Clunet 993 (1976), In this last case, the ICC arbitrators termed the gold clause as "exorbitant with respect to the common law."

12. *See* the partial award rendered on January 6th, 1989 by the ICC arbitrators in Case No. 5261, reprinted in 1989 Diritto del Commercio Internazionale 275 (1989), with a commentary by Draetta, *Interessi di mora e svalutazione monetaria, id.* at 276.

decide the amount of damages due to an Italian subcontractor from a Franco-American prime contractor with respect to a contract, the price of which was denominated in U.S. dollars. The Italian subcontractor performed in accordance with the contract, but the prime contractor was late in payment. There was no currency devaluation clause in the contract. The ICC arbitrators decided that the subcontractor was not entitled to compensation for the devaluation of the U.S. dollar against the Italian lira between the date of contract execution and the date the payment was due. They decided, however, that the subcontractor could in principle be compensated for the U.S. dollar devaluation with respect to the Italian lira occurring from the date the payment was due to the date the payment was actually made. The arbitrators' theory was that had the Italian subcontractor been paid in a timely manner, it would have converted the amount of U.S. dollars received in Italian lira. By converting into Italian lira the same amount of U.S. dollars at the time the payment was actually made, the subcontractor would have received a lesser amount of Italian lira. The arbitrators considered that this could constitute a loss additional to that intended to be covered by interest, for which the subcontractor could be in principle compensated. However, in so doing, the arbitrators applied the general principle according to which a party in breach of contract must be compensated for all the damages suffered as a consequence of such breach.[13]

B. Clauses Aimed at Adjusting the Contract to Unforeseen Changes of Circumstances

Contract provisions that seek to maintain the original value of a contract are not sufficient to deal with the adaptation of contracts to changed circumstances for several reasons. First, value maintenance clauses concern only the performance of obligations of a monetary nature, usually those of a purchaser or the owner. They do not afford the possibility of revising non-monetary obligations, usually those of a seller or contractor. Second, because value maintenance clauses often are structured with a complexity that lends credence to their analysis

---

13. On currency devaluation as an item of damages for late payment, *see* § 3.4 *supra*.

by economists, they are seldom of general utility. Third, these clauses sometimes encounter difficulties of enforcement because of public policy considerations in municipal law. Fourth, the automatic application of value maintenance clauses based on inflexible parameters, indices, and the passage of time, renders them inappropriate for most situations. Finally, because they operate only upon the occurrence of certain changes or variations expressly foreseen by the parties, such as the increase of costs or devaluation of the currency, the clauses do not offer a suitable adaptation for unforeseen changes of circumstance.[14]

Those who negotiate international business contracts thus seem to prefer clauses of the second type, which we have more broadly defined as adaptation clauses.

Most favored customer clauses belong to this category. The purpose is to extend to a contracting party more advantageous terms and conditions, which a party grants to third persons subsequent to the execution of a contract.[15] A variation of the most favored customer clause is the "second look," or "competing offer" clause. By such a provision, a contracting party is given the right to notify the other party of more favorable terms and conditions that another person has offered the notifying party with respect to the same transaction. The notified party then may grant the notifying party the more favorable terms and conditions, or terminate the original con-

---

14. For a more detailed criticism of these clauses, *see* Oppetit, *L'adaptation des contrats internationaux aux changements de circonstances: la clause de hardship*, 1974 CLUNET 797 (1974). The ICC Arbitration Case No. 3344, 1982 CLUNET 978 (1982), emphasizes the difference between clauses aimed at maintaining the original value of the contract and contract adaptation clauses, placing the accent on the mechanism that triggers the application of the clauses of the former type. *See* the comment from Derains, 1982 CLUNET 983–984.

15. *See generally* M. Fontaine, DROIT DES CONTRATS INTERNATIONAUX — (ANALYSE ET REDACTIONS DE CLAUSES) 295 (1989). Most favored customer clauses obviously are related to "most favored nation" clauses in treaties. As to the public international legal aspects of the latter, *see* generally Rossillion, *The Most-Favored Nation Clause in the Case Law of the ICJ*, 1955 CLUNET 3 (1955).

tract so that the notifying party can close the transaction with the third person.[16]

By far the most common contract adaptation clauses in international contracts are hardship clauses and force majeure clauses. The latter are discussed here in the broader application they have acquired in the lex mercatoria as opposed to the more restrictive traditional notion of force majeure in many municipal systems. In the traditional meaning of the term, an event of force majeure renders contract performance impossible, justifies contract termination, or acts as a limitation of liability for non-performance.[17] This concept evolved in international trade to include events that have the effect of rendering contract performance so onerous that an expectation of performance is unrealistic. In its broader meaning, force majeure gives rise to contract adaptation and not to termination.[18] When parties fail to agree on the terms of a contract adaptation, however, hardship situations occasionally permit contract termination.

In this way the internationalized concepts of hardship and force majeure have become very close. Both lead to contract adaptation. Adaptation normally, but not necessarily, consists of a price increase

---

16. For an analysis of "second look" clauses with respect to pre-bid agreements, *see* R. Lake & U. Draetta, Letters of Intent and Other Precontractual Documents 194, 217, 238 (1990).

17. § 3.2 *supra.*

18. *See* Brabant, Le Contrat International de Construction 311 (1981); Fontaine, Droit des Contrats Internationaux — Analyse et Redaction de Clauses 237 (1989). The evolution of the traditional notion of force majeure also can be seen in the definitions of force majeure and hardship given in ICC Publication (No. 421), entitled *Force Majeure and Hardship*: "The first [the force majeure clause] lays down the conditions for relief from liability when performance has become literally or practically impossible. The second [the hardship clause] covers the situation where changed conditions have made performance excessively onerous." The erosion of the traditional notion of force majeure, and its partial merger with hardship situations, results here from the reference to performance that has become *practically* impossible, i.e., not objectively but economically impossible. An excellent description of the evolution of force majeure can be found in Kahn, *Force Majeure et contrats internationaux de longue durée*, 1975 Clunet 467–469 (1975).

to offset the increased financial burden necessary to discharge a non-monetary obligation. Thus, the risk connected with the occurrence of unforeseen force majeure events is contractually allocated to a party that has a monetary obligation. The line between force majeure or hardship clauses and hardship clauses is thus a fine one, and it is often difficult to distinguish between them. Consequently, we will analyze the effects of the unforeseen change of circumstances on international contracts without distinguishing between changes due to "force majeure" or "hardship" in their more strictly defined meanings.

6.3 Contract Adaptation in Municipal Law

The rules of lex mercatoria regarding the adaptation of international contracts to changed circumstances evolved from a body of principles rooted in municipal law and public international law. The lex mercatoria rules are better understood in the context of these principles. After a summary of the municipal and international concepts, we will analyze the international application of contract adaptation concepts in an effort to arrive at a definition of the lex mercatoria on the subject.

Two concepts are at the heart of any discussion of contract (or treaty) interpretation and adaptation.[19] These are generally expressed by the Latin term "rebus sic stantibus," by which a contract must be adapted to unforeseen changes of circumstance,[20] and its opposite principle, "pacta sunt servanda," by which agreements must be performed in good faith in strict accordance to their texts.[21] The two concepts traditionally are thought to be in tension with each other, but they should in fact be seen as complementary concepts, and both have historically represented legal requirements worthy of protection.

---

19. *"Zwei Seelen wohnen in meiner Brust."* Goethe, Vor Dem Thor.

20. "Even when laws have been written down, they ought not always to remain unaltered." Aristotle.

21. Wotan: "den durch Verträge ich Herr,
               den Verträgen bin ich nun Knecht."
    [Wotan: "since by treaties I rule,
               by those treaties I am enslaved."]
    R. Wagner, *Die Walküre*, Act II, Scene 2

Some commentators have mentioned that there is no conflict between the two principles, since a rebus sic stantibus provision should be considered as implicit in any contract or treaty. In this view, the application of the pacta sunt servanda principle would always carry the possible enforcement of an implied rebus sic stantibus requirement. This is, however, an extreme thesis that rather begs the question. A potential tension between the two principles undoubtedly exists and the real issue, both in the municipal laws and international law, according to the majority of commentators, is to find the most equitable and fair compromise between them. From an historical point of view, no legal system, whether municipal or international level, has rigidly accepted one principle to the complete exclusion of the other.

Contract adaptation to changed circumstances is referred to in municipal laws as *imprévision, révision du contrat, bouleversement du contrat, Wegfall der Geschäftsgrundlage, eccessiva onerosità, presupposizione,* "frustration," and "contract adaptation," respectively in the French, German, Italian, and English languages. In public international law, the Latin expression "rebus sic stantibus" is used. In international trade law, the expressions "hardship" or "major economic dislocation" appear to be most favored. These terms are by no means synonymous, and they differ from each other by much more than nuance. They represent different legal concepts. In particular, none save the last expresses the conceptual difference between party agreed or judicially enforced changes in performance on the one hand and termination on the other.

Municipal laws deal with the problem of contract adaptation to changed circumstances by means of a wide range of statutory or judicial solutions.[22] Some conclusions may be drawn from a survey of the range.

---

22. *See generally* the excellent survey, Philippe, CHANGEMENT DE CIRCON- STANCES ET BOULEVERSEMENT DE L'ECONOMIE CONTRACTUELLE (1986), which analyzes French law (at 53–152), Belgian law (at 155–213), German law (at 215–328), English law (at 334–402), Italian law (at 405–483), Dutch law (at 486–553), and Swiss law (at 555–579) on the subject. *See also* FORCE MAJEURE AND FRUSTRATION OF CONTRACT (E. McKendrick, ed. 1991); 2 K. Zweigert & H. Kötz, AN INTRODUCTION TO COMPARATIVE LAW 208–228 (2d ed. 1987); Puelinckx, *Frustration, Hardship, Force Majeure, Imprévision, Wegfall der Geschäftsgrundlage,*

All the solutions offered by municipal law appear to lie between two extremes. At one pole are legal systems in which the principle of contract adaptation is contained in statutory provisions of a public order nature. At the opposite pole are legal systems that take a much less flexible approach to the issue of changed circumstances in the name of sanctity of contracts or pacta sunt servanda.

In the first group, Syria, Egypt, and Algeria deserve a special mention. The laws of these countries provide that all public and private contracts must be adapted after the occurrence of unforeseen changes of circumstance after execution, and that all contrary provisions are without effect. In particular, Article 148 of the Syrian Civil Code, Article 147 of the Egyptian Civil Code, and Article 107 of the Algerian Civil Code all provide that if discharging an obligation becomes excessively onerous because of exceptional and unforeseen events having an impact of a general nature, the courts have the power to reduce the extent of obligations to a more reasonable level.[23]

Articles 1467 to 1469 of the Italian Civil Code also contain a relatively expansive regimen to deal with situations where obligations become excessively onerous after execution of a contract (*eccessiva onerosità sopravvenuta*). The regimen only applies to (1) contracts

---

Unmöglichkeit, Changed Circumstances, 3 J. INT'L ARB. 47 (1986); Rapsomanikis, *Frustration of Contract in International Trade Law*, 1980 DUQ. L. REV. 551 (1980); Delaume, *Commercial Frustration: A Comparative Study*, (1967) TEX. INT'L L. FOR. 275 (1967); Smit, *Frustration of Contract: A Comparative Attempt of Consolidation*, 1958 COLUM. L. REV. 287 (1958); Rodhe, *Adjustment of Contracts on Account of Changed Conditions*, 1959 SCANDINAVIAN STUDIES IN LAW 153 (1959); Aubrey, *Frustration Reconsidered: Some Comparative Aspects*, 1963 INT'L & COMP. L.Q. 145 (1963); Schmiedlin, FRUSTRATION OF CONTRACT UND CLAUSOLA REBUS SIC STANTIBUS (1985); Horn, *Changes in Circumstances and the Revision of Contracts in Some European Laws and in International Law*, in ADAPTATION OF CONTRACTS IN INTERNATIONAL TRADE AND FINANCE — STUDIES IN TRANSNATIONAL ECONOMIC LAW No. 3, at 15 (1985).

23. On Algerian law, *see* Terki, *L'imprévision et le contrat international dans le code civile algérien*, 1982 DROIT ET PRATIQUE DU COMMERCE INTERNATIONAL 9 (1982).

that are not *aleatori*, i.e., those in which parties do not specifically undertake the risk of unforeseen events,[24] and (2) contracts that contemplate continuous or periodic, performance. When the performance of one of the parties to such contracts has become excessively onerous because of extraordinary and unforeseen events, the affected party may terminate the contract. The other party may avoid termination by offering to the first party equitable modifications of the contractual terms and conditions. The statutory provisions are not mandatory, however. Their application to a particular contract may be negated by common agreement of the parties.[25]

The laws of some other countries are patterned along the lines of Italian law. Such countries include Greece,[26] Hungary,[27] and Ethiopia.[28] In some of the formerly socialist countries in Eastern Europe, the hardship clause was codified with respect to international contracts only.[29]

Some legal systems contain statutory provisions contemplating the adaptation of specific types of contracts, normally construction contracts. Italian law, for example, provides for the appropriate revision of the price of a construction contract when the contractor's costs increase by more than one tenth with respect to the original forecast.[30] Similarly, Swiss law provides for the adaptation of the price of a

---

24. Option contracts for the purchase of shares on stock exchanges provide a ready example of aleatori contracts.

25. *See*, inter alia, Cottino, L'Impossibilità Sopravvenuta della Prestazione e la Repsonsabilità del Debitore (1955); Sacco, *I Rimedi Sinallagmatici*, in Trattato di Diritto Privato, Vol. 10: Obbligazioni e Contratti 530 (P. Rescigno, ed. 1983).

26. Art. 388 of the Civil Code.

27. Art. 241 of the 1977 Civil Code.

28. Art. 3.183 of the 1960 Civil Code.

29. This was the case in the former German Democratic Republic Law of February 5th, 1976 (para. 295).

30. Cod. Civ. Art. 1664. *See generally* Cagnasso, Appalto e Sopravvenienza Contrattuale — Contributo a una Revisione della Dottrina Dell'Eccessiva Onerosità' 145 (1979).

construction contract in the event of extraordinary and unforeseen circumstances negatively affecting the contractor.[31]

In another group of civil law countries, contract adaptation has been introduced solely by the judiciary. This has happened, for example, in Switzerland[32] and in Germany. In the latter, the civil code contains the concept of *Treu und Glauben* (corresponding broadly to "good faith" in common law systems).[33] Section 242 of the Code has been widely interpreted by the courts to include the possibility of adapting the contract to unforeseen changes of circumstance. This purpose has been achieved by considering the external circumstance as one of the *Geschäftsgrundlagen*, i.e., the fundamental elements of the contract, with the consequence that a dramatic change in such circumstances (*Wegfall der Geschäftsgrundlage*) justifies the termination or judicial adaptation of the contract.[34]

---

31. Art. 376.2 of the Swiss Code des Obligations. *See generally* Gauch, Der Werkvertrag 34 (1985). For an interesting application of Art. 376.2, *see* Perolini, *Contractor's Discharge From Contractual Fixed Price Risk by Judicial Intervention*, 1985 Int'l Construction L. Rev. 219 (1985).

32. Except for the specific instance of construction contracts mentioned above, there is no provision in the Swiss Civil Code comparable to Arts. 1467–1469 of the Italian Civil Code. " . . . [In] principle, no commitment is taken rebus sic stantibus." II Deschenaux, Le Titre Preliminaire du Code Civil Suisse, Traite de Droit Civil Suisse 185. Swiss courts, however, have introduced an extensive principle of contract adaptation to changed circumstances. *See, e.g.,* Engel, Traite des Obligations en Droit Suisse 528 (1973).

33. "The debtor is bound to perform according to the requirements of good faith, ordinary usage being taken into consideration." § 242 BGB.

34. This approach originated in two groups of cases dealing with the extraordinary economic conditions existing in Germany at the end of the First and Second World Wars. *See generally* 2 K. Zweigert & H. Kötz, An Introduction to Comparative Law 212–213 (2d ed. 1987); Business Transactions in Germany § 10.04[7] (B. Rüster, ed. 1986); Dawson, *Judicial Revision of Frustrated Contracts: Germany*, 63 B.U.L. Rev. 1039 (1987); Esser, Schuldrecht Vol. I, 226 (1970); Hay, *Frustration and its Solution in German Law*, 1961 Am. J. Comp. L. 345 (1961); Fikentscher, Die Geschäftsgrundlage Als Frage der

In Spain, the courts have applied the general principles of good
faith and equity to proceed to the judicial termination, suspension, or
revision of a contract when justified by new circumstances likely to
upset the fundamental balance between the obligations of the parties.[35]

Among civil law systems, French law,[36] together with Belgian law,[37]
which is largely inspired by it, is the most reluctant to adapt contracts
to changed circumstances. In France, a dual system of rules are in
place for the parallel French court systems, the civil courts and the
administrative courts. The civil courts deal with the law governing
commercial contracts between private parties, and the administrative
courts deal with the law governing "public contracts."[38] The civil courts
have followed rigidly the principle of the sanctity of the contract (pacta
sunt servanda),[39] and have refused to consider any request for contract

VERTRAGSRISIKOS 11 (1971); Philippe, CHANGEMENT DE CIRCONSTANCES ET
BOULEVERSEMENT DE L'ECONOMIE CONTRACTUELLE 215 (1986), with an
exhaustive survey of German case law on the subject.

35. S. Gonzales, *Note sull'eccessiva onerosità sopravvenuta nel diritto civile spagnolo*, 1960 RIVISTA TRIMESTRALE DI DIRITTO E PROCEDURA CIVILE
1053 (1960).

36. *See generally* CONTRACT LAW TODAY: ANGLO-FRENCH COMPARISONS (D.
Harris & D. Tallon, eds. 1989); B. Nicholas, FRENCH LAW OF CONTRACT
(1982).

37. De Page, TRAITÉ ELEMENTAIRE DE DROIT CIVIL BELGE II, para. 542 (3d
ed. 1964); Flamme, TRAITÉ THEORIQUE ET PRATIQUE DES MARCHES PUB-
LICS, 927 (1969).

38. As to French administrative law in general, *see* R. Von Mehren & C.
Gordley, THE CIVIL LAW SYSTEM 215–554 (1977).

39. The leading case in this respect is Canal de Craponne, decided by the
Cour de Cassation on March 6th, 1876. SIREY I, 161 (1876). The case
concerned a contract to deliver water that had been made in the 16th
century at a price that was derisory by the 19th century. The Aix Cour
d'Appel had revised the price to the then current level. There was no
force majeure because performance was still possible. There was no
lesion because the inequality was due to external events (the passage
of time) and not from inequality at the time of the contract. The Cour
de Cassation held: "[In] no case is it up to the courts, no matter how
equitable the decision could appear to them, to consider times and circumstances to modify the agreements of the parties and substitute new

adaptation to changed circumstances. There have been occasional cases of contract adaptation for circumstances that affect contracts in other than economic and financial ways, and there is some occasional mitigation of the sternness of the French rules.[40]

By means of the judicially developed *théorie de l'imprévision* (doctrine of the unforeseen events), the French administrative courts are prepared to adapt "public contracts," i.e., contracts performed in the public interest and subject to the public administrative law (as opposed to the general commercial law), to changed circumstances. The seminal case is *Gaz de Bordeaux*, which was the subject of a famous decision by the Conseil d'Etat (State Council) of March 30, 1916.[41]

In *Gaz de Bordeaux*, the Conseil d'Etat directly contradicted the Cour de Cassation. It held that the public interest in the performance of public contracts is more important than in purely private agreements in order to assure the continued supply of public services to the community. Contract adaptation thus is intended to avoid an excessive economic loss suffered by a party supplying such services endangering the orderly and timely performance of the "public contract." This objective generally is reached through a price revision agreed upon by the parties or, failing such agreement, determined by the courts.[42] The extra costs are assumed by the French government.

---

obligations to those freely accepted by them." The French civil courts have not changed this position, even for supervening events caused by war. *Id.*

40. These efforts of mitigation are found more often in the works of French scholars than in judicial decisions. *See, e.g.,* Weill-Terre, DROIT CIVIL — LES OBLIGATIONS 427 (1980), with respect to certain special situations, as well as Rouhette, *La révision conventionelle du contrat*, 1986 REVUE INTERNATIONAL DE DROIT COMPARE 370 (1986).

41. The *Gaz de Bordeaux* decision, where a supplier obtained a price revision following changed circumstances, can be found in 1916 SIREY, III, 17 (1916), with a commentary by Haurion. *See also* Devolvé, *The French law of "imprévision"*, 1981 INTERNATIONAL CONTRACTS, No. 3, 8 (1981); CONTRACT LAW TODAY: ANGLO-FRENCH COMPARISONS 231–232 (D. Harris & D. Tallon, eds. 1989).

42. The unforeseeable nature of the event that can justify a price revision is interpreted very strictly by the courts. The most minimal negligence in foreseeing an event makes the doctrine of *imprévision* inapplicable.

The common law countries have no general theory of contract adaptation. Certainly, the concept of rebus sic stantibus is not a part of the common law. The general rule is that of pacta sunt servanda.[43] In England, the effects of supervening changed circumstances are dealt with by the doctrine of frustration of contract; in the United States, by the very similar doctrines of impracticability and frustration. We have discussed both with respect to the ability of parties to use them as a basis to avoid liability for non-performance.[44] In this respect, frustration and impracticability presents certain points of contact with the civil law concept of force majeure, but they are conceptually distinct from it.

To what extent, however, do common law courts use theories of frustration and impracticability to adapt contracts? The simple answer is that a theory of contract adaptation is not only absent from the common law, but is so alien from the basis of contract in common law systems that the subject is rarely considered outside the law reviews. One might speculate that the relative political and economic stability of England and the United States have not made a theory of contract adaptation necessary, but the real reason probably has more to do with the common law concept of a contract being a bargained exchange that the law enforces, not a set of promises the parties must keep.[45] Contract adaptation in the common law countries is thus almost completely private. This is not to say that it never occurs, because the economic interests of both parties are often best served by ad hoc renegotiations to correct imbalances created by changes of circumstance.[46]

Mistake, frustration, and impossibility of performance are events that excuse performance of the otherwise strict obligation to perform.

Savatier, *La théorie de l' imprévision dans les contrats*, II Etudes de Droit Contemporaire 1 (1959).

43. Farnsworth on Contracts § 9.1 (1990).

44. § 4.1 *supra.*

45. § 2.1 *supra.*

46. Buxbaum, *Modification and Adaptation of Contracts: American Legal Developments*, in Horn, Adaptation and Renegotiation of Contracts in International Trade and Finance — Studies in Transnational Economic Law No. 3, at 31, 40 (1985).

The effect of a frustrating event is termination of a contract. Both English and U.S. law allow both parties to a terminated, frustrated contract to recover their restitution interests, and neither allows either to recover their reliance interest. The termination of the frustrated contract never has a retroactive effect. Consequently, termination often results in judges having to make assumptions about what parties would have done had termination not occurred in order to adequately compensate their restitution interests. The practical effect of this is sometimes not dissimilar to the judicial adaptation of the contractual terms in civil law countries.[47]

In English law, the courts have refrained from acting overtly to adapt contracts. Academic writers have urged that they do so, some arguing that existing law enables them to do so in some situations.[48] At least one English commentator has speculated that the influence of the European Community will cause English courts to begin to adapt contracts.[49] United States commentators have proposed a number of solutions to the inability of restitutionary damages awards to adequately compensate parties to frustrated contracts,[50] but the instances of actual

---

47. The problem with respect to contracts with long-term obligations is the same in civil law systems. *See* Ghestin, *L'effet rétroactif de la resolution des contrats à exécution successive*, MELANGES RAYNAUD 204 (1985).

48. The Law Reform (Frustrated Contracts) Act of 1943 gives courts the right to reform contracts in some situations. FORCE MAJEURE AND FRUSTRATION OF CONTRACT 156–157 (E. McKendrick, ed. 1991); CONTRACT LAW TODAY: ANGLO-FRENCH COMPARISONS 212–215 (D. Harris & D. Tallon, eds. 1989); Stannard, *Frustrating Delay*, 46 MOD. L. REV. 738 (1983).

49. FORCE MAJEURE AND FRUSTRATION OF CONTRACT 156 (E. McKendrick, ed. 1991).

50. These include taking an excused party's reliance interests into account, Fuller & Perdue, *The Reliance Interest in Contract Damages*, 46 YALE L. J. 373, 379–382 (1937); the courts' assuming a power of price adjustment, Speidel, *Court Imposed Adjustments Under Long-Term Supply Contracts*, 76 Nw. U. L. REV. 369 (1981); and the imposition of a good-faith requirement to negotiate adaptation, *id.*; Hillman, *Court Adjustment of Long-Term Contracts: An Analysis Under Modern Contract Law*, 1987 DUKE L. J. 1 (1987). *See generally* FARNSWORTH ON CONTRACTS § 9.9 (1990).

contract adaptation are very rare.[51] In practice, courts award generous restitutionary awards,[52] using "surrogate grounds of contract avoidance to achieve contract modification."[53]

6.4 Changed Circumstances in Treaty Law: The "Rebus Sic Stantibus" Clause

Before identifying how the lex mercatoria addresses the issue of adapting the contact to changed circumstances, it is essential to briefly describe which consequences public international law attaches to such change when it affects treaties or other international law obligations. From a historical point of view, the need for adaptation to changed circumstances arose with respect to international treaties much earlier than with respect to international contracts. It is not surprising, therefore, that the lex mercatoria is developing in this area around notions that find their roots in public international law and, more particularly, in the doctrine of rebus sic stantibus.[54]

There are two notions of rebus sic stantibus, which reflect two different theories under public international law. According to the first notion, rebus sic stantibus has a contractual nature, similar to the corresponding notions of frustration, hardship, *imprévision*, etc., with respect to contracts between private parties.[55] Acknowledging that for the interpretation of the treaties it is also necessary to search for the real intention of the parties, rebus sic stantibus is seen in this context as evidencing the parties' intention to consider the continuation of a given factual situation existing at the time of the treaty stipulation as

---

51. Aluminum Co. of America v. Essex Group, Inc., 449 F. Supp. 53 (W.D. Pa. 1980); Miller v. Campello Co-op Bank, 181 N.E.2d 345 (1962).

52. *Id.*

53. Buxbaum, *Modification and Adaptation of Contracts: American Legal Developments*, in Horn, ADAPTATION AND RENEGOTIATION OF CONTRACTS IN INTERNATIONAL TRADE AND FINANCE — STUDIES IN TRANSNATIONAL ECONOMIC LAW No 3, at 31, 40 (1985).

54. *See generally* A. Vamvoukos, TERMINATION OF TREATIES IN INTERNATIONAL LAW — THE DOCTRINES OF REBUS SIC STANTIBUS AND DESUETUDE (1985).

55. *See generally* J.L. Brierley, THE LAW OF NATIONS — AN INTRODUCTION TO THE INTERNATIONAL LAW OF PEACE 337–338 (6th ed. 1963).

essential for the continued existence of their obligations. Hence, a fundamental change of factual situation would justify the termination or revision of the treaty.[56]

Some of the supporters of this contractualistic approach to rebus sic stantibus shift the emphasis to the doctrine's objective elements, as opposed to the search for the subjective intention of the parties. According to them, the doctrine would operate in the sense of allowing the termination or revision of a treaty when its purpose can no longer objectively be achieved because of the change of the surrounding circumstances existing at the time of its stipulation.[57]

It is obvious that those who share this contractualistic view of rebus sic stantibus also conceive the international community of states as deprived of any effective authority, where relations are regulated by rules conventionally agreed upon between member states; in other words, they do not see, in the process of formation of international law the existence of any kind of authority, constituted by the overall community of states, eventually placed over and above individual states.[58]

Article 62 of the 1969 Vienna Convention on the Law of Treaties codified the above-mentioned contractualistic notion of the doctrine of rebus sic stantibus, and conceived it as applicable even if not expressly provided for by the parties.[59] According to the literal text of

---

56. *See* Morelli, NOZIONI DI DIRITTO INTERNAZIONALE 328 (1967) (asserting the existence, in public international law, of a general rule contemplating the treaty termination or adaptation in case of changed circumstances).

57. *See, e.g.*, De Visscher, THEORIES ET REALITES EN DROIT INTERNATIONAL PUBLIC 297 (1970).

58. *See, e.g.*, Westarp, *Die clausola "rebus sic stantibus" in heutigen Völkerrecht*, 1934 JURISTISCHE WOCHENSCHRIFT 20 (1934).

59. The text of Article 62 of the Vienna Convention is as follows:

1. A fundamental change of circumstances which has occurred with regard to those existing at the time of the conclusion of a treaty, and which was not foreseen by the parties may not be invoked as a ground for terminating or withdrawing from the treaty unless: (a) the existence of these circumstances constituted an essential basis of the consent of the parties to be bound by the treaty; and (b) the effect of the clause is radically to transform the extent of the obligations still to be performed under the treaty. 2. A fundamental change of circumstances may not be

Article 62, the consequences attached to the change in circumstances would be the termination or the suspension of a treaty, and not its revision. However, a majority of scholars contends that the threat of termination or suspension of a treaty almost certainly would open the way to negotiations, the results of which normally would be a treaty revision.[60]

The mere fact that the Vienna Convention codified rebus sic stantibus, stating that such clause is implied in all treaties, indicates that its drafters followed the objective, rather than the subjective, approach. This is also confirmed by the reference to the "radical transformation of the extent of the obligations," which is contained in Article 62.1 (b). Article 62.1 (a), however, also refers to the "essential basis of the consent of the parties," thereby conceding that the supporters of the subjective approach have merit to their position as well. Thus, it can be said overall that the Vienna Convention constitutes a reasonable compromise between the subjective and objective contractualistic approaches to the nature of rebus sic stantibus in public international law.

In any case, in order to trigger the revision or extinction of a treaty, the requirements of the radical nature of changed circumstances and unforeseeability both have been abundantly emphasized in the implementation practice of rebus sic stantibus.[61] It also has been stressed that no revision or termination effect can take place when the change of circumstances is attributable to the faulty behavior of the member state invoking such effect.

---

invoked as a ground for terminating or withdrawing from a treaty; (a) if the treaty establishes a boundary; or (b) if the fundamental change is the result of a breach by the party invoking it either of an obligation under the treaty or of any other international obligations owed to any other party to the treaty. 3. If, under the foregoing paragraphs, a party may invoke a fundamental change of circumstances as a ground for terminating or withdrawing from the treaty, it may also invoke the change as a ground for suspending the operation of the treaty.

The report by Fitzmaurice, on which Article 62 was based, is published in 1957 ANNUAIRE CDI, vol. II, 64–74 (1957).

60. *See, e.g.*, Sico, GLI EFFETTI DEL MUTAMENTO DELLE CIRCOSTANZE SUI TRATTATI INTERNATIONALI 296–297 (1983).

61. *See* the Fitzmaurice report, *id.* note 59 *supra*, at 36–38.

The second notion of rebus sic stantibus is advocated by those who see the international community of states regulated by an authority that is constituted collectively by the states themselves. According to this notion, rebus sic stantibus serves the purpose of replacing those rules of international law that become obsolete with others better reflecting the changed international situation and that of the parties to an international treaty. This would explain why the doctrine has been so widely invoked with respect to treaties imposed by force following a war, and consequently, related primarily to territorial boundaries, such as the Versailles Peace Treaties.[62]

This notion of the rebus sic stantibus clause, as a clause allowing the revision of rules of international law that become historically obsolete, was codified by Article 19 of the Covenant of the League of Nations, which provides: "The Assembly may from time to time advise the reconsideration by Members of the League of treaties which have become inapplicable and the consideration of international conditions whose continuance might endanger the peace of the world." This rule was aimed at replacing obsolete treaties with others better reflecting the changed political situation. Ironically, it was just a change in the political situation that caused the extinction of the treaty establishing the League of Nations itself, including Article 19.[63] One perhaps could argue that the mechanism contemplated by the above-mentioned Article 19 of the League of Nations' Covenant was never implemented, leaving the contractualistic notion of the rebus sic stantibus clause as the only one of real significance in public international law.

---

62. *See, e.g.*, A. Vamvoukos, TERMINATION OF TREATIES IN INTERNATIONAL LAW — THE DOCTRINES OF REBUS SIC STANTIBUS AND DESUETUDE 130–185 (1985) (citing invocation of the doctrine in state practice); D. Bederman, *The 1871 London Declaration, Rebus Sic Stantibus and the Primitivist View of the Law of Nations*, 82 AM. J. INT'L L., 1, 22–40 (1982) (on the relationship between rebus sic stantibus and pacta sunt servanda).

63. *See* Rousseau, I DROIT INTERNATIONAL PUBLIC 227–229 (1980); Verzijl, *Le principe rebus sic stantibus en droit international public*, FESTSCHRIFT SCHAETZEL, 515–529 (1960).

Based on the recent work of the International Law Commission and the 1969 Vienna Convention on the Law of Treaties,[64] it is appropriate to conclude that the doctrine of rebus sic stantibus is to be interpreted as an objective rule of law, without ignoring altogether the parties' intent.[65] Thus, "even in a case where the recourse to objective tests cannot justify an application of the *rebus* doctrine, one may reach the conclusion, by interpreting the treaty, that the changes are of such a [fundamental] nature that the continuation of the treaty would be incompatible with the original intention of the parties."[66]

6.5 Contract Adaptation in the Lex Mercatoria

To identify the lex mercatoria rules regarding contract adaptation to changed circumstances we will analyze:

1. International uniform laws determined by treaties;

2. Codification efforts by governmental and non-governmental international organizations;

3. The practice of the international business contracts; and

4. The precedents and practice of international arbitral tribunals.

The first three aspects will be discussed in Section 6.5, the last in Section 6.6.

The effects of uniform law on contract adaptation are minimal. Harmonization efforts have thus far dealt with contracts, such as sales contracts, which are performed in a relatively short period of time. The risk of unforeseen events is less serious for the parties, for they generally will have accepted them and are able to stipulate for them in a contract.

Article 79 of the 1980 Vienna Convention on Contracts for the International Sale of Goods only deals with situations in which a party

---

64. U.N. Doc. A/Conf. 39/27 (1969).

65. A. Vamvoukos, TERMINATION OF TREATIES IN INTERNATIONAL LAW — THE DOCTRINES OF REBUS SIC STANTIBUS AND DESUETUDE 214–216 (1985)

66. *Id.* at 24.

is not liable for a failure to perform in the event of force majeure.[67] The consequence of force majeure under Article 79 is termination of the contract without liability of the party that is unable to perform. There is no mention in the Vienna Convention of contract adaptation for changed circumstances, and Article 79 cannot logically be interpreted in a way to permit or require adaptation.[68]

The most significant codification efforts by international organizations for our purposes are the drafts of models of long-term international contracts. Articles 33 and 34 of the UNIDO Model Form for Turnkey Lump Sum Contracts for the Construction of a Fertilizer Plant[69] contain a broad notion of force majeure that includes a "duty to renegotiate" of the parties when a force majeure condition arises. This approach to force majeure resembles hardship, and it leads to a process of adaptation of a contract to an unforeseen change of the circumstances.

As for non-governmental international organizations, in 1985 the International Chamber of Commerce issued Document No. 421,[70] which included a model force majeure clause, as well as "drafting suggestions" for hardship clauses. These suggestions contain a number of alternative solutions for private agreement as to correcting imbalances created by unforeseen circumstances. Such alternative solutions include, inter alia, recourse to the *"ICC Standing Committee for the Regulation of Contractual Relations,"* established in accordance with the "ICC Regulation for the Discipline of Contractual Relationships."[71] This Regulation was drafted by ICC to afford a procedure for the adaptation of international contracts in hardship situations. It provides a

---

67. § 3.2.C. *supra.*

68. *See* J. Honnold, Uniform Law for International Sales under the 1980 United Nations Convention 442 (1982).

69. *See* the UNIDROIT publication of June 1983 reproducing the text of such model form.

70. Discussed in § 4.2.2. *supra.*

71. Its text is published in ICC Document No. 326, entitled *Adaptation of Contracts. See also* Mezger, *The ICC Rules for the Adaptation of Contracts,* in Horn, Adaptation of Contracts in International Trade and Finance — Studies in Transnational Economic Law No. 3, at 205 (1985).

mechanism for mediation by a third arbitrator, who, by virtue of a mandate received by the parties, is entitled to modify the contract as deemed appropriate.[72] Alternatively, the mandate to the mediator may simply authorize the mediator to issue a recommendation as to necessary contract modifications, which the parties agree to take into account "in good faith."[73]

As to contract forms prepared by industry associations, it will be recalled that the FIDIC clauses for civil works and electro-mechanical works deal with frustration.[74] As was previously mentioned, these clauses are largely inspired by the common law concept of frustration. In their effort to reconcile different systems and requirements, they end up providing a discipline that has been described as rather confusing.[75]

The treatment of the issue of changed circumstances in actual international business contracts provides perhaps the best insight into the developing lex mercatoria on the subject. The practice in this area is rich and highly articulated. It suggests a general view that the commercial entities that are parties to international contracts, especially long-term contracts, are unwilling to accept the risk allocation contained in the principle of pacta sunt servanda — that the party affected by them bear the consequences of changed circumstances. Rather, they prefer to redefine contract obligations to correct the imbalances possibly created by changes of circumstance.

The contractual provisions used to effect this redefinition generally are called "hardship clauses," or "(major) economic dislocation clauses." Irrespective of their nomenclature, however, they all contemplate a given procedure for the revision of the contract terms when unforeseen changes of circumstance cause an imbalance in the rights and obligations of the parties.

---

72. "Regulation for the Discipline of Contractual Relationships," Art. 11.3, ICC Document No. 326.

73. *Id.* Art. 11.2.

74. § 4.2.2. *supra.*

75. *See* Horn, *Standard Clauses on Contract Adaptation in International Commerce*, in ADAPTATION OF CONTRACTS IN INTERNATIONAL TRADE AND FINANCE — STUDIES IN TRANSNATIONAL ECONOMIC LAW No. 3, at 114 (1985).

Hardship clauses frequently are used in international contracts when both parties are entities of industrialized countries; they are used less frequently when one party is domiciled in a developing country. Their use is traditionally most frequent in the oil and natural gas industry, but recently they have been used in many other industry segments, including the financial industry.[76]

The inclusion of a hardship clause gives an international contract an evolutionary character. The negotiation phase does not end with contract execution, but recommences when changed circumstances cause an imbalance between the obligations of the parties. Thus, while the inclusion of a hardship clause creates some uncertainties in contractual relationships, it represents an advance compromise, which parties to certain types of international contracts appear to prefer to the risk of bearing the consequences of unforeseen events. With hardship clauses, the parties choose the continuation of a contractual relationship over a long time, through its continued adaptation to changed circumstances.

A typical hardship clause would read as follows:

> If during performance of this Contract there should arise economic, political or technical circumstances which were unforeseen by the parties and are beyond their control, and which make performance of the Contract so onerous (though not impossible) for one of the parties that the burden would exceed all the anticipatory provisions made by the parties at the time the Contract is signed, such affected party shall be entitled to equitable relief, and may request the revision of the Contract. The parties will discuss the matter, and if an amicable solution cannot be reached, the affected party may request arbitration of the matter in accordance with the arbitration clause of this Contract.[77]

Clauses of the above-mentioned type can be analyzed considering separately their three constitutive elements: (1) the events that trigger their application; (2) the consequences those events must have on the

---

76. *See* Asser, *The World Bank and the Renegotiation and Adaptation of Long-term Loans*, in Horn, *id.* at 253, as well as, with respect to the mining industry, Horn, *Standard Clauses on Contract Adaptation in International Commerce*, *id.* at 115–116.

77. For extensive surveys of the practice concerning hardship clauses, *see* the sources cited in note 2 *supra*.

parties' obligations in order for the contract to be adapted; and (3) the nature of the adaptation.

A. *The Events Triggering the Application of Hardship Clauses*

Events that typically are specified by hardship clauses are those that imply a change of the circumstances with respect to those existing at the time of execution. Thus, a delayed awareness of situations already existing at execution would not trigger the application of a hardship clause. For example, a typical hardship clause would not be triggered if after execution a contractor discovered particularly unfavorable sub-soil conditions, or sub-soil conditions different than those known at the time an offer was presented. One could, however, seek relief under various doctrines of mistake.[78] In addition to arising post-execution, events triggering the application of a hardship clause must be clearly unforeseeable. This element distinguishes hardship clauses from the price variation and devaluation clauses discussed previously, cost increases and currency devaluations clearly being foreseeable. Under some circumstances, of course, cost increases or the devaluation of the currency in which a contract price is denominated can constitute hardship events.[79]

The requisite of unforeseeability must not be interpreted too strictly. Conceptually, every event is foreseeable. Unforeseeability means the reasonable inability of parties to anticipate that a given event will occur, when it will occur, and the nature of its consequences. It is obvious that an "unforeseeable" event is not an "unforeseen" event. When the latter expression is used in hardship clauses, a not infrequent occurrence, a party may benefit from the clause even if it has been simply careless or imprudent in not anticipating events likely to happen. Furthermore, an "unforeseen" event is not the same as an event "beyond the control of the parties" because most hardship clauses

---

78. This situation is expressly contemplated by Article 24 of the FIDIC model form for mechanical and electrical works. Errors of this type, which French scholars call *sujétions imprévues*, are discussed, with specific reference to international construction contracts, in Brabant, Le Contrat International de Construction 324 (1981).

79. § 5.6 *supra*.

require the presence of both requisites. Clauses triggered only by events "beyond the control of the parties" without also being "unforeseeable" significantly broaden the scope of application.

When hardship clauses contain, as many do, a list of specific future events that the parties intend to qualify as hardship, one might wonder whether such a listing is compatible with the requisite of unforeseeability. It must be compatible, however, since contemplating the possibility of the occurrence of an event does not mean foreseeing that it could actually occur.

Finally, many hardship clauses contain some procedural requirements pursuant to which affected parties must give notice of hardship within a given time; failing such notice the right to invoke the clause expires.

B. The Impact the Events Must Have on the Parties' Obligations

The events triggering the application of a typical hardship clause must affect the parties in an alternatively or cumulatively qualified manner, according to specific objective or subjective criteria. From the objective point of view, hardship clauses often require that the effect of supervening events be such as to cause a "considerable," or "appreciable," or "substantial," or "fundamental" prejudice to the affected party.[80] From the subjective point of view, references sometimes are made to the disadvantage suffered by an affected party, which include notions such as "inequity" or "unfairness." It is not infrequent for hardship clauses to provide for third-party determination of whether a given event constitutes hardship sufficient to trigger the application of the clause. The same third-party arbitrator often determines the actual adaptation of the terms of the contract as well.

C. The Effect of Hardship Clauses

The effect of the application of hardship clauses is normally the revision of the terms of contract. The substance of the revision usually is left to party negotiation, at least in the first instance.

---

80. *See, e.g.*, Superior Overseas Development Corp. v. British Gas Corp., [1982] 1 LLOYD'S REP 262., in which the English Court of Appeal applied restrictive standard for the application of a hardship clause.

196

Hardship clauses often specify subjective or objective criteria to be used in effecting contract revision. The recourse to the concept of "equity" as a guiding criterion is very frequent. Equally frequent are formulae aimed at "de-localizing" adaptation criteria, such as reference to "principles of law generally applied," or to "the general practices in international trade." It is primarily these general references that have led some scholars to see in the practice of hardship clauses one of the most significant areas of development of the lex mercatoria.[81]

What if parties are unable to reach agreement as to the adaptation of a contract after an event triggers a hardship clause, and the clause itself is silent as to adaptation in such circumstances? First, it should be recalled that the obligation to renegotiate the terms of a contract is an *obligation de moyens*, and not an *obligation de rèsultat*.[82] Applying the general principles applicable to these different types of obligations, the contract continues in effect upon its original terms when no agreement is reached, assuming that the parties have negotiated in good faith.

The status quo, however, is not always acceptable to the parties, and hardship clauses thus often contain express provisions for the consequences of failure to adapt a contract. Sometimes, these consequences include termination, or at least the suspension of its effects for a given time. More often, however, the hardship clauses provide for recourse to the jurisdiction to which the contract is submitted, or to third parties specifically described.[83] These third parties are variously referred to as experts, arbitrators, mediators, referees, and interveners. It is

---

81. *See* Goldman, *La lex mercatoria dans les contrats et l'arbitrage internationaux: réalité et perspectives*, 1979 Clunet 488–489 (1979).

82. *See* the distinction in § 2.1 *supra*.

83. The various procedures in this respect are extensively described by Horn, *The Procedure of Contract Adaptation and Renegotiation*, in Adaptation and Renegotiation of Contracts in International Trade and Finance — Studies in Transnational Economic Law No. 3, at 173 (1985). Such procedures include recourse to the mediation mechanism established at the ICC, UNCITRAL, or ICSID level. The ICC mechanism has been discussed before in this paragraph; as to the two other procedures, *see* Herrmann, *The UNCITRAL Conciliation Rules: An Aid Also in Contract Adaptation and Performance Facilitation*, as well as B. Marcantonio, *ICSID a Forum for the Renegotiation and Adaptation of*

debated whether their role is of a jurisdictional nature, i.e., of settling disputes, or a contractual nature, i.e., of integrating the will of the parties. We will not expand on this issue, which has been dealt with exhaustively elsewhere.[84]

A more practical problem is the legal effect of a contract during renegotiation or while one of the adaptation procedures mentioned above is in process. Normally, hardship clauses contain a time within which renegotiation or adaptation procedures must be completed. Many provide that a contract is suspended during a renegotiation. Failing express provision, however, the only legitimate conclusion is that the contract will continue to be in effect during the renegotiation or the adaptation procedures.[85]

6.6 The International Arbitration Case Law

One of the most important arbitrations regarding contract adaptation is the well known *Société européenne d'études et d'entreprises v. Yugoslavian Government*.[86] The award was rendered by the arbitrators Ripert and Panchaud on July 2, 1956. The arbitrators had to decide whether a protection against currency exchange risk could be implied in a contract concerning the construction of a railway in Yugoslavia. The arbitrators stated that it was clearly the parties' intention, when they executed the contract, that their respective obligations be equiva-

---

Long-Term Loans, both studies being published in Horn, *id.* at 217 and 235 respectively.

84. *See* Loquin, L'AMIABLE COMPOSITION EN DROIT COMPARE ET INTERNATIONAL 348 (1980); Bernini-Holtzmann, *Les techniques permettant de résoudre les problèmes qui surgissent lors de la formation et de l'exécution des contrats à long term*, 1975 REVUE DE L'ARBITRAGE 18 (1975); Glossner, *Third Party Intervener in Contract Adaptation: the Référé Arbitral*, in Horn, ADAPTATION AND RENEGOTIATION OF CONTRACTS IN INTERNATIONAL TRADE AND FINANCE — STUDIES IN TRANSNATIONAL ECONOMIC LAW No. 3, 191 (1985).

85. *See* Bonell, *Arbitration as a Mean for the Revision of Contracts*, "Italian National Report to the Xth International Congress of Comparative Law," 221 (1978).

86. 1959 CLUNET 1074 (1959).

lent. On this basis, they decided that, *"s'agissant d'un contrat international, conclu sans intention spéculative, il y a lieu d'admettre que la garantie de dévaluation était voulue par les parties, sauf convention expresse"* (this international contract being concluded without a risk-taking intent, it must be admitted that the guarantee against risks of currency devaluation had to be implied in the contract, unless expressly excluded).

As to ICC arbitration practice, in a 1971 decision,[87] the arbitrators did not consider the 1965 conflict between India and Pakistan as an event sufficient to excuse performance. Specifically, they decided that the conditions for the application of the rebus sic stantibus clause contained in the contract in question were not met. The arbitrators searched for the real intention of the parties, applying the criteria of good faith and equity, and taking into account all the surrounding circumstances.[88] They decided that the parties could not be excused for non-performance in spite of the conflict. The arbitrators had not been requested to decide an issue concerning contract adaptation, but only questions dealing with exclusion of liability for non-performance. In this context, they did not rule out the abstract possibility that an international conflict could be a valid cause of force majeure justifying non-performance. They merely held that in the specific situation at hand, this did not seem to be the case.[89]

A similar attitude was taken by the arbitrators in a 1974 arbitration.[90] A purchaser had requested to be freed from its obligation to buy oil at an agreed fixed price because the world market price had

---

87. ICC Arbitration Case No. 1512, 1974 CLUNET 965 (1974).

88. This subjective approach is that taken by civil law courts in the determination of party intention. As to the attitude of civil and common law systems, *see generally* R. Lake & U. Draetta, LETTERS OF INTENT AND OTHER PRECONTRACTUAL DOCUMENTS 30–38 (1990).

89. This case often has been misinterpreted. *See, e.g.*, Kassis, THEORIE GENERALE DES USAGES DU COMMERCE 363 (1984), who concludes from it that the lex mercatoria generally denies the rebus sic stantibus rule. For a correct interpretation, *see* Goldman, *Lex mercatoria dans les contrats et l'arbitrage internationaux: réalité et perspectives*, 1979 CLUNET 495 (1979).

90. ICC Arbitration Case No. 2216, 1975 CLUNET 917 (1975).

decreased. The arbitrators decided that since the purchaser had negotiated a protection against *increases* of the oil price in the contract, the logical inference was that it had accepted the risk of *decreases*. Though their approach cannot be entirely shared, this arbitration provides an example of the normal application of criteria for the determination of the intent of the parties, and the tendency to preserve a contract in situations where the requested relief was termination, not adaptation.[91]

In another 1974 ICC arbitration,[92] the parties to an international contract for the long-term supply of oil had agreed to renegotiate its terms in the event of variation of the exchange rate of the currency in which the contract price was denominated. When a dramatic increase in the price of oil occurred, one party maintained that the price increase had to be considered as connected to the exchange rate variation provision so as to trigger a renegotiation of the contract. A renegotiation in fact occurred, but was inconclusive. The party affected by the price increase then referred the matter to arbitration, asking to be released from its obligation to perform. The arbitrators first decided that there was no connection between the price increase and the exchange variation clause. Furthermore, they stated that the only obligation the parties undertook was to renegotiate the contract in good faith. If the renegotiations failed, termination could not be ordered by the arbitral tribunal in the absence of an express contract provision to that effect.

In a 1975 ICC arbitration,[93] consistent with the award rendered by Ripert and Panchaud noted above, the arbitrators stated that "every commercial transaction is based on the balance between the respective obligations of the parties; denying this principle would imply rendering a commercial contract *"aléatoire"* [i.e., with the risk of changed circumstance borne by the affected party], based on the "spéculation ou le hasard" [i.e., risk or hazard]; it is instead a rule of the *lex mercatoria* that the obligation must remain balanced from an economic

---

91. Not even this case can be seen, therefore, as a negation of the rebus sic stantibus principle in the lex mercatoria, as some do. *See, e.g.*, Kassis, THEORIE GENERALE DES USAGES DU COMMERCE 363 (1984).

92. ICC Arbitration Case No. 2478, 1975 CLUNET 925 (1975).

93. ICC Arbitration Case No. 2291, 1976 CLUNET 989 (1976).

point of view."[94] The arbitrators added that: (1) international contracts must be interpreted in accordance with the principle of good faith; (2) consequently, each party is obliged to behave towards the other party in such a way as not to cause any undue prejudice to it; (3) it is customary to renegotiate an international contract in given situations; and (4) it would be against the good-faith obligations to refuse such renegotiation. In the specific case submitted to them, the arbitrators accepted the request for a price increase made by a party that had agreed to transport goods because the request was based on an increased quantity of goods transported than that originally agreed. They rejected a request of a price increase based on the increased weight of the transported goods because professionally competent transporters should have known the actual weight of the goods to be transported, and not simply relied on the weight stated in the contract.

In ICC Case No. 2404 of 1975,[95] the arbitrators refused to apply the rebus sic stantibus principle in favor of a party that wanted to be released from its obligation to purchase goods because of changed circumstances in the absence of an express contract provision. The arbitral tribunal again was confronted with a request for termination of the contract, not its adaptation. It stressed the need for applying the rebus sic stantibus principle only with extreme "caution and prudence" in the absence of an express hardship clause and also based its rejection of the party's request on the principle of the presumption of professional competence of the parties to international contracts.

In other ICC arbitrations, the arbitrators denied the application of the rebus sic stantibus principle because it conflicted with the provisions of the national law applicable to the contract.[96] In at least one case,[97] however, the arbitrators observed that in spite of such a conflict they could have been led to apply a less rigorous approach had the interested party supplied some more convincing evidence of the existence of a hardship situation.

---

94. *Id.*

95. ICC Arbitration Case No. 2404, 1976 CLUNET 995 (1976).

96. ICC Arbitration Cases Nos. 2708 and 2508, 1977, 943 and 939 respectively CLUNET (1977).

97. ICC Arbitration Case No. 2508, 1977 CLUNET 940 (1977).

In two other ICC arbitrations, the arbitrators had the power to decide according to equity, and stated that they did not believe they were entitled to proceed to a contract adaptation. In one of the cases,[98] however, the contract terms had not yet even been finalized, let alone implemented, so the arbitral tribunal was confronted with the need to formulate rather than adapt such terms. In the second case,[99] the arbitrators simply had to acknowledge the termination of the contract because of the failure of the parties to agree a suitable revision of its terms.

On the other hand, in cases where the parties have included express hardship clauses or other adaptation provisions in contracts, ICC arbitrators have enforced them, not by virtue of the rebus sic stantibus principle, but because of the pacta sunt servanda principle. They have, however, consistently interpreted extensively the parties' intention to proceed to a contract adaptation whenever such an intention was expressed, even if only partially or incompletely, in a contract. For example, in ICC Case No. 1990 of 1976,[100] the parties had contemplated that a distributorship relationship would be changed into a local manufacturing license relationship if the importation of certain goods became objectively difficult. The arbitrators not only decided that a 10 percent devaluation of the currency of the country of distribution was sufficient to trigger the change, but reconstructed the material terms of the manufacturing license agreement, which had only been roughly and incompletely sketched by the parties.

6.7 Conclusion

With this brief survey in mind, certain recurring aspects of international arbitration practice with respect to the contract adaptation to changed circumstances may be identified. We should start with the observation that academic commentators generally have concentrated on the question of whether a basic rule exists in international trade law: that contracts are to be interpreted in light of the rebus sic stanti-

---

98. ICC Arbitration Case No. 2694, 1978 CLUNET 985 (1978).

99. ICC Arbitration Case No. 3938, 1984 CLUNET 926 (1984).

100. ICC Arbitration Case No. 1990, 1974 CLUNET 897 (1974).

bus principle, and must, therefore, be adapted to changed circumstances even in the absence of an express contractual provision to that effect. Those who approach the issue in these terms generally conclude, on the basis of the results of international arbitration, either that no such basic rule exists, or that there are strong doubts as to its existence.[101]

In our opinion, the above approach misses the point. Any analysis of the international arbitration cases conducted solely from this perspective tends to be misleading. It should be emphasized that the real issue concerns contracts that do not expressly contemplate adaptation to changed circumstances. If they contain hardship clauses, the question confronting the interpreter is not one of applying the rebus sic stantibus principle, but the pacta sunt servanda principle.

At the present stage in the development of the lex mercatoria, however, one could not expect to find a harmonized statutory rule or treaty like those in many municipal systems that require or permit contract adaptation to changed circumstances. Such a rule can be introduced in the lex mercatoria only through the arbitration cases.

From the above survey, it appears that while the rebus sic stantibus principle has not been recognized in a general way, it has not been rejected in favor of a rigid application of the pacta sunt servanda principle. Instead, international arbitrators have proceeded in a very pragmatic way. They have avoided the enunciation of general principles, and have sought the intention of the parties as contract adaptation to changed circumstances on a case-by-case basis. In so doing, they have applied various interpretative criteria to reach their decisions.

In some cases, ICC arbitrators have used the presumption of professional competence of the parties, generally to exclude an implied principle of adaptation.[102] But they admitted that such a presumption could be rebutted, considering that its justification lies in the generalized use of hardship clauses. In other words, arbitrators appear to believe that since hardship clauses are so often used, the absence of a hardship clause in an international contract implies an intention contra contract adaptation. It is clear, however, that this attitude is in con-

---

101. *See* the observation by Derains, 1977 CLUNET 946 (1977), as well as Kassis, THEORIE GENERALE DES USAGES DU COMMERCE 367 (1984).

102. *See* the cases quoted by Derains, 1977 CLUNET 945 (1977).

flict with the very concept of customary usage, which implies that a concept in general use could be enforced even in the absence of an express provision.[103] Consequently, what has until now been more an element against the notion of an implied adaptation clause can become an element in its favor.

Similarly, when arbitrators become convinced of the risk-taking nature of an international contract, they tend to avoid the application of the rebus sic stantibus principle. They generally reach such conclusions in contractual situations where obligations must be performed immediately or within a very short time, as in sales contracts. Also, when a party uses a change of circumstances to be released from an obligation, as opposed to adapting the terms of the contract, arbitrators frequently opt for the principle of preservation of the contract. Finally, it must be mentioned that arbitrators appear generally reluctant to interpret their mandate so as to allow them to reconstruct new contract terms in the presence of changed circumstances, rather than simply adapting terms.

Other interpretative criteria play a role in the sense of making contract adaptation more likely to be enforced in international arbitrations. Among these is the non-risk-taking nature of the contract, which the arbitrators generally assume when confronted with long-term contracts. In these cases, the usual view seems to be that the intention of the parties was to preserve their original balance of rights and obligations in spite of changed circumstances, through a contract adaptation conducted according to the principles of good faith and equity. Many of the arbitral awards discussed above make express reference to such principles.

In conclusion, it can be said that the problem of contract adaptation in the lex mercatoria cannot be approached in terms of a choice between conflicting, mutually exclusive alternatives (rebus sic stantibus or pacta sunt servanda). Neither principle in an extreme formulation offers an adequate solution to the problem. It is rather through the application of the above-mentioned interpretative criteria that arbitrators reconcile the principles in specific cases. The same outcome occurs in those municipal legal systems where no authoritative legal

---

103. Kassis, THEORIE GENERALE DES USAGES DU COMMERCE 367 (1984).

regime regarding contract adaptation exists, though with an important difference. Since international arbitrators must decide within the limits of the mandate conferred upon them by the "terms of reference," in some cases they have been reluctant to effect a contract adaptation because they believed that an adaptation would be outside the scope of their mandate. Domestic courts do not have such a limitation.

In defining the lex mercatoria, it may be concluded that the formulation of international business contracts is evolving in the direction of providing for contract adaptation to changed circumstances. ICC arbitrators increasingly appear to be adopting interpretation criteria by which non-risk taking contracts, i.e., practically all long-term contracts, must be appropriately revised when an unforeseen change of circumstances creates a substantial imbalance between the obligations of the parties.[104]

---

104. *See* Kahn, *L'interprétation des contrats internationaux*, 1981 Clunet 19 (1981); Oppetit, *L'adaptation des contrats internationaux aux changements des circonstances: la clause de hardship*, 1974 Clunet 799 (1979).

Chapter 7. Unilateral Contract Modifications

7.1 Change Clauses in International Construction Contracts

In Chapter 6 we discussed cases where the content of the parties' obligations contained in international contracts may change either judicially or by the action of the parties because of changes in the surrounding circumstances. Modifications also can occur, however, as a consequence of the unilateral action of a party, particularly when such a party is the "owner" in an international construction contract.

This chapter deals with those clauses that relate to "changes," "variations," "alterations," or "additions." All such clauses generally contemplate that a contractor's "scope of work" may undergo certain qualitative or quantitative modifications upon the request of an owner. The rationale behind these provisions is the owner's desire for the scope of work to be adapted to reflect technical evolutions during the execution period or merely to its own changing requirements.

Change clauses sometimes are proposed by contractors because they seek flexibility as to the scope of work in order to ensure its correct execution. However, in order to become contractually binding and entitle the contractor to compensation, these changes must be accepted by an owner. Consequently, they fall outside the general category of unilateral contract modifications.[1]

The change clauses analyzed here are those that entitle one of the parties, normally the owner in an international construction contract, to unilaterally impose a change in the scope of work, with the result that a contractor must perform the change even before agreement is

---

1. This aspect of international construction contracts is the source of many disputes, particularly with reference to turnkey contracts. With respect to such contracts, owners tend to conceive the obligation of a contractor as an *obligation de résultat*, requiring contractors to do whatever is necessary to produce the result desired without additional compensation. A contractor's usual view is that the agreed compensation is for an agreed scope of work, so that any change in the scope of work that becomes necessary must imply a price adjustment. Disputes often center around the very concept of turnkey contracts.

reached as to the economic impact of a modification and even if a change does not imply a price adjustment.[2] The fact that the economic consequences of a change are undetermined at the time a contractor becomes obligated to effect them makes these clauses different from option clauses.[3]

The presence of change clauses in international construction contracts is more the rule than the exception.[4] The FIDIC model forms for civil works (Articles 51 and 52) and for electro-mechanical works (Articles 31.1 to 31.5) both contemplate the right of the engineer to order "alterations, additions, omissions" on behalf of the owner.[5] A typical change clause in an international construction contract would read as follows:

> The Owner may, at any time, by written order designated or indicated to be a change order, make any change in the work within the general

---

2. *See* Kahn, *Unilateral Modification Clauses in Long-Term Contracts*, 1986 INT'L TRADE L. REV. 146 (1986): "Typical of these contracts [long-term contracts] are the exceptional provisions, surprising when first met, that one party, the customer, can unilaterally impose a change on the other party, and that if necessary *the change must be acted upon before the consequences, including price adjustment, are agreed up*" (emphasis added). *See also* Fresle, *Variation and Escalation Clauses*, in Horn, ADAPTATION AND RENEGOTIATION OF CONTRACTS IN INTERNATIONAL TRADE AND FINANCE — STUDIES IN TRANSNATIONAL Economic LAW No. 3 149 (1985).

3. Option clauses in construction contracts give an owner the right to request some changes *at an agreed upon price*. Unlike unilateral change clauses, such option clauses are not "pathological" aspects of international contracts, because they provide a contractor the right to condition its commitment to perform the changes to an agreement being reached as to price adjustment.

4. Some statutory provisions in municipal laws expressly contemplate the right of the owner to impose changes upon the contractor (jus variandi). Article 1661 of the Italian Civil Code, for example, prescribes that the owner has the right to request changes from the contractor up to one-sixth of the price agreed upon, provided that such changes do not substantially alter the nature of the works to be performed.

5. The reference in the model forms is to the third edition, 1987. *See generally* Wallace, THE INTERNATIONAL CIVIL ENGINEERING CONTRACT 94 (1974).

scope of the contract, including but not limited to, changes: (a) in the specifications; (b) on the method or manner of performance of the work; (c) directing acceleration in the performance of the work. If any change under this clause causes an increase or decrease in the Contractor's cost of, or the time required for, the performance of any part of the work under this contract, an equitable adjustment shall be made and the contract modified accordingly.

Such a clause typically is followed by procedural provisions regarding the submission of claims (in the form of "Requests for Change Order" (RFCO) or "Objections to Change Order" (OTCO)) by the contractor.

The practice of international construction contracts has, however, established a number of widely accepted limitations on the right of the owner to order changes. First, a quantitative or qualitative change in the work to be performed must be kept "within the scope of the contract."[6] This determination may be difficult in given instances. For example, owners have argued that the request for a fence to be built around a power plant was "within the scope" of the contract concerning the construction of such a plant. Such a request is probably rightly "within the scope." Other owners, probably wrongly, have argued that the construction of a mosque naturally would fall within the scope of a contract for the construction of an airport in a Muslim country.

Second, a change must be reasonable in its entirety, so as not to become what in the jargon of international construction contracts is called a "cardinal change." In this respect, many change clauses contemplate a ceiling for the value of total changes. Such ceilings normally are established in terms of a percentage (approximately 20 percent) of the total contract price, and an owner may request changes only within their limits.

Third, a time limit beyond which no requests for changes are allowed is also often expressly contemplated. Such limits normally coincide with the issuance of a "substantial completion" or "provisional acceptance" certificate by an owner. The justification for time limitations is the need for a contractor to execute changes while still on-site and not yet demobilized. Otherwise, the performance of a change order

---

6. *See* Kahn, *Unilateral Modification Clauses in Long-Term Contracts*, 1986 INT'L TRADE L. REV. 148 (1986).

would require a re-mobilizing of a contractor's resources and would be equivalent to a new job.

Finally, the issue of change orders is generally subject to a detailed procedural regime, which includes formal decisions by an owner, which are duly and timely notified to a contractor. As an exception, "constructive changes" are admitted.[7]

Change orders issued within the above-mentioned limits determine a contractor's obligation to perform them. However, contractors are entitled to compensation, the calculation of which is not without problems. Many change clauses simply refer to an "equitable adjustment" of the contract price. The practical effect of such a provision is that a contractor's compensation is established by the owner. If a contractor disagrees with an owner's determination of compensation, the dispute resolution mechanisms of the construction contract are the only recourse. This solution, of course, may not be fair to a contractor, who must perform without knowing the extent of compensation.

Much more preferable from a contractor's perspective are change clauses that contain a schedule of unit rates, or a bill of quantities, to be used in determining the price of the work that is the subject of the change order. In these situations, a contractor may rely on objective criteria for determining the level of compensation. Some change clauses obligate a contractor to perform changes without compensation, provided the value of the extra work is kept within a given percentage (usually 10 percent) of the total contract price.[8]

A change clause is usually part of a turnkey contract that contemplates a lump-sum payment. However, the setting is different when a contractor is paid on a "cost-plus" basis (e.g., reimbursement of documented costs plus a fee).

Since change orders typically affect the completion schedule contractually agreed upon, they normally entitle the contractor to a

---

7. As to the notion of "constructive change," *see* Kahn, *Unilateral Modification Clauses in Long-Term Contracts*, 1986 INT'L TRADE L. Rev. 152.

8. The most recent practice of international construction contracts seems to require that all extra work be compensated. Article 52.3 of the FIDIC model (3d ed. 1987) contemplates that if the value of changes exceeds 15 percent of the total contract value, the contractor is entitled to an increase in its general overhead costs.

suitable extension of the delivery term.[9] Finally, a change order may imply the need for revising the payment terms under the original contract.[10]

7.2 "Termination for Convenience" Clauses

Unilateral contract modification also occurs under "termination without cause" or "termination for convenience" (i.e., convenience of the owner or buyer), or "termination without fault" (i.e., fault by the contractor or seller) clauses. Such clauses typically are inserted in long-term international contracts, mainly construction contracts. Their purpose is to enable an owner or buyer unilaterally to terminate a contractual relationship at any time it deems its interests not to be served by the contract.[11]

There is no obligation that such a decision be based on fault or non-performance. To illustrate, Article 23 of the 1987 FIDIC model contract for electro-mechanical works and Article 40 of the 1987 FIDIC model contract for civil works provide for the right of an owner simply to suspend the performance of the works. Termination for convenience is provided for as "default of the employer."

Like unilateral change clauses, termination for convenience clauses are more the rule than the exception in long-term international contracts. A typical clause is as follows:

The execution, completion and maintenance of the Works under the Contract may be terminated by the Owner in whole or from time to time in part whenever the Owner shall determine that such termination

---

9. This aspect of the change clauses is not without problems. Suffice to consider that if a change order consists of a free-standing addition to the works originally contemplated, it may have a completion term of its own. Furthermore, a delay in the original works cannot only be the direct consequence of the changes, but also of the possible redeployment of the contractor's resources necessary to perform such change.

10. Kahn, *Unilateral Modification Clauses in Long-Term Contracts*, 1986 INT'L TRADE L. REV. 156 (1986).

11. The unilateral modification of the contractual obligations in these situations consists of the fact that contractual obligations are terminated with-

is in the best interest of the Owner. Any such termination for convenience shall be effected by delivery to the Contractor of a Notice of Termination specifying the extent to which performance of work under the Contract is terminated and the date upon which such termination becomes effective. After receipt of a Notice of Termination and except as otherwise directed by the Owner, the Contractor shall as soon as possible: (a) stop work under the Contract on the date and to the extent specified in the Notice of Termination; (b) place no further orders or contracts for materials, services, or facilities except as may be necessary for completion of such portion of the Works under the Contract as is not terminated; (c) terminate all orders, contracts, and Subcontract Agreements to the extent that they relate to the performance or work terminated by the Notice of Termination; (d) assign to the Owner in the manner, at the times, and to the extent directed by the Owner, all of the right, title, and interest of the Contractor under the orders, contracts, and Subcontract Agreements so terminated, in which case the Owner shall have the right, in its discretion, but not the obligation, to settle or pay any or all claims arising our of the termination of such orders, contracts, and Subcontract Agreements and the Owner shall indemnify the Contractor against any further liability with respect to any such claims to the extent the Contractor's right, title, and interest pertaining thereto under such Sub-contract Agreement may have been assigned to the Owner; (e) take all necessary steps to resolve or settle all outstanding liabilities and claims arising out of such termination of orders, contracts, and Subcontract Agreements with the prior approval of the Owner to the extent it may require; (f) transfer title to the Owner and deliver in the manner, at the times, and to the extent directed by the Owner (i) Construction Materials not located at the Construction Site, title to which is not vested in the Owner on the date of the Notice of Termination, in any manner connected with the performance of the work terminated by the Notice of Termination and (ii) the completed or partially completed plans, drawings of any type, information, and other property which, if the Works had been completed in full, would have been required to be furnished to the Owner; (g) take such actions as may be necessary, or as the Owner may direct, for the protection and preservation of the property related to the Contract which is in the possession of the Contractor and in which the Owner has or may acquire an interest.

---

out breach of a contract by either party. Termination based on defective performance is beyond the scope of the clauses discussed here.

Such a clause then typically contains a detailed regulation of the calculation of the compensation due to the contractor.

Many municipal laws contemplate a similar right of the owner in domestic construction contracts.[12] The practical effect of these provisions is not dissimilar to that deriving from a breach of contract by an owner. It is important to note that under domestic laws, public interest is not necessarily the legal basis of termination for convenience clauses, as any change in the owner's schedule can give rise to a termination.

In international practice, the clauses under discussion generally contain detailed provisions regarding the compensation rights of a contractor. Typically, when a termination for convenience notice is received, a contractor must cease performance of a contract and initiate measures to minimize damage. For example, it promptly must terminate its contractual relationships with its suppliers and subcontractors. It is not unusual for owners to reserve the right to intervene in the severance of the ties between the contractors and their subcontractors, suppliers, and vendors to protect its interest in minimizing damages.

On the other hand, if a contractor is able to pass on a termination for convenience provision to its subcontractors on a pari passu basis, the negative impact of a termination, in terms of damages to be paid by a terminating owner, can be somewhat contained. This is not always the case in practice, however, and disputes on the matter are frequent.[13]

---

12. *See, e.g.*, Art. 1794 of the French Civil Code and Art. 1671 of the Italian Civil Code. Both contain such rights. In the United States, termination for convenience provisions were pioneered by the procurement regulations of the U.S. government. 41 CFR §§ 1-8.70–1-8.706; as well as § 24 of the General Provisions of the U.S. Army Corps. of Engineers. *See generally* S. Stein, Construction Law § 4.13[3] (1988); Niagara Mohawk Power v. Graver Tank & Mfg. Co., 470 F. Supp. 1308 (N.D.N.Y. 1979).

13. The problems deriving to the subcontractors as a consequence of the modifications of the U.S. space and defense programs are illustrative. See Aydin Corp. v. Grumman Aerospace Corp., Memorandum of Order, dated November 14, 1986 in Civil Action No. 86–5244 before the U.S. District Court for the Eastern District of Pennsylvania.

As a matter of principle, the compensation due to a contractor in the case of a termination for convenience should be similar to that recoverable in the case of a breach of contract by the owner. In practice, the clauses vary substantially, and show a tendency to limit the contractor's right to damages. The loss of profit generally is recognized as a reimbursable item, although sometimes it is determined on a lump-sum basis. It is not infrequent that a contractual payment system is modified after a contract is terminated for convenience with respect to the portion of the works already performed. For example, a cost-plus payment method typically would replace a lump-sum system. In this case, a contractor must produce evidence of its costs up to the time of the termination, and it would be entitled to a reimbursement of such costs, plus a fee for general overhead and loss of profit. Title of the work already performed passes at the time of the termination.

As a final observation, drafters of international contracts should not consider a termination for convenience clause as part of the "boilerplate" clauses, the practical relevance of which is minimal. At a time of general deterioration of the worldwide economy, such clauses are likely to find more than occasional practical application.[14]

---

14. Suffice to quote the effects of the termination for convenience by ARAMCO in 1985 of the complex of contracts concerning the Quassim refinery in Saudi Arabia.

TABLE OF CASES

[References are to page numbers.]

ENGLISH CASES

FRENCH CASES

GERMAN CASES

INTERNATIONAL COURT OF JUSTICE

ITALIAN CASES

UNITED STATES CASES

INDEX

Leges Genuenses, 11
Leonine Clause, 105, 114, 141
Letters of Intent, 39
Lex Rhodia, 11
Liability, 33–35, 62, 64, 69, 73, 75–76, 79–80, 96, 99–100,
    103–111, 120–121, 153–155, 165, 177, 185, 192, 199, 212
Libya, 23, 139
Limitations and Exclusions, 83–155
Liquidated Damages, 83, 110–119, 122–123, 144, 155, 157
Lord Mansfield, 11
Loss of Profit, 74, 76, 79, 214

M

Merchant Judges and Courts, 11
Mexico, 104
Mirror Image Rule, 140

N

New York Convention of June 10, 1958, 20

O

Objections to Change Order (OTCO), 209
Objective Liability, 106
Obligations de moyens, 36, 38–39, 41–45, 50, 52–53, 55, 83, 96,
    105, 117, 160
Obligations de résultat, 36, 38, 41–47, 49, 52, 83, 96, 105, 116
Obligations of Dare, 43

P

Pacta Sunt Servanda, 14, 22, 178–180, 183, 185, 193, 202–204
Penalty Interest, 119
Portugal, 113
Principia Mercatoria, 8
Proper Law, 149–150
Provisional Acceptance, 209
Punitive Damages, 38, 62

Q

Quantification of Damages, 57–82, 107

R

Reasonable Foreseeability, 64–65